Metaphor Sound and Meaning
IN BRIDGES'
THE TESTAMENT OF BEAUTY

ROBERT BRIDGES

Metaphor Sound and Meaning

IN BRIDGES'

THE TESTAMENT OF BEAUTY

By

Elizabeth Cox Wright

Philadelphia

UNIVERSITY OF PENNSYLVANIA PRESS

LONDON: GEOFFREY CUMBERLEGE

OXFORD UNIVERSITY PRESS

1951

1|72

PREFACE

Robert Bridges' *The Testament of Beauty* has received much scattered comment, but very little sustained study. Several essays, Elton's *Robert Bridges and The Testament of Beauty* is among the best, a small but indispensable volume of explanatory notes by Smith, *Notes on 'The Testament of Beauty,'* McKay's *A Bibliography of Robert Bridges,* and a host of reviews, make up the bulk of the written criticism. Three chapters on the poem in Guérard's *Robert Bridges* are an admirable introduction to its philosophical meaning and to some of its poetic elements, necessarily brief in a book which discusses all of Bridges' poetry. So important and so fine a poem, still too little read but growing in familiarity, will receive in the future both the detailed study and revised judgment of quality it deserves; however, the field is still largely unworked.

The present book is an experiment. Students of literature have recently been both developing new critical attitudes and reëxamining scattered poems and limited aspects of novels and plays in their light. There has been much private study, but only a limited amount of publication of results, however. Until the appearance of Wellek and Warren's *Theory of Literature,* 1949, there had been no summing up of various conclusions or reconciliation of them with sound traditional ideas and procedures. No long poem, no single novel, no play, has been subjected to minute analysis of its stylistic and structural elements for the purpose of determining the degree and character of its aesthetic unity and its subtle, indirectly expressed meanings. The following study

v

has attempted chiefly this particular task. The development of theory in Chapters I and XIV, highly selective and pointed to its limited purpose, is merely a guide to the basic idea behind the detailed analysis of the long poem. The choice of *The Testament of Beauty* as a practical example for critical analysis, although surprising no doubt to many, needs no apology. This poem is a major work of art; to present it as such, proportioned, consonant in its tone and idea, expressing aesthetically far more than its ideological statements and signifying far more than its incidental "beauties," has been a vastly rewarding labor. If successful to any degree, such a presentation will be the beginning of a new treatment of philosophical poetry. However tentative the method and results, the attempt may show students of poetry its far-reaching possibilities.

Full indebtedness to previous writers is difficult to trace in a book of this kind. Reading all the major contributions to each part of the thought developed throughout has been the goal, but there have no doubt been serious omissions. The books expressly referred to are, however, only those which were pertinent to the writing rather than to the study of the subject. No further bibliographical data are given than the details of place and date of publication of each title the first time it appears in a footnote.

Personal acknowledgments are equally hard to make complete. I should not be satisfied, however, to refrain from pleasing myself by the following. Robert E. Spiller, friend over many years, could not have been more encouraging. Dorothy Koch Bestor gave the manuscript its first and most complete textual criticism. Bruce Dearing, Stephen E. Whicher, and Monroe C. Beardsley wrestled with the obscurities of my generalizations to more effect than is apparent. Henry Seidel Canby very generously gave me for the frontispiece, the portrait which had been presented to him by Bridges. The President and Board of Managers of Swarthmore College have been generous with leave of absence and with a grant for stenographic help. The students of the College have been a constant and incalculable stimulus and check. My family has given strong support and hours of practical help.

ELIZABETH COX WRIGHT

Swarthmore College,
Swarthmore, Pennsylvania,
March 1, 1951.

ACKNOWLEDGMENTS

The quotations from *The Testament of Beauty, Poetical Works,* and *Collected Essays, Papers, etc.,* by Robert Bridges, are used by kind permission of the Clarendon Press, Oxford; those from *Correspondence of Robert Bridges and Henry Bradley* are used by permission of Sir Edward Bridges as the author's executor, and of the Clarendon Press, Oxford.

I have been generously granted permission to use other copyright material as follows:

By Messrs. Faber and Faber, Ltd., the Harvard University Press, Harcourt, Brace and Company, Messrs. Jackson, Son and Company, Ltd., and Mr. T. S. Eliot for quotation from *Selected Essays, The Use of Poetry and the Use of Criticism,* and *The Music of Poetry;* by The Macmillan Company for quotation from *The Name and Nature of Poetry* by A. E. Housman; by Macmillan and Company, Ltd., for quotation from *Form and Style in Poetry* by W. P. Ker; by Harcourt, Brace and Company for quotation from *To the Lighthouse* by Virginia Woolf; by J. M. Dent and Sons, Ltd., for quotation from the Temple Classics edition of Dante's *Paradiso* and from the preface to *The Nigger of the Narcissus* by Joseph Conrad; by E. P. Dutton and Company for quotation from the Temple Classics edition of Dante's *Paradiso.*

CONTENTS

ROBERT BRIDGES   *Frontispiece*
  Photograph by Will Stroud

Chapter   *Page*
   I Introduction   1

            PART I   THE SOUND
  II The Invention of a New Metre   13
 III The Theoretical Justification of the New Metre   28
  IV The End-Pause   47
   V The Voices Revealed   77

            PART II   THE IMAGERY
  VI The Properties and the Keeping   103
 VII The World in Space   120
VIII The World in Time   137
  IX The World of Man   159
   X The Dominant Metaphors and Symbols   174

            PART III   THE STRUCTURE
  XI The Study of Structure   195
 XII The Inner Logic   205
XIII The Poetic Structure   256

 XIV Conclusion   300

CHAPTER ONE

INTRODUCTION

I, 8

> 'Twas late in my long journey, when I had clomb to where
> the path was narrowing and the company few,
> a glow of childlike wonder enthral'd me, as if my sense
> had come to a new birth purified, my mind enrapt
> re-awakening to a fresh initiation of life. . . .

This reawakening came to Robert Bridges at a time of life when visions are rare; he was nearly eighty. By 1929, when he published his long poem, *The Testament of Beauty*, he was eighty-five, and we may share the surprise he expressed at its end:

IV, 1297

> for my tale was my dream and my dream the telling,
> and I remember wondring the while I told it
> how I told it so tellingly.

His vision was one of experience ordered and so estranged by beauty that he scarcely recognized it,

I, 39

> and yet was nothing new to me, only all was vivid
> and significant that had been dormant or dead:
> as if in a museum the fossils on their shelves
> should come to life suddenly, or a winter rose-bed
> burst into crowded holiday of scent and bloom.

His vision held also the certainty of spiritual evidences "supreme in themselves, eternal, unnumber'd" (I, 35) crowding through the portals of the sensuous world, "activ presences, striving to force an entrance." (I, 683) The content of the tale of his dream is different from most visions, but the psychological effect on the man was the same as the experi-

1

ence of St. Francis, and of William Wordsworth, and of George Fox. This vision set the poet forward on a new track, with joy in his heart. The old, the accustomed, could no longer hold him. In *The Testament of Beauty* he created a new form to express the vision vigorously and organically.

Bridges' vision of truth is embodied in human history, its physical origins and machinery, its psychological motive power, its recorded events, its prophecy of achievement, its constant tragedy. The poem is an adventure of the mind, a consideration of all the experience he knows; this experience has its limitations, as will be shown hereafter, but it is remarkably inclusive. It is the experience of the flesh, of knowledge, of joy and grief over earthly things, and of vision. Whatever he knows of all this is spread out before him for arrangement, comment, and assessment. First, origins, scientifically known. The experience of man as science interprets it seems to him to have its source in the earliest conditions of existence. He disentangles three kinds of responses to these conditions, responses of equal validity and equal potentiality, but of different character. These responses in Bridges' words are labeled Selfhood, Breed, and Ethick. We may paraphrase them baldly: the urge to get along oneself, to unite with another, and to develop *being* according to ultimate evaluations. They all spring from forms of life so ancient and are duplicated in still-existent forms so primitive and simple, that they may be described in physical and chemical, as well as biological, terms. The second, third, and fourth books of *The Testament of Beauty* discuss these three urges inherent in the physical universe and explicit in man. The first book is in thought chiefly a consideration of the claims of man's reason to judge of these matters.

Second, man's history. The poem is the incarnation in words of the great moments of man's past and the terrible ones alike; all are parts of his historical evolution. Socrates by the grassy banks of the Ilissus, St. Francis sick in Damian adoring the Sun, Spinoza grinding his lenses, science com-

forting men's bodies, the fashioning of well-toned viols by Amati and Stradivari, are all man's experience. So too are the murder of the attendants in the tomb of Ur, the blind misery and massacre of the Second Crusade, our modern Industry badly fed and shut out from the sun, and War in its modern development become fratricide. These many things represented by the experience of individuals have happened to multitudes, over countless epochs. In the way of Art, the attempt is made

II, 676
      to explore, estimate and accumulate
  those infinit dark happenings into a single view. . . .

There is finally the third plane of experience which Bridges writes into his poem. On a strictly scientific base of the habits of electrons and the flux and change toward complexity of the evolutionary current, he sees man to have developed the potentiality, if rarely the achievement, of the highest spiritual grace, or vision, as he constantly uses the word. But this achievement is so miraculous and the potentiality so universal that the substance of all life appears spiritual in principle. Yet the physical facts of life are always presented as the base, not, as in the Platonic sense, as the shadows of reality:

IV, 5
      ev'n as in a plant
  when the sap mounteth secretly and its wintry stalk
  breaketh out in the prolific miracle of Spring. . . .

The content of each book in turn celebrates this miracle, reiterating that

III, 1002
   From blind animal passion to the vision of Spirit
  all actual gradations come of natur, and each
  severally in time and place is answerable in man.

To recreate man's past and to interpret scientifically his present Being in the light of revelation, is new in vision literature, although it is with *The Divine Comedy* and *The Vision of Piers Plowman* that *The Testament of Beauty* should be grouped. An understanding of Bridges' problem must lie behind a discussion of the form of the poem. Some of its material is traditional in poetry; natural beauty and an extravagant joy in it, religious fervor and even moral contemplation are contained in the greatest poems. But scientific information, for instance the physics, chemistry, and biology of sex, or even reasoning through the persistent problems of philosophy, have little traditional justification. However, Bridges' vision and his spiritual elation embraced science and philosophy as well as the beauty of nature, and love, and religion, and it was the character of the vision that determined the soul's language of the poem. (I, 678) Its expression required an invention comparable to that of *The Divine Comedy* in complexity and unifying power. Its satisfactory expression, to bring *The Testament of Beauty* into the company of those great poems men are not willing to let die, required a similarly commanding poetic imagination.

The successful accomplishment of his great task has not been allowed Bridges. His poem has many loving readers, and it is recorded that reading it aloud to diverse groups is remarkably successful, but comment usually concludes with some variant of the opinion that "It is by individual passages that Bridges' poem will live."[1] The metre is condemned as too loose, its effect chaotic or monotonous, its structure not only "philosophical" and unpoetic, but disorganized and illogical; its philosophy is called banal or unoriginal or amateurish, its spirit insular and class-ridden. But there are apparently some passages, and in general opinion, a great many passages so moving, so vigorous, and so profound that no one writing about poetry can afford to neglect at least a passing reference. *The Testament of Beauty*, if one follows currents of opinion, is gaining steadily in importance; if one follows critical comment, it is a store of colorful material, a

[1] Thompson, Edward. *Robert Bridges* (Oxford, 1944), p. 111.

personal document of learning, wit, and remarkable flexibility, and an anthology, with much filler that may be skipped over, of wonderful short sections, but not a poem.

It is not really strange that this long poem needs propaganda of its interest and richness. Even qualified readers who give it a good word in passing apparently find it a little dull. Writing and music alike may seem dull if the details are not observed; new kinds of detail in new arrangements take time for their perception. *The Testament of Beauty* has not yet become a known idiom, a familiar melody. Neither an inherited understanding, such as in a sense we have for *Paradise Lost,* nor, for most people, a long acquaintance with the poem, has yet brought the details to brightness. However one may judge of the theory of accumulation of popular knowledge as a source of wisdom, there is some sort of accumulation over the years of understanding of works of art which stands a reader in good stead. It will be only a matter of decades before the reader of *The Testament of Beauty* will be as competent in his judgment as he is today with *King Lear,* if, in Bridges' phrase, he have a peduncled eye and not a fixed one. But at present there is considerable misunderstanding of the poem.

The man on the street has always been sure that what he cannot read like a hymn tune and as clearly understand as the hymn is not poetry. Although the sound of *The Testament of Beauty* pleases him if it is read correctly, he cannot really follow it orally and when he sees the printed page he can make nothing of it. But we do not have to stop for him. A more challenging fact is that some of the best of modern critical principles have been invoked against the poem. These principles have been developing from the base of the best traditional criticism; they are not revolutionary, in the sense that they overturn what has been considered established, but radical in the sense that they have grown from established roots, expanded by writers who themselves are fine poets, and austere in their standards of thought. It would seem, then, that the adverse criticism of those writers who mention *The Testament of Beauty*, is likely to be sound. Shall we go on reading the fine passages, trying to dodge the eccentricity of the total attempt, enjoying the enthusiasm and the learning with apology to our more critical selves? Many will, no doubt, and the number who read merely for their enjoyment is increasing. But the alternative is not to set it aside eventually as an interesting failure; the very principles which appear to reduce its stature, when carefully and freshly applied, raise it to the ranks of the very few great long poems of the world.

What are these principles? They cannot be enumerated in an orderly way and applied like a blueprint to specific poems. They spring from the questions which arise when we are faced with the unfamiliar and the displeasing, and from certainties which we feel when we are satisfied in our reading. They bear on poetry as an art among the other arts, rather than on the relationship of a poem with literary or social history, or with the poet. They are being used by students of the novel and by students of Shakespeare, and the results are equally interesting and valuable. They are, however, as yet hardly principles at all. One cannot find any full account of the ideas, nor the extensive application of them to any poem. Present-day critics are working toward the same objective, but they contradict one another frequently both in theory and judgment. Their studies have been restricted to short poems, or inevitably, considering the whole purpose of their books, to incomplete studies of longer ones. Two things are needed for the fuller understanding and use of these views: a reconciliation of all this antecedent critical writing about novels, plays (especially those of Shakespeare) and poetry, and an attempt to bring some one long poem forward in an analysis that considers all its demands. This book is the latter attempt, the analysis of a poem which apparently these writers believe to suffer from such treatment.

The clue to be followed lies in Eliot's now famous remarks

on the metaphysical poets. "When a poet's mind is perfectly equipped for its work," he says, "it is constantly amalgamating disparate experience; the ordinary man's experience is chaotic, irregular, fragmentary. The latter falls in love, or reads Spinoza, and these two experiences have nothing to do with each other, or with the noise of the typewriter or the smell of cooking; in the mind of the poet these experiences are always forming new wholes. . . . The poets of the seventeenth century, the successors of the dramatists of the sixteenth, possessed a mechanism of sensibility which could devour any kind of experience."[2] The usefulness of this idea is manifest, and the term "mechanism of sensibility," a fine tool. But as a psychological power, critics are no longer inclined to restrict the possession of such a mechanism, which Keats would have called the imagination, to the poets of any particular century. Eliot's restriction of it to the immediate successors of the Elizabethan dramatists[3] suggests that he had in mind not only a mechanism of *sensibility* (a psychological power) but a dramatic technique for the creation of a poem, an aesthetic whole, from the disparate experiences or materials the poet wishes to incorporate in it. This mechanism (never a very happy choice of word and by repetition offensive) for "making a union of emotion and thought" has been assumed to be that of "thinking in images and thus bringing a living body" to ideas.[4] Eliot himself was probably thinking of his "objective correlative," which he conceived of as being not only "a set of objects," but also "a chain of events" as "formula" for the particular emotion to be expressed.[5]

It is interesting in this connection that Bridges quotes Santayana's view that literature must dramatize: " 'To turn

[2] Eliot, T. S. "The Metaphysical Poets," *Selected Essays, 1917-1932* (London, 1932), p. 273.

[3] Implied in his *The Use of Poetry and the Use of Criticism* (Cambridge, Mass., 1933), *passim*.

[4] Matthiessen, F. O. *The Achievement of T. S. Eliot* (New York, 1947), p. 68.

[5] "Hamlet," *Selected Essays*, p. 145.

8 *The Testament of Beauty*

events into ideas is the function of literature. . . . It looks at natural things with an incorrigibly dramatic eye, turning them into permanent unities (which they never are) and almost into persons, grouping them into their imaginative or moral affinities and retaining in them chiefly what is incidental to their being, the part they may chance to play in man's adventures.'"[6] In *The Testament of Beauty* Bridges is constantly doing this.

It is perhaps for the psychologist to settle the question of what really the shaping spirit of imagination is. Coleridge and Keats had intuitions about it and their phrases still linger in our minds, as in the metaphor in the preceding sentence. Keats speaks of "the innumerable compositions and decompositions which take place between the intellect and its thousand materials before it arrives at that trembling delicate and snail-horn perception of beauty."[7] He says of a passage in *Endymion* that it was "a regular stepping of the Imagination towards a truth."[8] But if the critic uses the word *mechanism* he must use it to describe technique. The significant question for criticism then becomes: What mechanism or mechanisms has the poet used to devour or amalgamate or fuse the various kinds of experience he wishes to put into his poem?—using *mechanism* neither as a criterion of mental health nor an alternative to the much-abused word *imagination*. Most poems use several mechanisms, not one, and the poet must be free to emphasize or exclude as he likes.

Bridges has called on all the resources of his poetic power to amalgamate what are indeed the very disparate experiences of his poem: argument, scientific knowledge, facts of history, speculation concerning the nature of man, physical satisfaction, religious mysticism; these words hardly suffice to sum up the variety. The purpose and procedure of this

[6] Bridges, Robert Seymour. "George Santayana," *Collected Essays, Papers, etc.* (Oxford, 1927-33), p. 161, quoting Santayana's *Little Essays*, p. 138.
[7] Forman, H. Buxton, Ed. *The Letters of John Keats* (London, 1895), p. 114.
[8] *Ibid.*, p. 77.

book is to show how the sound, imagery, and structure of
The Testament of Beauty have done their work. In the study
of these elements, as will be seen, many new meanings and a
new perspective for the whole poem emerge; the result is
a conviction that the poem is profound and significant in a
way demanded by all those who do not ask of a work of art
that it confirm their own special beliefs. However, the object
and the chief matter of the following pages is the examination of the aesthetic unity of *The Testament of Beauty,* a
unity which includes the homogeneity of seemingly disparate
parts and the relationship of parts to the whole.

Because of this limitation of purpose, the study of each of
the elements, sound, imagery, and structure, has a particularly pointed and not a more appreciative or rhetorical flavor.
The whole question of the sound of a poem includes of course
consideration of incidental beauty, of assonance and alliteration, for instance, and of separable passages of exceptional
sonority or subtlety. Because of the confusions in previous
criticism about the proper rendering of the poem, most of
the section on sound deals with the versification, which has
hitherto been so misunderstood as to have caused the most
careful students with few exceptions to consider it too loose
for full poetic power. It is only with the recognition of the
characteristics of the metre, that the subtle variations may
be heard. With proper reading, one comes to understand an
important device in the dramatizing of the poem, that is,
its sound.

I am particularly aware of the limited significance of the
section on the imagery and metaphor of the poem. Bridges'
metaphorical sense combines the skill with which he trans-
fers feeling to fact, and the subtlety of those relational elements between sense and idea which create metaphors of the
highest quality. This success in metaphor is a study in itself,
and fully developed would push the examination of the unity
of the poem out of focus. What is here presented shows the
consistent colorings of the image surface of the poem, and

the transfusion of the poem with the repeated metaphors, or symbols, of the dream vision.

The section on the structure of the poem is more nearly all that can be said of the principles of its organization, of its cohesion and its proportions. By thought, by pervasive and progressive metaphor, and by the fiction of a journey in a dream to the vision of truth, its multifarious materials are shaped to a whole. In this embodiment lies the reason for the connecting sections of the poem, set apart by even the most sympathetic of Bridges' readers as "the harder passages . . . that (no doubt) choke the verse."[9] It also justifies the peculiarity of the sequence of thought; the circular movements, so puzzling to the philosophically trained, exist over and around a carefully executed inner logic; they are psychologically appropriate to the framework of the vision chosen by Bridges. Future students of his method of bringing unity to the content of that vision will find further nicety of detail, but even this first examination makes impressively certain the shaping power of his imagination and the fine appropriateness of his means to the end of Art. "Never was symbol more deftly devised" (III, 1128) than the structure of this poem.

[9] Elton, Oliver. *Robert Bridges and The Testament of Beauty*, English Association pamphlet No. 83 (November, 1932), pp. 4, 14.

PART I

THE SOUND

CHAPTER TWO

THE INVENTION OF A NEW METRE

Aesthetically speaking, a poem is badly condemned if it is said that there is in it too much intellectual paraphrase, that its versification is too free and careless, and that its structure is loose and disorganized. Such criticisms lead directly toward condemnation of the vigor and significance of the poem's life as an independent being. To consider them, we must take up the positive study of *The Testament of Beauty*. The first criticism spreads wide; the philosophical and the scientific parts "choke the verse"; they are statement, they are undramatic,[1] they are separable from the great lyric passages. We should make no attempt to dodge these parts, either as reader for pleasure or as critic. They are in the poem, and if they are blemishes, they must be serious ones. The second criticism at first glance seems very separate from this one, but it is in fact, bound up with it, as every critical question must be with every other one, if one is dealing with a poem with pretensions to being a work of art throughout. If the versification is limp and careless, it will not have been used as a means to fuse those harder parts with the passages expressing the emotional values of personal experience. Its carelessness will be another cause of the falling apart of the poem into its different kinds of material; it will be another symptom of the loose organization, to turn ahead to the third criticism. Much depends on the versification of *The Testament of Beauty*, then, and it has been very incompletely understood.

---

[1] Elton. *Robert Bridges and The Testament of Beauty*, p. 14; Tillyard, E. M. W. *Poetry Direct and Oblique* (1st ed.; London, 1934), p. 269; Matthiessen. *The Achievement of T. S. Eliot*, pp. 67, 80.

One has to be both born and trained an authority in metrics. Fundamentally, the ear should be sensitive, no doubt as sensitive as the poet's; it should be trained in music; it should be trained in the musical effects of the best English poetry, and of classical and modern European poetry, especially Italian and French. The mind should be trained by study of a literature of metrics that is chaotic and unself-critical; it should learn to use the resources of the psychological laboratory. But it is not necessary to do for Bridges' prosody what he did for Milton's. Such a complete study should someday be made, but here the chief concern has been with the proper reading of the poem, since only by proper reading can one perceive that its sound is one of the most important of its means of unification. Once heard, in its variations, of course, but also in its consonant tones, the sound and movement of the lines make a composition of the elements usually considered separable.

But the proper reading is not just the reader's business; it was the poet's business to begin with. Reports are various and contradictory in evaluation. Is this the poet's fault or the reader's? Did Bridges choose inadvisably to break from the English iambic pentameter tradition for a long philosophical poem? Did he invent a metre that is unsound in theory, and ineffective as a whole in execution? Or does the belief that he can be so criticized spring from incomplete understanding of the verse form of the poem? To understand the "neo-miltonics," the "loose Alexandrines," requires that we consider the questions of the break from tradition, the inventing and executing of a new metre. What are the problems of versification in a long philosophical poem; what are the features of this new metre; what are the effects Bridges gained by them?

Unless he is experimenting, the poet tells us that he does not so much deliberately choose his verse form, as feel the preliminary rhythms along with his initial idea for a poem.[2] To liberate his poem, he must already know how to use a suitable form. "One cannot originate a poem in an unknown metre, for it is familiarity with the framework which invites the words into their places."[3] After years of experimentation with quantities in English verse, and exhaustive analysis of Milton's poetry, Bridges was ready by 1913 to take the step that Milton had just stopped short of. "It struck me that Milton had freed every foot in his blank verse . . . except the last. . . . By having 'freed the feet' I mean that in his metrical system there was no place in which any one syllable was necessarily long or short, accented or unaccented, heavy or light."[4] He wondered what the effect would be to free the last foot and to exclude the extra-metrical syllable, "and determined to experiment on it."[5] "I had had for many years a poem in my head which had absolutely refused to take any metrical form. Whenever I had tried to put it into words the metre ruined it. The whole poem was, so far as feeling and picturing went, complete in my imagination, and I set to work very readily on it, and with intense interest to see what would come. I was delighted to find that the old difficulty of metering it had vanished and it ran off quite spontaneously to its old title *The Flowering Tree*, which is dated in my book Nov. 7, 1913."[6] This metre turned out to be the basis for that finally developed over the next ten years, to be ready in 1924 for what was later used as the first seven lines of *The Testament of Beauty*.[7]

With a long poem, the period of gestation must spread over a considerable period, and the element of choice in the metre used is dominant. Further, the conditions of choice

[2] Among other accounts, one may call on Housman, *The Name and Nature of Poetry* (New York and Cambridge, 1933).
[3] Bridges. "Note to *New Verse*," Collected Essays, Vol. 7, No. xv, p. 88.
[4] *Ibid.*, p. 87.
[5] *Ibid.*, p. 88.
[6] *Ibid.*, p. 88.
[7] *Ibid.*, p. 86. M.M.B.'s note.

are severe. Primarily, if there is any order of necessity, the versification of a long poem must be interesting enough, and effective enough in other ways, to justify the presentation of the material in verse rather than prose, with its greater variety of rhythms and its lesser demand on the reader. It must, however, not be so interesting in itself as to be peculiar, and to fatigue the reader by its peculiarities. It must be forgettable as well as memorable. Blank verse has proved very successful in this respect. The line is long enough not to be restless, in the first place. It is long enough and may be simple enough to fade out of the consciousness as verse, and make its impression as speech. Bridges' intention in using the twelve-syllable line freed of regular metrical accent was to meet the same conditions. The verse form of a long poem must be flexible enough to follow the changes of the material, as well as the flow and shift of feeling that is required likewise in a lyric. Both plays and narrative poems need such flexibility, and blank verse has been found an admirable instrument for it. Flexibility may be further increased by shifts from one metre to another or from verse to prose, but to balance this need there is the need for a versification firm enough to hold the poem together. This is especially necessary when the poem has not got a swift and closely knit narrative to hold it together. Bridges called this quality or function of metre its carrying power, a better characterization than the words "machinery" or "mortar."[8] He believed that it should harmonize whatever the poet had to deal with.[9] He found this power preëminent in the metre of *The Divine Comedy*, although in English, no doubt, the complexities of the *terza rima* might prove a stumbling block in not being sufficiently forgettable.

Many readers would insist that an important condition of choice of metre in a long poem is that it should not be monot-

[8] "Humdrum and Harum Scarum," *Collected Essays*, Vol. 2, No. ii, pp. 48, 49.
[9] *Ibid.*, p. 50.

onous. However, this is an ambiguous word. The versification of *The Testament of Beauty* has been accused of monotony because of its freedom, and that of *The Essay on Man* because of its regularity. Readers use the word rather to express their own state of inattention (which, of course, may be caused by the poem, as well as their own limitations) than a real quality of the poem. *Monotonous* really means written in a monotone; by all criteria of art criticism the variety in the unity is essential to its power. Therefore we may say that one of the conditions of choice for the long poem is that the versification should not be monotonous. But only in a narrow way is monotony caused by the principle of the versification; regular rhyming, and a short line, are perhaps the chief dangers. Otherwise, monotony is a matter of ineffective use of a metre, not of choice of metre. If the poet can compel his metre to many and significant variations, he has avoided monotony, although the reader still may not like it. However, Guérard is critical of the metre of *The Testament of Beauty* on the ground that "the principle of perpetual variety in meter usually leads to monotony."[10] Whether the perpetual variety is the characteristic of the principle or the rendering of the metre will be discussed later.

There is another kind of consideration observed by the poet in his choice of metre, although I am not sure of its validity. This is the question as to whether or not a metre can become outworn, whether its use with complete success exhausts its possibilities for another poet or another generation. Certainly, after a great poet or a great period of poetry has exploited a verse form, it becomes easy for minor poets to achieve good effects in it; these effects, however, may have little power to move us to wonder or delight because we are tired of them. Whether this is a literal exhaustion of the possibilities of a form matters little if the poet believes it to be true. If he does, he will avoid the old and try something fresh. The poets of the romantic period avoided the rhymed

---

[10] Guérard, Albert. *Robert Bridges* (Cambridge, 1942), p. 246.

couplet. Bridges avoided not only the five-foot line, but also
the accentual pattern of blank verse. Although a little cau-
tious in subscribing to a theory of exhaustion in "Humdrum
and Harum Scarum,"[11] in his essay on Wordsworth and
Kipling he says, "It is true in all art that when a great master
appears he so exhausts the material at his disposal as to
make it impossible for any succeeding artist to be original,
unless he can either find new material or invent some new
method of handling the old. . . . Any one may see that serious
rhyme is now exhausted in English verse, or that Milton's
blank verse practically ended as an original form with
Milton. There are abundant signs that English syllabic verse
has long been in the stage of artistic exhaustion of form
which follows great artistic achievement."[12] Feeling as he
did, it is no wonder that he threw his energies into exploring
the possibilities of classical quantitative verse and then of
the line he developed from Milton's. The freedom of the
latter miraculously took hold of *The Flowering Tree*, and
continued to produce very rich and varied rhythms which
delighted him.[13] By the time he was faced with the need to
choose his metre for *The Testament of Beauty*, he had gained
competence in it and some degree of recognition for its
beauty. His friend Mackail had written him, on reading
Noel in *The Times*, "What is this lovely new metre?"[14] Seven
or eight years later, Sir Walter Raleigh was able to read
Poor Poll correctly without the help of punctuation; he
thought well of the poem, *qua* poem, and both Newbolt and
Conway were well pleased also.[15]

By the time *Poor Poll* was written, it is clear that much
of the foundation work for the ideas and the metre of *The
Testament of Beauty* had been done. The verses to his parrot

[11] *Collected Essays*, Vol. 2, No. ii, p. 36.
[12] *Collected Essays*, Vol. 7, No. xiii, p. 30.
[13] *Collected Essays*, Vol. 7, No. xv, p. 89.
[14] *Ibid.*, p. 89.
[15] *Correspondence of Robert Bridges and Henry Bradley* (Oxford, 1940),
p. 156. Letter dated only provisionally 1920; *Poor Poll* was published in 1921.

and other poems in *New Verse* are already exploring the naturalistic base for man's scientific and spiritual developments, and considering the details of his recorded history in relation to his evolutionary past and future.[16] It is, finally, the demands of these interests, the very impulse and driving power of the poem itself, that determined its versification. The polysyllabic words of science, the homely phrases of everyday living, and the highest reaches of his expressive power as equally parts of his experience, all needed a metre that would invite them into place and accommodate them with ease, elegance, or force, whichever might be appropriate. In the prefatory note to *New Verse* Bridges explains this:

I saw that all the old forms of 12-syllable verse, the Greek iambic, the scazon, the French Alexandrine &c., would be admitted on equal terms. It was partly this wish for liberty to use various tongues that made me address my first experiment to a parrot, but partly also my wish to discover how a low setting of scene and diction would stand; because one of the main limitations of English verse is that its accentual (dot and go one) bumping is apt to make ordinary words ridiculous; and since, on theory at least, there would be no decided enforced accent in any place in this new metre, it seemed that it might possibly afford escape from the limitations spoken of. And thus I wrote *Poor Poll*.[17]

The lack of pretense behind this new venture is very pleasing; in the poem itself, Bridges laughs at the whole idea: To the parrot he says:

I am writing verses to you & grieve that you sh'd be
absolument incapable de les comprendre,
Tu, Polle, nescis ista nec potes scire:—
Alas! Iambic, scazon, and alexandrine,
spondee or choriamb, all is alike to you—
my well-continued fanciful experiment
wherein so many strange verses amalgamate
on the secure bedrock of Milton's prosody:
not but that when I speak you will incline an ear

---

[16] *Poetical Works of Robert Bridges, excluding the Eight Dramas and The Testament of Beauty* (London, 1936).
[17] "Note," *Collected Essays,* Vol. 7, No. xv, p. 90.

in critical attention lest by chance I might
possibly say something that was worth repeating:
I am adding (do you think?) pages to literature
that gouty excrement of human intellect
accumulating slowly & everlastingly
depositing, like guano on the Peruvian shore,
to be perhaps exhumed in some remotest age
(piis secunda, vate me, detur fuga)
to fertilize the scanty dwarfd intelligence
of a new race of beings the unhallow'd offspring
of them who shall have quite dismember'd & destroy'd
our temple of Christian faith & fair Hellenic art
just as that monkey would, poor Polly, have done for you.
                    (*Poor Poll*, lines 76 f.)

Considering all these things, Bridges seems justified in his
choice of a long-lined, unrhymed metre which would permit
him to use diction ranging from the old poetic words through
everyday words to scientific polysyllables, and to create
rhythms echoing both past great poetic utterance and all
manner of speech-rhythms as well. But even Guérard, who
on the whole feels that the metre is successful and recognizes that it has a part in the "youthful gusto and imaginative
fertility"[18] of the poem, hedges in saying that "a more vertebrate meter, such as blank verse, would have helped the
average reader considerably."[19] Running through the adverse
criticism, and there is a good deal of it, is a strain of doubt
whether the choice of metre was well advised. It is nearly
always impossible quite to distinguish between a criticism
of the metre itself and of Bridges' handling of it; perhaps
one need not. It is enough to point out an uneasy sense that,
wonderful as it is from time to time, the poem meets an
insuperable barrier to greatness in its versification. These
criticisms come from the very writers whose view of literature and whose development of principles of criticism one
finds helpful and necessary in understanding poetry. They
know fine poetry, they are poets of distinction, many of them,

[18] *Robert Bridges,* p. 246.
[19] *Ibid.,* p. 246.

yet even when they admire *The Testament of Beauty* and love it, they are qualified in their praise of the versification. Winters, who believes Bridges and Hardy to be "the two most impressive writers of poetry in something like two centuries,"[20] remarks, "*The Testament of Beauty,* by Robert Bridges, offers one other experiment toward a carry-all form, which I should like, but am unable to admire."[21] Tillyard implies that the metre is not enough to give "the something behind the statement" which is needed for the best poetry.[22] Thompson says that the metre "falls readily into a kind of jog-trot. . . . Its rules depend so completely on the poet's own sense of speech-rhythms, that, if this sense momentarily flags, caprice seems to take a hand . . . sometimes too much is huddled into a line—or, contrariwise . . . a line is left loose and the voice must therefore pad it. . . . He was concerned with his message, and rhythm and verbal music or power were secondary, and not always that."[23] Guérard feels that "this belated freedom" must be regarded "with mixed feelings. If it permitted an almost unparalleled vivification of wide learning . . . it also admitted lines as pedestrian as any in English poetry."[24] Stauffer finds the lines of *The Testament of Beauty* wavering, billowing, and irregular.[25] The most sweeping disapproval comes from Eliot: "I would give all his ingenious inventions for his earlier and more traditional lyrics."[26]

This is a formidable battery of criticism from some of the finest of our vanguard critics, including some whose reading of the poem has obviously been careful and devoted. A dissenting voice can hardly forbear to fall back on Charles Williams' rather plaintive query, "But how can any one

[20] Winters, Ivor. "Robert Bridges and Elizabeth Daryush," *The American Review,* VIII, 353.

[21] Winters, Ivor. *Primitivism and Decadence* (New York, 1937), p. 139.

[22] Tillyard. *Poetry Direct and Oblique,* 1st ed., p. 117.

[23] *Robert Bridges,* pp. 108, 109.

[24] *Robert Bridges,* p. 245.

[25] *The Nature of Poetry* (New York, 1946), p. 212.

[26] Eliot, T. S. *The Music of Poetry* (Glasgow, 1942), p. 12.

prove that the lines of the poem are effective, when his opponent has merely to deny?"[27] He himself gives a rousing yes and no: "though the rhythms of that poem [*The Testament of Beauty*] are anything but prosaic, yet perhaps its total conclusion leaves us more directed toward the dominion of prose than poetry."[28] Many readers, however, have felt the poem to be regular in its rhythms, measured, and patterned, although one looks in vain for satisfactory explanation of its versification.

Bridges himself has helped to establish the heresy that after decades of traditional verse-writing and constant experimentation he threw humdrum to the winds and proceeded into the harum scarum of free verse. His remarks about it are unassuming in the extreme. His lines he calls "loose Alexandrines" (II, 841); to his experimental procedure he gives almost a hit-or-miss character: "I had no notion how the thing would hold together when thus apparently freed from all rule. It was plainly the freest of free verse."[29] But one should note that he says "apparently," and must remember that behind these casual remarks lie years of plotting to arrive "at very rich and varied rhythms" by means of "a very definite form of marked effects and possibilities."[30] One should not be deceived by the atmosphere of carelessness created by the absurd use of the word "thing" to indicate the prosody he finally evolved. He carefully distinguished between free verse and his experiments in "Humdrum and Harum Scarum": "In carrying on Milton's inventions in the syllabic verse there is better hope of successful progress than in the technique of free verse as I understand it."[31] There may be a kind of wit behind his deprecating ways, just as

27 Williams, Charles. *Reason and Beauty in the English Poetic Mind* (Oxford, 1933), p. 92. He was not talking of *The Testament of Beauty*.
28 *Ibid.*, p. 172.
29 "Note," *Collected Essays*, Vol. 7, No. xv, p. 90.
30 *Ibid.*, p. 89.
31 *Collected Essays*, Vol. 2, No. ii, p. 55.

there surely is in *Poor Poll's* likening of accumulating literature to accumulating guano. Certainly Bridges had the utmost technical skill, and the most sensitive ear, trained by
years of music study, and it is unreasonable to suppose that
he would have let a poem go from his hands before it had
satisfied that ear in all its parts. That the metre is capable
of beautiful effects, all have admitted, and Tillyard, at least,
has seen something positively good in turning away from
traditional versification: "Apart from the great beauty of
isolated passages, what most matters is the prosodical
courage."[32]

Can we say exactly what this metre is? For several years
after the poem was published, there was a certain amount
of articulate disagreement as to its rules. This kind of misunderstanding went back to the appearance of its early form.
Bridges tells us: "The reason for my writing this [the *Note*]
is that the strict construction of the verse is not likely to be
understood without my explanation. On its first appearance,
for instance, there was a learned account of it in the *Times*
by the Secretary of the British Academy, which was altogether wrong."[33] There still lacks a full account of its character, although as far as he goes, Guérard is so clear and
accurate that one may summarize his conclusions.[34] Specifically, there is an unalterable rule that each line must have
twelve syllables, except for the two dozen or so that have
ten chiefly as a kind of punctuation at paragraph ends. The
rules of elision followed by Milton and amplified in one
respect by Bridges, may be called upon to reduce to the
required twelve whatever extra syllables we might count up
on our fingers. This, Guérard calls the one rule, expressing
negatively the other two characteristics that are important.
These twelve syllables are not arranged by feet, and the

[32] Tillyard. *Poetry Direct and Oblique*, 1st ed., p. 270.
[33] *Collected Essays*, Vol. 7, No. xv, p. 87.
[34] *Robert Bridges*, pp. 281-84.

accents are speech stresses, not metrical, that is, counted, accents. Since there are no feet to measure syllabic quantity, there can be no quantity, in the classical sense.

This description of the prosody of *The Testament of Beauty* is so meagre that it cannot possibly account for the power of the poem, but to cut from the preliminary statement all the usual verbiage of iambic and trochaic, pentameter and hexameter, falling rhythm and rising rhythm, substitution and feet, is so important that it bears repeating: the line consists of twelve syllables, and there are neither divisions into feet, nor other evidence either of metrical accent or syllabic quantity as the traditional English and classical prosodies use those words.

This meagreness undoubtedy has puzzled critics of *The Testament of Beauty*. As to previous writers in the science of metrics, they would declare that either *The Testament of Beauty* had no metrical system worth mentioning or that the analysis of it must be incorrect. Probably Saintsbury would have been the liveliest critic of the theory, although one cannot doubt that he would have read the poem correctly. Whether he would have gone back on his basic assumption that you simply cannot have poetry without feet, is another matter. Possibly that mysterious something he had with the power of determining feet, would have found them in *The Testament of Beauty*. There may be very sound objections to a metre having only the rule of twelve syllables, certainly. It is doubtful whether the ordinary ear can detect temporal values in a syllabic rule without recognized rules of quantity or some other means. Bridges tried by years of experimentation to transplant quantitative measures on the Latin model into English poetry, and discarded the attempt long before he came to *The Testament of Beauty*. The very greatest metrical skill and the keenest listening ear would be needed to create and detect regularity in mere count of syllables in English. More obvious to the listener as a measure, is the regularity of accent present or assumed in traditional English versification and in such experiments as Hopkins'. Without rules of quantity, without a pattern of accent, without rhyme, Bridges had to find another rule to make his metre vertebrate.

It was probably Bridges' classical training and his fine musical ear that caused him to write along Patmore's line of thinking about metre. To Patmore, metre's chief function is to measure off equal time intervals, "isochronous intervals," he calls them.[35] He never quite specifies that these intervals may be lines, as well as feet, but without doubt he applies the rule to lines. He insists that the short line is lengthened by the requisite pause, to fill out the time of his long line, and that the time length chosen is established early in the poem.[36] Bridges never specifies that his "twelves," as lines, are measured in isochronous intervals, either. He had learned, however, "to *think* in quantities."[37] This statement makes most sense when it is read to mean that he had learned how to adjust the twelve syllables of various duration into lines of equal duration. He had learned to do this without crushing (or rushing) an overbalance of long ones, or expanding artificially in reading, an overbalance of short ones. In other words, by ear and ear alone, he had learned to write twelve-syllable lines that are measurable by time, without an artificial system of quantity such as Greek and Latin poetry depends on.

Now this may be possible for the poet, if his time sense is very acute. But what about the reader? It seems clear that some criticism of *The Testament of Beauty* is based on a reading that does not recognize these isochronous intervals. When they are recognized, *The Testament of Beauty* has the steady pace, with full and even movement, that is the quality of nonaccentual syllabic or quantitative verse in

---

[35] Patmore, Coventry. "Essay on English Metrical Law," in *Poems by Coventry Patmore* (3d collective edition; London, 1887), II, p. 219, and *passim.*
[36] *Ibid.,* p. 239f.
[37] *Poetical Works,* Note to *Poems in Classical Prosody,* p. 408.

foreign languages. We know very little as yet about equal time intervals in English poetry. Bridges observed in a footnote to the "Letter to a Musician": "Indifference to quantity is the strangest phenomenon in English verse. Our language contains syllables as long as syllables can be, and others as short as syllables can be, and yet the two extremes are very commonly treated as rhythmically equivalent."[38] But however indifferent the theory of English verse may be to quantity, in practice it seems probable that poets have expected readers to observe time intervals more than is realized. A full examination of this factor for definitive results is a technical matter for the psychological laboratory.

Although much of this is speculative, the hypothetical conclusion may be formulated that the twelve-syllable rule for *The Testament of Beauty* is amplified by a strict rule of equal time length for every line, the equal lines being marked always, but with varying strength and a great variety of phrase "end-of-line pause." Specifying such a pause is the means. These means will be lumped inaccurately under the necessary complement to Guérard's analysis, and it is assumed as a reading device, if not a metrical one, by Smith. He cautions readers to observe "that pause, often infinitesimal, which is implied by the ending of each line."[39]

Although Bridges himself calls his line an Alexandrine, loose, to be sure, it is not a true French Alexandrine, with all the authority of that metre. However, he was aware of, and considered deeply the possibilities inherent in, French prosody. In a letter to Bradley, commenting on the poems of Jammes, he shows that during the period of preparation for the writing of *The Testament of Beauty*, French poetry was in his mind: ". . . he makes me despair of finding out how to get English rhythms to do that which the French does so admirably."[40] Guérard, without drawing the conclusion to

[38] *Collected Essays*, Vol. 7, No. xv, note 1, p. 74.
[39] Smith, Nowell Charles. *Notes on 'The Testament of Beauty'* (Oxford, 1931), p. xxxiv.
[40] *Correspondence of Robert Bridges and Henry Bradley*, p. 153.

its end, and neglecting the fact apparently that the syllables in the French are regularly long and short, remarks: "... the meter is identical with the French Alexandrine."[41] The use of the word "Alexandrine" is, however, welcome here, with its suggestion of French prosody which is at least as formal and regular as any prosody in English. One could wish, nevertheless, that Bridges had put into words the second important part of this regularity; he assumed the syllabic regularity, and also specified it. He did not specify the temporal regularity, nor the end pause, as one may assume them in the French.

[41] *Robert Bridges,* p. 183.

CHAPTER THREE

THE THEORETICAL JUSTIFICATION OF
THE NEW METRE

Why should it be necessary to establish the theoretical base of the metre of *The Testament of Beauty* and the fact of the end-of-line marker with finality? In a complete study of any poem, no details are out of place, but this book is limited to the discussion of its unity. All details must be used to show how Bridges had unified and enlivened disparate experiences, from outbursts of wonder and joy to scientific fact and philosophical reasoning. The justification lies in the nature of the adverse criticism that many of the most sensitive and sophisticated students of poetry have aimed at this poem. These critics believe that the sound of a poem, which is based on its metre, is a primary factor in creating movement of idea and feeling and in giving shape, direction, and completeness to diverse material. They have not apparently heard, however, the variations of tone and expression which, when imposed on a firm and regular metre, prevent the "disconsolate patches" Bridges deplores in free verse,[1] nor appreciated the "rhythm of fluctuating emotion"[2] firmly based, as a structural element. Stated concretely, they cannot have read the poem as Smith advised: "Read it aloud, with no attention to anything but the sense and that pause, often infinitesimal, which is implied by the ending of every line."[3] And the reason that they have not, is that they have not recognized this end-pause as the essential indication of the metric regularity, in principle as well as practice. Not

[1] "Humdrum and Harum Scarum," *Collected Essays*, Vol. 2, No. ii, p. 49.
[2] Eliot. *The Music of Poetry*, p. 18.
[3] Smith. *Notes . . .* , p. xxxiv. Guérard considers that the rhythm "overrides the barrier of the line end." *Robert Bridges*, p. 247.

recognizing it, and being serious students of prosody, they would not yield readily to the suggestion that they read without paying any attention to the versification.

There is obviously a confusion here between the reading of a poem and the understanding of its prosody. But the confusion is not cleared up by separating the two; they are inextricably bound together. The relation, of course, between the way various people read a poem, and the metric structure of the poem itself, is not a clear one. Good poetry-reading is like violin-playing, requiring all the resources and experience of the reader for the best results. But good reading cannot make bad poetry good, although the hypnotic affect of a warmly sympathetic voice emphasizing regular rhythms not actually there has often been noted. If a poem does not compel the voice, then it is the virtuoso who is creating its effect. Thompson has said that the voice must pad some of the lines in *The Testament of Beauty*.[4] However, although it is certainly true, as Guérard points out, that "the prosodial explanation of a line defines its basic structure, not the way in which it is read,"[5] the relation between the basic structure and the reading is very close and flows both ways. The metre must compel the reading, but a misunderstanding of its prosodic principles may weaken its compulsive power. The mind is recalcitrant, and, clinging to preconceived ideas, it directs the voice so energetically that the poem loses out. Unfamiliarity with the prosody of a poem is the greatest handicap to its full understanding, as Bridges himself points out: "Now the limitation of metres . . . offers a form which the hearers recognize and desire, and by its recurrence keeps it steadily in view. Its practical working may be seen in the unpopularity of poems that are written in unrecognizable metres, and the favour shown to well-established forms by the average reader. His pleasure is in some proportion to his appreciation of the

4 *Robert Bridges*, p. 108.
5 *Robert Bridges*, p. 270.

problem."[6] But to speak away from the general reader to the advanced student of poetry who is perfectly aware of these possible barriers to his understanding: "Apart from the desire which every artist must feel to have his work consistent in itself, his appeal to an audience would convince him that there is no chance of his elaborate rhythms being rightly interpreted unless his [prosody] is understood. Rules must therefore arise and be agreed upon. . . ."[7]

Some of the previous discrepancy of report on the success of the metre of *The Testament of Beauty* arises from the fact that those who have read it correctly have not fully or correctly analyzed it, including Bridges himself, and those who have analyzed it best, have based their analysis on an incorrect reading. A good example of the former is Smith, who, perfectly aware of the invariable end-pause, pays tribute to the rigorous discipline of the versification[8] without mentioning the end-pause in his analysis of the prosody. Guérard is an example of the latter; his accurate analysis stops short of the essential because he has not heard the line-end barrier. But it is extremely important not to be content with counterstatement because it is on serious critical principles that careful objection to the versification of *The Testament of Beauty* has been made. These principles involve the complex question of the aesthetic values of elaborate rhythms and how they are created. The position is admirably expressed by Guérard: "The absence of a fixed scheme of feet and accents deprived him of the opportunity to introduce various subtle metrical substitutions which a poet working in blank verse, for instance, may use."[9] This principle has come to be expressed by the word "counter-

[6] "The Necessity of Poetry," *Collected Essays*, Vol. 10, No. xxviii, pp. 221-22.

[7] "Letter to a Musician," *Collected Essays*, Vol. 7, No. xv, p. 64. I have omitted the words "treatment of syllables" and substituted "prosody" for them, Bridges' definition of prosody in this essay being "the treatment of syllables."

[8] *Notes* . . . , pp. xxxiv-xxxvi and p. 95.

[9] *Robert Bridges*, p. 246.

point." It is of course a musical, not a literary, term, first used, I think, by Patmore, and given currency in our day by interest in Hopkins' use of it to explain the effects of his sprung rhythm. The word "substitution," used by Guérard, is the more exact and limited word, and it stems from Saintsbury's explanation of Coleridge's practice in *Christabel*. Bridges was well aware of the function in fine poetry, and uses the word "counterpoint" to cover the effects. First, he speaks of its value in ornamentation:

A great deal of our pleasure in beauty, whether natural or artistic, depends on slight variations of a definite form. Fancy if all roses were as similar in shape as all equilateral triangles! The fundamental motive of this pleasure may be described as a balance between the expected and the unexpected—the expected being a sedative soothing lulling principle, and the unexpected a stimulating awakening principle. Too much of the type would be tedious, too much of the unexpected would worry. The unexpected stimulates the consciousness, but you must also be conscious of the type. Or this *balance* may be regarded as a *strife* between two things, the fixt type and the freedom of the variations: and metre gives the best possible opportunity for this kind of play, which is really comparable to Nature's, for no two lines of a poem are exactly alike: they differ much as do the leaves of a tree: and a pleasure arises from our knowledge of the normal rhythm (the type) beneath the varieties which the poet delights to extend and elaborate: his skill in this sort of embroidery being to push its disguises as far as he dare without breaking away from the type.[10]

If it were not for the use of the word "strife" in this passage the matter of the infinite variations on the metre would seem to be merely a matter of ornament. With the idea of a real struggle between two forces, that overcoming of obstacles which is the special beauty of art (II, 495) comes the secret of the significance of counterpoint, a significance that lies in the bloodstream of poetry. For all poets of dramatic tendency, no doubt, both Shakespeare and Donne, for instance, and in the minds of several of today's outstanding

10 "The Necessity of Poetry," *Collected Essays*, Vol. 10, No. xxviii, p. 222.

poets, the counterpoint that matters arises from the struggle
of the rhythms of speech with the metred rhythms of verse.
Bridges is explicit about this. First, he insists that there is a
"tyranny" in speech-rhythms, and that "one of the difficulties
in writing good verse is to escape" from it.[11] Some of our
present critical thought seems to suggest that it is in the
complete liberation of the speech-rhythms that the greatest
poetic values emerge. But with our best contemporary poets,
Bridges believed that the tension between the two produces
the finest effects when it is at its most taut. And he believed
this to be true in classical verse as well as modern English:
"If we take verses by Virgil, Dante, or Milton, who were all
of them artistic geniuses, we find that their elaborate rhythms
are a compound, arrived at by a conflict of two separate
factors, which we may call the *speech-rhythm* and the *metric
rhythm*."[12] The speech-rhythms he insists "were always
present; they constituted in classical verse the main variety
of effects within the different metres, but they were *counterpointed*, so to speak, on a quantitive rhythm, that is, on a
framework of strict unaccented time."[13] But this counterpoint is not merely that of one rhythm "floating" over another
or "mounted" upon the other,[14] but a real tension, in which
the metre must set up a fairly strong opposition. The metric
rhythm is the abstraction, the pattern, which is established
in our minds; it creates expectancy of repetition. The speech-
rhythm is the surprise factor; it depends upon what the poet
has to say for which we are waiting; we do not know what
he will say before he says it. The balance between the two
creates the poetic effect, that effect being at its strongest
when the opposing forces are nearly equal. The belief that
Bridges' metre does not set up a sufficient antagonism to his
speech-rhythms, lies at the heart of the criticism which is

[11] "Humdrum and Harum Scarum," *Collected Essays*, Vol. 2, No. ii, p. 51.
[12] "Letter," *Collected Essays*, Vol. 7, No. xv, p. 56.
[13] *Ibid.*, p. 72.
[14] *Poems of Gerard Manley Hopkins* (3d ed., edited by W. H. Gardiner, New York, 1948), p. 7. (Hopkins' preface.)

expressed by Stauffer in the words "billowing," "wavering," and "irregular."

The theoretical question as to whether the metre of *The Testament of Beauty* is capable of this true counterpoint, depends then on whether the rules of syllable number and end-pause are really prosodic rules; the practical question depends on whether it provides sufficient regularity to combat the tyranny of speech-rhythms. That the metre is both sound and sufficient must therefore be established. First, is it sound in theory? Does it agree with recognized metrical principles of which Bridges himself was aware? Second, is it really true to the text of the poem that each line is composed to end with a pause of some degree?

As to the theoretical foundation of this metre, it must be confessed that nowhere in either Bridges' or other prosodists' writing can a full justification be found for it. The basic, though incomplete or unexplained, assumptions that accent must be the prime factor in English verse, and that end-of-line pause is a reading device, not a metrical one, are not accepted by all metrists, but the disagreements among them have scattered the fragments of thinking to the winds. Ker remarked of them: "They do not seem to care whether any one listens to their teaching; they seldom listen long to one another."[15] The result is that there are many crevices into which this new metre may fit, but a consistent theory of it must be worked out from the beginning.

There are four questions on whose satisfactory answers depend confidence in the versification of *The Testament of Beauty*. First, can accent be abandoned in English as a prosodic measure? Second, must all lines in English poetry be divisible into feet? These questions are related by the fact that normal English accentual metre depends on division into feet to establish the lighter and heavier accents by which it is counted. The next two questions are related also,

[15] Ker, W. P. *Form and Style in Poetry*, a review of Saintsbury's *History of English Prosody* (London, 1928), p. 317.

in this case by the factor of time, or duration. Third, what are the theoretical relationships of syllables-quantity-time in English verse? Fourth, can pause be considered a prosodic device, or is it merely a reading device? There is disagreement on all these points in the literature of versification; the answers were sought wherever possible, but are in the following pages worked out essentially from Bridges' own writing. The chief documents are his "Letter to a Musician" (1909), the notes to *Poems in Classical Prosody* (1916) and to *October and other Poems* (1920), "Humdrum and Harum Scarum" (1922), and the "Explanation of the Prosody of My Late Syllabic 'Free Verse' " (1923).

First, the relation of accent to metrical structure in English verse. There is a very strong tendency to assume that a regular accentual pattern is essential to English verse; its absence in *The Testament of Beauty* has led several critics to ask for a variation from a kind of norm not attempted or even taken for granted, as it is by Hopkins in his sprung rhythm. There is no logical reason for this assumption, although the practical reason lies in the fact that the English language has a strong speech-stress. Bridges sheds light on this problem in a letter to Henry Bradley, written at the time when he was experimenting with William Stone's system of English quantity. He is struck by the fact that in Latin verse there is "a nearly uniform accentual pattern for the ends of the hexameter and pentameter." Searching for a reason, he concludes: "I may be wrong in my explanation, but I have supposed the reason to lie in the fact (now very widely acknowledged) that Latin, unlike Greek, had a fairly strong stress-accent, and that in consequence the identity of rhythm in a long quantitative verse was obscured unless it was reinforced by some accentual regularity at the line's end." In writing quantitative verse in English, he considers using the same device: "As English has a stress-accent probably even stronger than that of Latin, the reasons for an accentual fixed type at the end of the line, if they were valid for Latin, ought to be still stronger for English. But it does not follow that the pattern ought to be the same in English as in Latin."[16] More than twenty years later, Bridges discarded not only the Latin pattern for accentual regularity, but accent itself as a marker, however effective he found it to add expression to the line. The requirement, he apparently came to see, was merely that some sort of reinforcement of the rhythm of a long time-measured line was necessary. There is no hindrance here to assuming that "a nearly uniform," indeed, an invariable, end-pause would equally well provide such reinforcement.

It is true that in 1909, Bridges' theory leaned heavily on accent as a metrical necessity. He said that "every metre has a typical accentual rhythm of its own,"[17] and even in discussing Dante and Virgil he identifies prosodic metre with rhythm of accent. However, he makes it very clear, by a most amusing experiment with choirboys and organ, that quantity, and quantity alone, is responsible for rhythm; he found that pitch and loudness (the usual determinants of accent) were inefficient for this purpose.[18] This is confirmed by Lanier: "No rhythm is possible without quantity."[19] That is, accent is not essential to rhythm, but quantity is. He distinguishes finally, of course, when he is talking of metres which are repeated rhythms, between the quantitative metre, where the quantities are fixed and the accents free, and the accentual metre, where the accents are fixed and the quantities free.[20] His position in 1909 (not a very revolutionary one, but making some interesting distinctions sometimes slurred over) is, then, that quantity is sufficient in prosody,

[16] *Correspondence of Robert Bridges and Henry Bradley*, pp. 14-15. Letter dated 23 January 1902.
[17] "Letter," *Collected Essays*, Vol. 7, No. xv, pp. 65f.
[18] *Ibid.*, pp. 59-63.
[19] Lanier, Sidney. *Science of English Verse* (New York, 1880), p. 67.
[20] "Letter," *Collected Essays*, Vol. 7, No. xv, pp. 65-66.

but accent is a useful and, in some way not quite clear, a parallel, device in metre, even though presumably quantity must still be the essential rhythmic factor.

By the time he comes to his explanation of the versification of *Poor Poll*, however, the evaluation of accent has changed. The "Note" to *New Verse* says nothing about accent as a determining or even necessary factor in metre. It expressly disclaims accents: "because one of the main limitations of English verse is that its accentual (dot and go one) bumping is apt to make ordinary words ridiculous; and since, in theory at least, there would be no enforced accent in any place in this new metre it seemed that it might possibly afford escape from the limitations spoken of."[21]

Consideration of the question in the light of Bridges' own remarks on prosody, then, gives us leave to believe that although he held that a pattern of accent might be present in quantitative verse, it was unnecessary, even in English where quantity in the classical sense was not possible. And further we find that its absence might be a virtue under some circumstances. He had discovered the tendency to alternate accent to be "the norm and bane" of syllabic verse.[22] It is likely that the absence of accentual pattern seemed a virtue to Bridges when he discarded it later under the circumstances of his long poem, *The Testament of Beauty*. He would not have apologized for turning from it on either theoretical or practical grounds, because he would have been confident that he had produced some of those rich and varied rhythms he felt lay ahead and unexplored after his experiments in classical prosody, although he had learned that it was impossible to transplant classical quantities into English.

To move on to the second question, the assumption that there should be a norm of accentual pattern in English verse includes the idea that the accentual pattern itself is deter-

[21] "Note," *Collected Essays*, Vol. 7, No. xv, p. 90.
[22] "Letter," *Collected Essays*, Vol. 7, No. xv, p. 69.

minable by the arrangement of the syllables into feet. The two hang together first because, as Guérard points out,[23] the metrical accent is noted within the foot, as the most pronounced of the syllables of that foot, and not merely as the more pronounced of the syllables scattered in the line. They hang together, also, no doubt, on the analogy of quantitative prosody, where the long and short syllables are measured within the foot. That Bridges has discarded the foot, however, as part of his metre in *The Testament of Beauty*, is affirmed by Guérard. He says, it will be remembered, that "the *differentia* of Bridges' meter is its abandonment of the accentual-syllabic division of the line into feet."[24]

Nevertheless, in the "Letter to a Musician," Bridges' very definition of prosody assumes division into feet: prosody "primarily denotes the rules for the treatment of syllables in verse, whether they are to be long or short, accented or unaccented, elidible or not, etc., etc. . . . Then the syllables being fixed, their commonest combinations (which are practically commensurate with word-units) are defined and named; these are called *feet*. And after this the third step of Prosody is to prescribe metres, that is to register the main systems of feet which poets have invented to make verses and stanzas."[25] This is certainly the traditional view, and no doubt the view of most poets past and present, as well as prosodists.

There are indications, however, that even as early as 1902, Bridges did not think it necessary to work toward preserving the foot. During his experiments in classical quantities, he wrote to Bradley, "Nothing wd. induce me to make the feet show too plainly."[26] And in "The Letter to a Musician" he points to the break-up of the foot *de facto* in Milton. "For all Milton's free speech rhythms, which are the characteristic beauty of his verse, and by their boldness make his original-

---

[23] *Robert Bridges,* p. 270.
[24] *Robert Bridges,* p. 284.
[25] "Letter," *Collected Essays,* Vol. 7, No. xv, p. 65.
[26] *Correspondence of Robert Bridges and Henry Bradley,* p. 17.

ity as a rhythmist, are confined by a strict syllabic limitation, viz., that the syllables which compose them must . . . be resoluble into so many 'iambs.' But these so-called iambs are themselves now degraded to nothing, for the disyllabic unit which still preserves that old name has no definition: it has lost its quantities, nor are its lost quantities always indicated by accent or stress; its disyllabic quality, too, is resoluble by the old law of Latin elision into trisyllabic forms."[27] He comes to call the iambs "fictive iambs." But the final logical step of discarding the conception of feet in his prosodic theory was not taken in the various notes to his volumes of poetry. Although in "Humdrum and Harum Scarum" he gets along very well without mentioning feet, one cannot assume thereby that he has discarded the principle implied by the word. Throughout even the note to his *New Verse* the word appears, "six foot" being interchangeable with "twelve syllable." However, in summary of his practice, there is an interesting shift in terminology: "This 12-syllable verse then is written by the rules of Milton's Prosody with only this difference, viz. that it forbids the extra-metrical syllable *at the end of the verse*."[28] The last phrase has been italicized to point to the fact that finally Bridges himself has stopped talking about feet. Of course, it would still be possible to say that in his twelve-syllable line one must consider every other syllable as the first syllable in a foot, but it would be indeed a fictive foot to match Milton's fictive iamb.[29] Guérard's idea that the foot no longer applies in discussing the metre of *The Testament of Beauty* is preferable. The theoretical question, however, as to whether such a practice is prosodically sound, is not settled. As an aid in composition and in reading to measure off isochronous intervals, the ear holding a specified number of small units as the large rhythmic unit better than the larger rhythmic unit itself, it has

---

[27] "Letter," *Collected Essays*, Vol. 7, No. xv, pp. 72-73.
[28] "Note," *Collected Essays*, Vol. 7, No. xv, pp. 90-91.
[29] "Letter," *Collected Essays*, Vol. 7, No. xv, pp. 72-73.

proved useful if not invariable throughout the history of poetry. But with another aid, the end-pause, say, why is it necessary either in theory or practice? Apparently Stauffer is working toward this idea, although he does not quite state it.[30]

The two questions so far discussed have been related in their usual connection; accent and feet are established terms in metrics. The next two are equally important and are related because they both refer to that kind of analysis which deals with time as a basis. First, what is the relation of time to syllables and quantity? Second, can pause be a metrical factor in versification?

The fundamental question here really is whether a verse form can be based on the principle of equal time units measured by the line, without reference to rules of syllabic quantity. Classical prosody creates lines of equal time length by adding up equal numbers of feet, which are in turn constructed according to a system of syllable length making each foot equal in duration. It does not admit that the lines can be equalized in any other way. Patmore, so far as I know, was the first to suggest that the important thing is the temporal line length; he goes to the point of saying that the measurement of the lines of his odes included the length of time necessary to pronounce the words, plus the pause, which is lengthened by ear to fill up the isochronous interval. Whether in normal accentual verse the psychological laboratory will show either kind of equal line lengths remains to be seen. In Bridges' essays and notes, his thought moves toward a statement admitting "quantity" in the sense of clock time measured by lines, not syllables, as a possible fundamental for a metre in English verse, but the statement is never made. It is always necessary to push what he says, and he says it frequently in the prose under examination, a step further than he goes. It is possible that he might consider this splitting hairs; it is also possible, as some readers of this discus-

[30] *The Nature of Poetry*, p. 221.

sion may feel, that he never meant anything he said to indicate his belief that equal line lengths could be the basis of a sound prosody; the third possibility is the true one, I think, that at the time he discussed these matters most fully, he did not himself see where his experimentations would lead him, or what the final step in theory would be.

There is a good deal of relevant quotation to support this interpretation, but to somewhat monotonous effect. Most of the key ideas are in "The Letter to a Musician." The notes to the several volumes are less significant, but it will be necessary to show from the final explanation of his "free verse" that no contradictory ideas are there.

In the first place, the idea of quantity in English verse was a matter of great importance to Bridges in the period which extended approximately from the publication of *Shorter Poems,* in five books, in 1894, to the second edition of *Poems in Classical Prosody* appearing in 1916. During the period, he had been experimenting with William Stone's theory of quantitative verse, following at first Stone's determination of lengths of English syllables, but gradually amending them. By the end of the period he had given up this strict discipline, but recognized its great value: "Though the difficulty of adapting our English syllables to the Greek metres is very great, and even deterrent—for I cannot pretend to have attained to an absolutely consistent scheme— yet the experiments that I have made reveal a vast unexplored field of delicate and expressive rhythms hitherto unknown in our poetry."[31]

It was during this period that "The Letter to a Musician" was written, and it reflects conspicuously Bridges' interest in quantity, whatever he meant or might come to mean by that word. He shows quantity to be the only indispensable quality of sound for rhythm in poetry, an idea supported by his choirboy and organ experiments. In discussing the three

[31] *Poetical Works,* p. 408.

distinct systems of prosody shown us by the history of European verse, the quantitive, the syllabic, and the stress, the
theory of the quantitive system (of the Greeks) is the only
one given a clear bill: it "was scientifically founded on quantity, because they knew that to be the only one of the three
distinctions of spoken syllables which will give rhythm of
itself."[32] He finds in the syllabic system no "definite prosodial
principle"[33] because modern European prosodies have not
developed artificial systems of quantity and their verse does
not demand a pattern of long and short syllables.[34] It is also
subject to the assertion in it of "different and incompatible
principles, indiscriminately overriding each other's authority."[35] He finds (in 1909) that the stress verse had no
recognized prosody.[36] But, and this is significant, "I have
experimented with it, and tried to determine what those
rules must be, and there is little doubt that the perfected
Prosody will pay great attention to the quantitive value of
syllables, though not on the classical system."[37]

If it were not for two points, we might find here a basis
for Bridges' later versification. These two points are, (1)
that quantity is clearly applied to syllables, and (2) that he
suggests that the future of English verse lies in the realm of
stress prosody. It may almost be assumed from the context,
however, that he is referring to a prosody dealing with
speech-stresses, not metrical accent, and he actually specifies
that great attention must be paid to quantity.[38] In the second
place, there are hints that "quantity" is considered as an
actual time measurement, in contrast to its artificial character
in the Greek system.[39] He has already said that their system

[32] "Letter," *Collected Essays,* Vol. 7, No. xv, p. 66.
[33] *Ibid.,* p. 67.
[34] *Ibid.,* p. 70.
[35] *Ibid.,* p. 67.
[36] *Ibid.,* p. 74.
[37] *Ibid.,* p. 74.
[38] *Ibid.,* p. 74, note 1.
[39] *Ibid.,* p. 67.

was actually founded on the fact that duration is the basis of rhythm.[40]

To understand these hints, we may pick up the references to Milton's versification. They are rather confusing in relation to our knowledge of Bridges' admiration for Milton which had already been fully presented in his book *Milton's Prosody*. The course of ideas is as follows. In discussing the syllabic system he has called it "a wretched skeleton"[41] in itself, although he admits that perhaps the greatest variety is possible over the simplest base.[42] But the suggestion is that the varieties overran syllabic verse when syllables lost their specified quantities:

In the syllabic prosody in which the prosodial rules were so much relaxed, [these] speech-rhythms came in the best writers to be of the first importance and in Milton . . . we can see that they are only withheld from absolute authority and liberty by the observance of a conservative syllabic fiction, which is so feature-less that it needs to be explained why Milton should have thought it of any value.[43]

He goes on to elaborate that the "so-called iambs are themselves now degraded to nothing." But there is no explanation of the value of this fiction, although the later poetry of Milton is called "carefully composed"[44] and "the secure bed-rock of Milton's prosody"[45] is considered in the essay "Humdrum and Harum Scarum" more hopeful for the future of English poetry than free verse.[46]

Bridges does not clear up this difficulty in any of his theory, and it is dangerous business to say what a writer probably meant when, so careful in analysis and practiced in composition, he leaves an idea apparently at loose ends. But the whole problem is solved if one may imagine the

[40] "Letter," *Collected Essays*, Vol. 7, No. xv, p. 66.
[41] *Ibid.*, p. 70.
[42] *Ibid.*, p. 71.
[43] *Ibid.*, p. 72.
[44] *Ibid.*, p. 73.
[45] *Poor Poll*, line 83.
[46] *Collected Essays*, Vol. 2, No. ii, p. 55.

possibility of extending the time unit from the syllable (and the foot made up of measured syllables) to the line (made up of a strict count of syllables). Thus stated, this does not sound like a rash extension. Even as far back as 1909 one may find a statement which, interpreted in the light of this extension, provides the prosodic authority for *The Testament of Beauty.* He says that in classical verse, speech-rhythms "were counterpointed, so to speak, on a quantitive rhythm, that is, *on a framework of strict (unaccented) time,* which not only imposed necessary limitations, but certainly in Latin, to a great extent determined their forms."[47] This could not have referred to the versification of *The Testament of Beauty,* but the base of that versification could hardly have been expressed better. It remains only to consider whether the marker for the reader of this framework of strict time, not its determination by the poet, because that is a matter of ear, could have been conceived by Bridges to be what is here called the end-pause.

Nothing is clearer than that he never said so. The caesura, of course, is recognized as a rule in the Anglo-Saxon and the Middle English of *Piers Plowman,* for instance, and in classical and regular English hexameters. Bridges deliberately dropped the caesura in his 1921 experiments, following the precedent of Milton. "I saw that these twelves, or Alexandrines, had in Milton's practice no title to a fixed caesura. In all his work from earliest to latest he delighted in the Alexandrine without its hemistichs."[48] But there is in the "Note" nothing further about pauses, and from first to last, nothing about pauses at the end of the line to mark a regular interval that the ear would have difficulty in detecting without more help than a rule of twelve English syllables.

There is indeed apparently some primary difficulty in the study of pause. Prosodists generally accept the essential importance of pause to rhythm, it is true. Lanier believed that

---

[47] "Letter," *Collected Essays,* Vol. 7, No. xv, p. 72.
[48] "Note," *Collected Essays,* Vol. 7, No. xv, p. 90.

constantly in beautiful verse, "the rhythm is absolutely dependent on measured silences, or rests, instead of measured
sounds."[49] Baum stresses the dangers of sing-song and jog-
trot when regular pause is overused.[50] Perhaps it is significant that Bridges' report is affirmative. In "The Letter to a
Musician," having said that to express the rhythm of English
verse one freely uses the only three means at one's disposal,
quantity, loudness, and pitch, he continues: "There is nothing else you can do towards expressing rhythm, except that
(and especially in elaborately written verse) you will have
relied a great deal on pauses or silences of suitable duration.
These pauses are essential to good reading."[51]

The contradictions among writers concern matters of fact,
frequently, and stem from the inability of the ordinary un-
aided ear to make accurate judgments about time intervals.[52]
The question as to whether pause may compensate for
omitted syllables to fill out a line, is a case in point. Patmore's
reliance on pauses to regularize his line lengths has never
found much favor as a metrical theory, although in practice
readers tend to lengthen the shorter lines either by slower
reading or by end-of-line pause.

Whether by actual clock-time equal time units are really
achieved for each line, as Patmore contends, must be a matter
of laboratory measurement. Snell, in a study of pause made
in the psychological laboratory, quotes Omond as developing the theory of compensating pauses most fully. But she
believes her own experiments to discredit it. Her conclusion
is that "in the construction of metrical units, or feet, pause
may take the place of omitted light syllables; but pause does
not consistently make up the time of omitted syllables and
cannot therefore be a compensating element."[53]

[49] *Science of English Verse*, p. 101.
[50] Baum, P. F. *The Principles of English Versification* (Cambridge, Mass.,
1922), p. 61f.
[51] "Letter," *Collected Essays*, Vol. No. xv, p. 58.
[52] Snell, Ada L. F. *Pause; a study of its nature and its rhythmical function
in verse, especially blank verse* (Ann Arbor, 1918), p. 65 and *passim*.
[53] *Ibid.*, p. 84.

It is especially confusing that the relation between metrical, grammatical, and reading pauses has not been cleared up. Bridges makes the distinction briefly, but does not stop to develop the subject fully. He finishes with the remark that discussion of metrical pauses belongs "to a more advanced treatment of the subject."[54]

This section of the otherwise admirable "Letter" is, indeed, not very clear. Bridges has recognized the complexities and subtleties of metrical pauses, but perhaps in his avoidance of explanation, there is a reluctance to embark on something he has not yet thought out. The clearest statement of differentiation of pauses is given by Baum:

(1) The *logical* pause is that cessation of sound which separates the logical components of speech. . . . (2) the *rhythmical* pause separates the breath groups of a sentence and therefore concerns language chiefly as a series of sounds independent for the most part of logical content or symbolism. . . . (3) *Metrical* pause is primarily independent of the other two, but most frequently falls in with them. It belongs to the formal metrical pattern, and serves usually to mark off the line units. There is thus theoretically a pause at the end of every line, and a greater pause at the end of every stanza.[55]

Even though Bridges himself gives only a parenthetical page and a half to pause in his "Letter to a Musician," the soundness of his understanding of the principles of poetry, and the care and logic with which he usually works out his statements, make it possible to interpret his remarks on pause to illuminate his practice in *The Testament of Beauty*. The relationship he detects between the metrical pause and the grammatical pause is the relationship which contributes most to the fine effect of the versification of that poem.

First there are the metric pauses, which merely isolate balancing sections of verse-rhythm. Then there are the grammatical pauses or stops: these are interruptions of the metric rhythm, which are either condoned for the sake of the sense, or are observed to

[54] "Letter," *Collected Essays*, Vol. 7, No. xv, p. 59.
[55] *Principles of English Versification*, pp. 61-62.

indicate and separate the ever-varying sections of the speech-
rhythm (being thus to speech-rhythm what metric pauses are
to metre).[56]

If the definition of metric pauses is shorn of its qualification
"merely," it stands as good theory behind *The Testament of
Beauty.* "The metric pauses isolate balancing sections of
verse-rhythm," that is, in *The Testament of Beauty*, the balancing sections, which are lines, are isolated, separated, by
markers which bear close relation to pauses of all sorts. But
by delicacy of ear and technical proficiency in reconciling
idea, feeling, grammar, and twelve-syllable units, the grammatical pauses are not interruptions of the metric rhythm to
be condoned; they do indeed indicate and separate the sections of the speech-rhythm, enforcing thereby the metrical
pattern of isochronous intervals measured by line length.
Once embarked on his long poem, Bridges wrote no more on
metrical theory.

[56] "Letter," *Collected Essays,* Vol. 7, No. xv, pp. 58-59.

CHAPTER FOUR

THE END-PAUSE

Nothing stands in the way of accepting the theoretical soundness of the metre of *The Testament of Beauty*, I think, except *a priori* views about the nature of the relation of the English language to poetry. It may be said that accentual verse corresponds with the accentual nature of spoken English, but if Bridges is correct in his assumption that Latin also had "a fairly strong stress-accent" (he must have meant speech-stress), certainly a stressed language may be molded into poetry by a quantitative system. It is true that English verse lines cannot be measured by quantitative rules which do not exist, but they can be measured by ear, and marked by the poet as a guide to readers whose time-sense is less acute than his. Syllable number and duration of line provide sufficient regularity in classical verse and French and Italian verse, and, in theory, may provide regularity of versification in *The Testament of Beauty*. The second question must now be considered: Is it true that each line is composed to end with a pause, marking equal line-lengths? It is indeed true that the question of whether each line of the poem actually takes the same number of seconds to be read, can only be answered after experimentation in a psychological laboratory, where even the techniques for this sort of thing are still in their initial stage. But the attempt must be made to establish the recognition of the end-pause as a true perception of the dominant factor in the versification of *The Testament of Beauty*.

There are three difficulties here, and the first is that proof of the fact of pause at the end of any unpunctuated line is impossible. The individual may certainly read as he likes.

47

Secondly, figures in literary criticism seem remote to many
people, even to students, and valueless. As Bridges said, "the
grammar of any art . . . seems unrelated to the magic of its
delight."[1] Even more its arithmetic. Figures, the method
here used, are indeed less accurate and prove less than some
of their proponents would contend. But many critics use
the authority of figures, or at least proportions, without the
justification of making as good a count as they can. For instance, the most impressionistic critic might say (if he believed it) that "most" of Bridges' lines have an end-pause.
Smith even went so far as to say that "each of them" has such
a pause. One can be much more explicit. In spite of a margin
of error and indecision from reading to reading, there are
figures which, if followed by the reader, will point out quite
conclusively that the basic pattern of the versification is set
by the end-pause. The third difficulty is with the term itself.
The complications of the terminology are important enough
to stop for in some detail, and explanation of them is necessary for the proper understanding of what follows.

In the meaning of the psychological laboratory, the word
"pause" ought not to be used here at all, nor is it to be
equated with the phenomenon of the rest in music. It is thus
defined by Snell: "Pause is a cessation of sound; but this
cessation is of two sorts,—a cessation of sound with the vocal
organs in motion and a cessation with these organs at rest."[2]
The study from which the definition is taken deals with the
latter only, but as a marker at the line-end, both are considered here. Further, Snell's records show that her readers
often mistook greater intensity, unusual duration of the
word, or a fall in pitch, for pause; they also show that punctuation did not always command a pause from her readers.[3]
In the laboratory, then, the phenomenon here discussed is

[1] "The Necessity of Poetry," *Collected Essays*, Vol. 10, No. xxviii, p. 193.
[2] Snell. *Pause*, p. 4.
[3] Snell. *Ibid.*, p. 12, note 1, and p. 19, note 1. Noted also by Patmore.
Essay, p. 240.

not one phenomenon, but several, and should not be desig-
nated by the word "pause." "End-of-line-marker" would
probably be a safer term to use, but it is awkward. Further,
the end-of-line-marker may be equivalent to a rest in music;
if *The Testament of Beauty* is ever tested in a recording
apparatus that can measure the clock time of its lines, perhaps it will be shown that the time units from the beginning
of one line to the beginning of the next, that is, line plus
pause, are identical. Without such scientific measurement, no
such identity can be assumed. It is probable that the equal
time units predicated here are merely marked off by the
pauses, which in themselves may be of varying duration. It
is possible, however, that like the musical rest, they are
added to the line, line and pause then making a duration
equal to that of the next unit.

In this investigation it was found that the pattern of pause
in Bridges' versification is (1) set by the lines whose sense
demands the pause, (2) confirmed by those whose sense
encourages it, and then is (3) varied and embellished for the
greater beauty of the poem by the movement of those lines
in which the issue of pause is placed somewhat in doubt. In
these last, the sense asks for a run-on line and the sound of
the words used, or some syntactical inversion, requires a
pause.[4] It will be recognized as reasonable that the most
pronounced pauses are of course those which are demanded
by sense, and that the easiest to achieve by aesthetic means
are those at least encouraged by sense. There are a few lines
probably which are for meaning best read without an end-
pause; sense and syntax encourage the *enjambement;* perhaps some of these may run on without metrical hindrance.
However, from one reading to another, it is never quite
certain that the sound does not ask for a slight lengthening
out and slowing, or even hesitation at the end, to prepare for
an accent or a dental at the beginning of the next. Snell has

[4] Snell's recording confirms the possibility of this. *Pause,* pp. 14, 48.

found, in corroboration, that once a rhythm is established, her readers paused for no other reason.[5]

But that the basic pattern of the verse is set by the proportion of lines with a marked end-pause is clear. First, there are lines actually stopped by punctuation marks, comma, dash, brackets, semicolon, colon, or period; there are 2,035 of them, nearly half of the 4,374 lines of the poem. The regularity is established further by the 806 added lines where the sense clearly asks for a pause and where a fussy punctuator might even have placed a comma, although it would sometimes be annoying. Bridges, a light punctuator, preferred to omit the comma, but the sense demands the pause. This final number of lines, about five-eighths of the poem, is surely a positive element in the pattern.

As to the remaining 1,583 lines, if the poem is read as Smith advises, all of them come to a pause, even if it is infinitesimal. But such a statement of course only begs the question. To try to answer it, a system of punctuation tapering off in intensity from the comma must be used. This system divides the unpunctuated lines into four groups. The first group has already been accounted for: there are 806 whose sense so clearly asks for a pause that commas would be possible. Here is an example:

III, 221
                    as once with Dante it was [,]
      who saw the grace of a fair Florentine damsel . . .

The second group has 522 lines. These lines are clearer, mean more, and sound better when a perceptible pause is given. For instance, in the continuation of the above lines:

III, 221
                    as once with Dante it was [,]
      who saw the grace of a fair Florentine damsel [,]
      as WISDOM UNCREATE. . . .

[5] *Pause*, pp. 25-26.

A pause after "damsel" permits a stress on "wisdom" that improves that line in sound and sense. And also:

II, 173
> —nay, incommunicable and beyond all compare [,]
> are the rich influences of those moments of bliss. . . .

A pause after "compare" permits the whole next line to be read as a unit, in marked contrast of tune with the first.

The remaining thousand lines (the count cannot continue to be exact) include two classes, those lines which can be read to advantage in sound, with no interference from the sense, if they are given the benefit of the doubt, and the last group already defined as doubtful and varying from reading to reading. As suggested, the first group is by far the largest. In the examples, the slight pause is indicated by the slur ⁀ :

III, 297
> provide tales of despair, ⁀
> disease and madness; melancholy tragedies
> of ignobility unredeem'd, to scare mankind.

Here it is best perhaps to lengthen out the second half of the line; in any case, the *ies* of *tragedies* can stand time for a kind of meditation, with emphasis on *unredeem'd* easier to realize. The following lines show the two degrees of pause, the end of the second line, as indicated, belonging in the above group. The third line has to my ear the lightest of all the pauses.

II, 7
> Thus Plato recordeth—how Socrates told it
> to Phaedrus on a summer morning, as they sat [,]
> beneath a lofty plane-tree by the grassy banks
> of the Ilissus, talking of the passions of men.

(There are two others of this kind, one ending like this one with *banks* and the other with *embankments*.) Here at first, the *enjambement* seems complete; the sense is clearly "banks of the Ilissus," and the vowel in *of* and the anapaestic movement of *of the Ilissus* enforce it. But if the whole passage, the first ten lines of Book II, are read with the pause acknowledged up to this point, even these lines contribute to the ordered serenity if the very slightest pause be allowed.

But this is so much a matter of intangibles, or possibly even, inaudibles, that one is reluctant to put a figure to the number of such lines. When the pattern of sound in the ear is imposed by the dominance of the unavoidable or preferable pauses, no one single line can be set aside without some hesitation; yet there may be considerable variation in readers' willingness to accept this pattern. At the most, however, there are only about sixty lines (seven in Book I and approximately eighteen in each of the other three) about which there should be serious quarrel. It seems very clear that Bridges has set the pattern of end-pause with finality.

The metrical regularity of *The Testament of Beauty* was based on prosodic theory toward which Bridges himself was obviously moving, although he did not analyze the poem's versification after he had finished it; a close examination of every line shows how the metre was worked out. This regularity has been felt by many sympathetic readers, some of them, Smith and Elton, for instance, quite aware of "the strict construction"[6] which Bridges claimed for it. Others, and probably the majority, have felt the regularity because they have heard the pause in their own or another's proper reading. In coming to a consideration of the effects of this metre, the reader of the preceding pages may well wonder whether such invariable rules as twelve syllables and end-pause may not be monotonous and mechanical. However, the positive value of the sound elements permitted and caused by the metre are so strong as to make the negative criticism unimportant. Positively approached, the prosody creates effects beautiful in themselves, and vital in their fusing and

[6] "Note," *Collected Essays,* Vol. 7, No. xv, p. 87.

structural influence on the whole poem. First, some of the familiar music of accentual metres is allowed to appear from time to time, the use of both accentual pattern and end-pause giving special emphasis to these lines. Second, there is a constant play of variation in the marking of the end-pause comparable in richness to the more usual kind of counter-point in English poetry.[7] But most important of all, this metre permits the inclusion of all the poem's disparate experience in appropriate idiom and inflection by liberating the speech-rhythms under the discipline of isochronous lines. By this, a voice emerges as the auditory evidence of a dramatic figure, which with range of utterance sufficient to encompass all the material, nevertheless unifies the poem into a kind of interpreted story of mankind.

Once the reader's ear has caught this voice, charges that the verse of *The Testament of Beauty* is monotonous and mechanical seem empty. As to monotony, oddly enough it has been attributed not to the regularity, but to the "perpetual variety" of the metre.[8] However, in reading with an end-pause, the effect is monotonous only if the voice is allowed to drop. Snell testifies that her subjects frequently accompanied a pause with a drop in pitch.[9] This must be avoided almost as rigorously in *The Testament of Beauty* as it is to be avoided in French poetry: the pause should be observed either by a lengthening out of the voice with pitch unchanged, or by a rise in pitch varied by the emotional context. So read, the lines completely avoid monotony.

No careful, responsible reader of *The Testament of Beauty* could for long believe it to be mechanical in its versification. However, there is some theoretical objection to both the end-stopped line and the line measured by an invariable number of syllables. Objection to the former appears especially in

---

[7] Guérard is aware of effects that parallel normal metrical substitution, but does not, of course, attribute them to variations of the end-pause; *Robert Bridges,* p. 246.

[8] Guérard. *Robert Bridges,* p. 246.

[9] Snell. *Pause,* p. 47.

the historical treatment of literary matters, as in the orthodox statements concerning the end-stopped line versus the run-on line. Saintsbury, for instance, calls both the middle- and end-pause in blank verse "a prosodic go-cart to the infant."[10] Keats's epithet "rocking horse" for Pope's metre is the classic objection to the monotony felt in end-stopped lines. But how reasonable is the idea that in increasing the number of his run-on lines the poet automatically shows his skill and improves his verse? It is true that as Shakespeare needed greater flexibility to express his deepening psychological insight, he gradually but steadily increased the proportion of run-on lines. He did not thereby increase their music, and it will be recognized that where his purpose is essentially poetic as distinguished from psychological or dramatic, the end-pause is emphasized. The poets of the romantic period certainly opened up the iambic pentameter line for new purposes beyond the desire of Pope if not beyond his scope, by their use of the *enjambement*. But however Keats's verse benefited by this freedom, and much of its beauty depends on it, he returned to the pattern of Dryden in *Lamia*, a far more muscular verse resulting. In theory, there should be no party line about end-stopped and run-on lines, except that a poet should use, or rather practiced poets do use, sufficient regularity to allow diversity, the relation of the two being the condition of interest or beauty called counterpoint. In blank verse, with its expectancy of five accents and even more in the heroic couplet with its added rule of rhyme, the rigidity must indeed be mitigated by considerable flow from line to line. Without rhyme, or regular accent, the lines of *The Testament of Beauty* must hold themselves to their established time unit by some other means and make it clear that they are doing so.

The great need, when the regularity is assured, is to avoid the mechanical, either the dot-and-go-one bumping possible

10 Saintsbury, George. *History of English Prosody* (London, 1906-10), I, p. 410.

in accentual verse, or the rocking horse of the couplet, or the mere chopping up of prose into lines of twelve syllables. Bridges' techniques for avoiding the mechanical in his use of end-pause will be spoken of later; here will be considered the possible objection that the syllabic measurement, "always to the count of ten," as Shapiro calls it in Milton,[11] is merely subjecting sentences to a sausage machine set at the measure of twelve syllables. Primarily, reading experience is sufficient evidence from within, and a knowledge of Bridges' proficiency in writing a great variety of metres, corroboratory evidence from without, that there was nothing mechanical about the use of this metre. We can further trust Bridges' own account of the writing of *The Flowering Tree*, where he first used it. "It ran off quite spontaneously," he said.[12]

But perhaps forty years and more of writing verse develops such facility that such writing in itself may be called mechanical. This accusation would not be made by the responsible critic, but the mere statement of the poet's experience is not really more than interesting here: the problem is, whether there is or is not something essentially *poetic*, that is, from this point of view, alive and organic, rather than mechanically contrived, in the lines of *The Testament of Beauty*. Can one isolate in any way the movement of these lines from the poetic idea, or the poetic diction, or the poetic quality of the metaphors, and say that some part of the effect is traceable directly to the rhythmic pattern arising from the versification? This is what one would always like to do to support one's perceptions, but one must acknowledge that the final demonstration is impossible. However, something may be learned from the close comparison of certain passages from *The Testament of Beauty* with parallel passages in the lecture on poetry delivered in 1929 as the first of the Broadcast National Lectures.[13] The ideas of the separate passages

[11] Shapiro, Karl. *Essay on Rime* (New York, 1945), p. 187.
[12] "Note," *Collected Essays*, Vol. 7, No. xv, p. 88.
[13] "Poetry," *Collected Essays*, Vol. 10, No. xxix, p. 243.

are identical, their diction and syntax almost identical; yet one is prose, emotional and inspired, to be sure, and the other poetry. There are at least half a dozen of these sections long enough and close enough to provide comparison. In the lecture, Bridges starts off with the question how he can satisfy his listeners by speaking worthily on a great subject: "I do not say that I should take stock of my spiritual aspirations; or set out a shop window of my philosophy of life; but in some sort I should systematize my aesthetic faith . . ."[14] His following remarks may be set parallel with a verse paragraph in Book IV of *The Testament of Beauty:*

Lecture, p. 243f.

and in the field of emotion discriminate those subtle psychic influences,

whereby man comes

to awareness of eternal things, and by glimpses of mysterious vision is drawn within the attraction of that creative energy which is the source of all Being whatsoever.
    (5 lines omitted)
while Science, patient Science, toiling apart in the workshop, is intent on her OWN, other Invisibles; and, working back to the Atoms, wil handle and harness them as she is doing for us tonight,

in serviceable obedience to Man's material needs.
Nor is Science to be interrupted in her devotion nor called off her task; for she too dreams amid the

The Testament of Beauty, IV, 660f.

Delicat and subtle are the dealings of nature,

whereby the emotionable sense
    secretly is touch'd
to awareness and by glimpse of
    heav'nly vision drawn
within the attraction of the
    creativ energy

that is the ultimat life of all
    being soe'er:

While Science sitteth apart in her
    exile, attent
on her other own invisibles; and
    working back
to the atoms, she handleth their
    action to harness
the gigantic forces of eternal
    motion,
in serviceable obedience to man's
    mortal needs;
and not to be interrupted nor
    call'd off her task,
dreaming, amid the wonders of
    her sightly works,

[14] *Ibid.,* p. 243.

wonders of her sightly works
by her own INFINITESIMALS to
arrive herself at the unsearchable Immensities of Creation.

thru' her infinitesimals to arrive at
last
at the unsearchable immensities of
Goddes realm.

There is not much to point to in the analysis of these passages in proof that one is prose and the other poetry; the
differences are too subtle to assign to very precise causes.
However, the first test is to see whether the lines of the lecture may be set up verbatim, as twelve-syllable lines. They
cannot, taking the passage as a whole. Taking it in parts,
there are a few sections that can be so divided, using of
course the same rule of elision as Bridges would use in poetry
when necessary. One sets out this way:

And in the field of emotion discriminate
those subtle psychic influences whereby man comes

(eliding *emoshun* and *influ nces*).
Here the division into twelve-syllable units is stopped: the
next line is broken at *glimp* before *ses*. Then let us try this:

discriminate those subtle psychic influences
whereby man comes to awareness of eternal things

(no elision in *influences;* elide *to awareness*) and continue:

and by glimpses of myster(i)ous vis(i)on is drawn
within the attraction of that creativ energy

and we find that the last line here is like the poem, with
"thatt" substituted for "the," which changes the stress. And
the next clause, "which is the source of all Being whatsoever,"
is impossible to divide.

Further, the prose, highly rhythmical as it is, runs to longer
units of rhythm than the poetry, and the units are not repeated. In "Humdrum and Harum Scarum," Bridges speaks
of these differences: "in the verse you have a greater expectancy of rhythm, and that comes of the rhythms being

more marked and predetermined and confined . . ."[15] And further along, "and since there is no short speech-rhythm in prose which might not be used as a metrical rhythm or a part of some metrical system, the only difference would seem to be that in prose the rhythms were not evident or repeated; if repeated you would come to expect them,"[16] and also, the units of the rhythm in the prose, as most readers will agree, are different from each other in length. When it comes to the passage in *The Testament of Beauty*, the matter will lie in doubt with many. This passage is one that must be practiced to be read with the marked separation of lines as rhythmic units; it is a passage whose counterpointed rhythms are strong, where the tensions between the two are achieved by reliance on most of the devices Bridges had at his command for the final victory of the line, the most important here being the requirements of breathing. It will be noticed that in the fourteen lines quoted, there are only two which end in a strong grammatical and meaning pause, indicated by period and semicolon. Unless the breath is manipulated skillfully, it is impossible to read the passage to give value to both meaning and sound. If it is manipulated skillfully, it will be found that the two may be made to balance. Lines 461 to 463 and line 467 are the most difficult to manage, but practice will produce an effect that will impress even a very skeptical listener.

It is clear, then, that something has happened to the prose of the lecture "Poetry"; prosodic skill has turned the material into verse. A full analysis of the sound of *The Testament of Beauty* shows the degree of this skill, but this book has the limited intention of showing only the unity of the poem. Therefore this section on the prosody will develop fully only the way that characteristic which contributes to the rule of isochronous lines, marked at the line-end, is handled with

---

[15] "Humdrum," *Collected Essays*, Vol. 2, No. ii, p. 38.
[16] "Humdrum," *Collected Essays*, Vol. 2, No. ii, p. 39. *See also* "Letter," *Ibid.*, Vol. 7, No. xv.

complexity and grace, and second, the way the speech-rhythms, permitted but molded by the lines, become audible as a human voice.

There are, however, aside from this prime function, many other effects of sound created within the metrical pattern. Too many friendly readers of the poem speak, for instance, of the familiar accentual patterns to allow this aspect of the music to be entirely ignored. Nothing is more certain than that *The Testament of Beauty* is not written in an accentual metre: if one tries to read any page, or even any five lines, with an accentual base in mind, chaos comes again. But there are accentual patterns discernible, and usually one may find good reason for them where they are. Sometimes, not always, when there is traditional lyric material and feeling, the movement of individual lines is traditional. The passage descriptive of the mounting wildness of the storm, and the peace of its passing, begins with two iambic six-foot lines, with traditional substitutions:

I, 277

  The sky's unresting cloudland, that with varying play
  sifteth the sunlight thru' its figured shades, that now . . .

and ends with two:

I, 295

  and the immortal fireballs of her uttermost space
  twinkle like friendly rushlights on the countryside.

The intervening lines slide in and out of the pattern of six iambs, the variations usually being in the same way analyz-able as traditional substitutions. This, however, is an unusu-ally long passage with such movement. Sometimes, a line which has no enrichment from sensuous or metaphorical words is brought into the canon of poetry by the familiar music, as in the following:

II, 660

  and with rich thought atone the melancholy of doom.

The second of the two lines called by Thompson "the greatest lines ever written"[17] is clearly composed in six iambic feet:

I, 35

> things supreme in themselves, eternal, unnumber'd
> in the unexplored necessities of Life and Love.

Further, a fairly consistent use of four speech-stresses to the line may be noted, although concentration on them destroys the full subtlety of sound to be heard when stress is understated. The presence of whatever accentual pattern there may be found is not evidence of "more than one metrical structure," although this condition may account for the beauty of some English poetry, according to Eliot.[18] Beneath the additional accentual music, the firm base of the metre goes on unaffected. And it is over this firm base that the most interesting variations play.

The discovery of the firm base of the metre was in itself interesting, but far more rewarding was the growing perception of the variety of methods used to achieve it, and the aesthetic effect of the gradations of the degree of pause. An examination of the many ways Bridges has achieved the end-of-line marker brings out his skill and originality and at the same time will show what justification, if not necessity, there is for the metric pause. This examination will not include the extremes of pause, the actually punctuated and the uncertain lines, in spite of the fact that this begs the question of both extremes. As to the first, Snell believes that her experiments give no support to the "once popular notion that punctuation always indicates a pause,"[19] and as to the second, the very critical reader would wish proof above all of the debatable lines. But these doubtful lines depend so much on the ear of the reader, that for demonstration of variety of method and effect, those lines only where the base is clear over which is "woven a seamless web of invisible strands"

[17] *Robert Bridges*, p. 116.
[18] *The Music of Poetry*, p. 12.
[19] *Pause*, p. 19, note 1.

(I, 727) can be used. It is true, however, that so talented a poet as Bridges meets the problems of the extreme lines with equal skill. Even in the punctuated lines, he was not content with an unadorned sense pause, and the effects are of the finest when his resources are most taxed by the contention of the aesthetically contrived pause with a thought flowing from line to line.

Even reducing the number of lines to be discussed by omitting the punctuated and the questionable pauses, there remain about fifteen hundred. There is a considerable problem of how to deal with these, when the shadings and variations are so many and so subtle that each one could be treated in itself. The following are merely convenient groupings of methods for setting the end-pause: there are pauses created by (1) syntax, (2) use of long syllables or juxtaposition of consonants, and (3) demands of breathing.[20]

There is extraordinary variety in the sentence structure of *The Testament of Beauty*, a variety which expresses intricacies of thought and shifts of feeling, as well as giving texture and accent to the sound of the whole. By means of this variety, Bridges has created a movement to his verse regularly measured by syntactical end-pause that is never awkward or obtrusive. Among the syntactical variations, the following will be illustrated; most of them spring from some sort of inversion of the natural order of the simple sentence. They are: (1) the inclusion of a quotation ending at a line-end, or the introduction to indirect discourse; (2) the inclusion of qualifying material; (3) its opposite, its omission by ellipsis; (4) a pronounced accent on the last syllable, to give emphasis to the meaning; (5) complex structure; (6) balanced structure. All of these are emphasized, when not created, by the established rhythm. They are readily detectable and may be illustrated profusely. They are of course

[20] Snell found similar determinants of the pauses her readers made in their reading of *Paradise Lost*. *Pause*, pp. 14-15.

at bottom, pauses to elaborate or clarify meaning; in a metic-
ulously careful reading for the exact sense of the passages,
the pauses, although not essential to understanding, help a
great deal. These structural pauses or markers for emphasis
show how subtle Bridges has been. He has taken his least
"poetic" factor, the elaboration of his thought, and put it to
the service of his fundamental prosodic device. In most
poetry whose complexity of meaning is important, there is a
war going on with poetic form. Here they are allies in "a
living compact." (II, 826) The distinctions among them,
made for arrangement's sake, are often faint, and were after
all created by the ear of the poet, not by his analytical mind.
Therefore the critical analysis is artificial, if clarifying, and
it is ear, not mind, that has detected the differences.

One of the most obvious of these pauses is that called for
but rarely punctuated, before and after a quotation. Before
the quotation:

IV, 898
>   thatt old proviso [,]
>   *nisi ipse intellectus* is futile to me. . . .

After the quotation:

II, 355
>   or when, tho' *summer hath o'erbrim'd their clammy cells* [,]
>   the shorten'd days are shadow'd with dark fears of dearth. . . .

Between the verb and the statement in indirect discourse:

IV, 538
>   rather say I [,]
>   that as man realizeth his higher energies . . .

and IV, 878
>   Now seeing the aim of Socrates we must inquire [,]
>   what the Mind's cóntents are; how disorder'd; and why [,]
>   ther should in the good mind be any disorder at all.

Marking an ellipsis which would be filled out in prose:

I, 50

>   I felt at heart
> a kinship with it and sympathy, as children wil [,] [feel]
> with amicable monsters . . .

I, 198

> our hope is ever livelier than despair, our joy [,] [is]
> livelier and more abiding than our sorrows are . . .

III, 770

>   suddenly escaped the visibles
> are changed to invisible; the fine-measured motions [,]
>   [are changed]
> to immeasurable emotion; the cypher'd fractions [,]
>   [are changed]
> to a living joy that man feeleth to shrive his soul.

Related to the ellipsis is Bridges' habit of not marking with a comma, but implying one, between items in a series, and not putting either "and" or a comma between two adjectives:

I, 365

> Not emotion or imagination ethick or art [,]
> logic of science nor dialectic discourse . . .

III, 172

>   with unlimited power
> to vary the offspring in character, by mutual [,]
> inexhaustible interchange of transmitted genes . . .

Of the pauses demanded by some inversion of a straight declarative sentence, of course complex structure is the most obvious. Bridges' use of a preliminary clause, exactly measuring a line, seems simple and easy in the extreme, and so it reads:

IV, 582

> Forever on the asses bridge and in the ship of fools [,]
> life is agog . . .

II, 502

> Beneath the spaceless dome of the soul's firmament [,]
> he liveth in the glow of a celestial fire . . .

The less expected inversions give a particular tone to Bridges' style in general, an elaboration and decoration which occurs often in those passages picked out by adverse critics for their bareness and starkness. That they are perhaps numerically the most constant determinant of the end-pause is the point made here; they occur in several different sorts:

IV, 656

    and once again on this wise, "If ther be any sin [,]
    "unpardonable even in the wide compassion of God" . . .

III, 407

    because of the two love songs which pedantry hath saved [,]
    of Sappho's complisht artistry . . .

III, 824

    he would make shipwreck, and of mere brutality [,]
    fall to pieces . . .

IV, 183

                     while some
    belittle also our Ethick, saying the subject is [,]
    of matter unknowledgeable in scientific sense . . .

Grammatically, of course, these inversions suggest a pause, by separating essential parts of the sentence. Another kind of separation of parts which needs to be marked with a pause, is the use of qualifying material, such as phrases in apposition, or elaborate adjectival or adverbial phrases. A long substantive:

III, 288

    Thus oft the full majesty and happiness of love [,]
    is found in lovers whose corporeal presences . . .

Phrase or clause in apposition:

III, 827

    and with faith in his hope and full courage of soul [,]
    realizing his will at one with all nature,
    devise a spiritual ethick for conduct in life.

Noun separated from verb by qualifying or explanatory material:

IV, 854
> nay, see the starry atoms in the seed-plot of heav'n [,]
> stripp'd to their nakedness are nothing but Number . . .

A final group should be called rhetorical rather than grammatical, the pauses asked by balanced structure or pronounced accent:

I, 379
> cruel and tenderhearted, truthful and perfidious,
> imaginativ or dull—one man how loveable [,]
> another how hateful, alike man, brutal or divine.

IV, 1084
> whose Being is thatt beauty and wisdom
> which is to be apprehended only and only approach'd [,]
> by right understanding of his creation . . .

The device of accent occurs with a final word as in *not at all* (II, 84), *again* (II, 400), *to us* (II, 672), *for-why* (IV, 138), and as it is here:

I, 675
> nor is discerptible in logic, but is itsélf [,]
> an absolute piece of Being. . . .

Nearly always these structural pauses are reinforced by juxtaposed consonants difficult to pronounce without a gap between them, or by lengthened syllables made of labial or liquid consonants and long vowels which inevitably slow the enunciation. This seems elementary, but illustrations will show the need for pauses so induced. Beginning readers of *The Testament of Beauty* are struck forcefully and delightedly by the realization that they are not supposed to rush over the difficulties of the rough consonants, or underemphasize the long smoothness of the vowels. One has only to read a page or two, observing the terminal and initial syllables, to find how invariably the words emphasize, suggest, or make easy an end-pause which may or may not be created by other means.

A long passage will show the full effect of the end-pause on rhythm and sense better than a number of short examples:

IV, 1268

'TWAS at thatt hour of beauty when the setting sun
squandereth his cloudy bed with rosy hues, to flood
his lov'd works as in turn he biddeth them Good-night;
and all the towers and temples and mansions of men
face him in bright farewell, ere they creep from their pomp
naked beneath the darkness;—while to mortal eyes
'tis given, ifso they close not of fatigue, nor strain
at lamplit tasks—'tis given, as for a royal boon
to beggarly outcasts in homeless vigil, to watch
where uncurtain'd behind the great windows of space
Heav'n's jewel'd company circleth unapproachably—
'Twas at sunset that I, fleeing to hide my soul
in refuge of beauty from a mortal distress,
walk'd alone with the Muse in her garden of thought,
discoursing at liberty with the mazy dreams
that came wavering pertinaciously about me; as when
the small bats, issued from their hangings, flitter o'erhead
thru' the summer twilight, with thin cries to and fro
hunting in muffled flight atween the stars and flowers.

This is a passage with line-ends exceptionally unmarked by the demands of sense; as in other more lyric passages the thought flows from line to line as it does not when there is a more complex syntax for the expression of thought subtlety. But this smoothness and pace is suitable to the emotion of the passage. The smoothness is apparent even when the lines end in dentals: *flood-his, night-and* because the next lines begin with vowels; the following are less smooth, *watch-where, head-thru'*; finally, there is a definite pause needed between *thought* and *discoursing.* However, it will be found that even where the consonants do not stop the lines, their movement is modulated by the long vowels of *night, eyes, strain, boon, space, soul, dreams, fro,* and *flowers.* This is clearly an exceptionally flowing passage, but the music is emphasized and the whole made more lyrical, when the pause allowed by the vowels and consonants is given a value slightly more than called for by the sense.

These effects are repeated in all passages where the sense itself is more active, those in the following illustrations being especially fine. The slur mark rather than a bracketed comma is used to emphasize that it is the sound, not the sense, which is to be remarked.

IV, 55

ev'n by the common folk, that none the less pursue

their common folly interminably, and more and more
pamper despair that is the giant sorrow of earth ...

I, 16

a landscape so by beauty estranged
he scarce wil ken familiar haunts, nor his own home,
maybe, where far it lieth, small as a faded thought.

Many times, lines end with polysyllables with light terminal accents, and a vowel:

III, 949

and impute precocious puberty
to new-born babes, and all their after trouble in life
to shamefast thwarting of inveterat lust.

IV, 4

attempteth every mortal child with influences
of her divine supremacy. ....

III, 297

provide tales of despair,
disease and madness; melancholy tragedies
of ignobility unredeem'd, to scare mankind.

In an unrhymed poem, the occasional rhymes emphasize an end-pause:

II, 513

and ever as to earth he neareth, and vision cleareth

of all that he feareth, and the enemy appeareth
waving triumphant banners on the strongholds of ill. . . .

These pauses create a music as of melody, as well as constantly reaffirming the basic pattern of line-end pause. The pauses caused by dentals, sibilants, hard labials at the end of one line and the beginning of the next, often reinforced by accent (iamb-trochee) or the accent of sense (itsélf), give the needed variety and positive articulation. They are more often than not accompanied by a sense pause, which gives them less the effect of artifice, though artifice is there. Dentals:

IV, 334

sacrificed
to accompany their lord . . .

Dental and guttural:

IV, 505

who is apt
kindly to judge of good by comfortable effect.

Sibilants:

IV, 568

the unparagon'd nobility of the great virtues
standeth without controversy among them that know . . .

Nasals:

IV, 1132

In truth, "spiritual animal" wer a term for man
nearer than "rational" to define his genus . . .

Labials:

IV, 684

if but the teacher be himsélf
virtuous or musical . . .

This pause is also emphasized by accent, and in the following, the final iamb and the initial trochee are very definite:

III, 241:
     and lived thereafter in Love, by the merit of Fa<u>íth</u>
     <u>t</u>oiling to endow the world. . . .

We come now to those pauses which are created or accentuated by the demands of phrasing, as vocalists call it, phrasing based on a normal breathing unit. There is nothing completely forced about this, and the pauses may not be detected unless the reader has become particularly sensitive to the music established; in this group are some of the most beautiful lines in the poem. On the general possibility of relationships between poetic rhythm and respiration or heart-beat intervals, Stauffer has something to say in *The Nature of Poetry,* but his assurance that there are relationships is not of specific value here.[21] However suggestive the results may be, no very exact correlations are likely to be found in the psychological laboratory between poetic measurement and the physiological rhythms, though large-scale experimentation with reading verse paragraphs may reveal a normal speed and rhythm for reading. But in the individual reader of the specific poem there is probably a very individual adjustment, and versification in all its aspects must work to force the reader to approach the adjustment natural to the poet. If the versification is weak, or if the reader refuses to be bound by the metrical pattern, listeners will not be impressed by the regularity of the rhythms. Both Smith and Thompson testify to great success in reading *The Testament of Beauty* to bring out the dominion of poetry, and untrained readers soon catch on to the steady pace of the long lines read as separable units. The cause of this success must be Bridges' compelling metre: the subtle and minute quarrels between the verse rhythms as written and the individual's physiological rhythms are obviously settled in favor of the poem.

[21] *The Nature of Poetry,* Chap. vi.

The problem of the breathing unit and Bridges' line unit works out with many people as follows:

More than two lines cannot easily be read without a new breath; if a pause is required by the sense at the end of each line, a line to a breath is possible although the effect is monotonous; finally, a line and a half seems the best interval for breathing. When a passage is read in this breathing rhythm, the sense and the sound of the words pull against the regular pause that would otherwise come in the middle of every other even line, and the end of alternate odd lines. When the breath pause would naturally come in the middle of the line, Bridges has by sense pause or by aesthetic means mitigated its force. When the breath pause comes at the end of the line, the pause varies very considerably from line to line. Because this subject of reading techniques is inevitably a matter for the individual reader, illustration may not be immediately convincing, but an analysis of the following passage will show specifically how the above works out.

III, 64

> —a thing overlook'd
> among the agreeable superfluities of life,
> trifles good in themselves, and no more censurable
> than the fine linen of Ulysses and the brooch
> that Penelope gave him, nor the rangled shroud
> that she wove for his sire, nor any work of price
> that humbly doeth honor unto any temple of God. . . .

The effect of breathing in this passage, is to emphasize the pause at *censurable* where it is already asked for by the polysyllable with accent on the first syllable. The breath has come through the line and a half from "a thing overlook'd," where the breath was taken because of a dash. Line 69 also comes to a pause for the same reason. This determinant is stronger than the commas in the middle of lines 66, 68, and 69, and it is enforced further by the consonantal halt between *brooch* and *that,* and *price* and *that,* and the balance of the repetition of *that* in the three lines. The interweaving of these factors, the balance of the weights, the equalizing of the thrusts, causes the fine effect of these lines.

The assumption that most readers will finally read the crucial lines 66 and 69 with a pause, because their breathing demands it, is confirmed by other factors emphasizing the pauses. The smoothness of line 66 separates it from the preceding and following lines; in lines 65 and 67 the emphasis is on *n* (with the light *i* and *e* of *linen* and *Ulysses*). This leaves the last eight syllables of line 66 outstanding with the full m's and l's, with the wider vowels of *no* and *more* and *able*. This considerable lengthening, added to the drawnout *censurable*, combines with the breathing for a very distinct pause. To continue the passage, the abrupt word *brooch* demands a rest as in music, so that one may read on with "that Penelope gave him." The same is true of *shroud* followed by *that*, although the pause here is modified (and is thereby less monotonous) by the softer sound of the *d* after the *ch* of *brooch* and the longer vowel *ou* than *o*. These two *thats* following the dentals lead the ear to expect the pause after *price* and before *that* in line 69. However, the main element of pause here is breathing.

Another example will show that sometimes the breathing interval creates the pause when all other factors are against it:

IV, 785
> Suchlike co-ordinations may be acquired in man
> with reason'd purpose consciently, as when a learner
> on viol or flute diligently traineth his hand
> to the intricat fingëring of the stops and strings. . . .

Here the line and a half breath unit ending with *consciently* must be extended to two lines, because of the far greater difficulty of extending the breath over the two and a half lines from *as when* to *strings*. This is the kind of passage that has to be read several ways before the best one is found; the above way satisfies both sense and sound better than any other, and so read the lines have a very interesting movement, with considerable inflection and quality.

A somewhat briefer discussion of another passage will bring out another kind of effect produced by Bridges' handling of the end-pause. Here the reader is called upon to exercise his judgment, and with some practice he will find a poetic power he may have missed before. In several lines of this passage, the sense asks for the lines to be run-on, and they will be so read if the reader is not sensitive to the peculiar music, or the need to follow very flexibly the lead of syntax as guide to shades of feeling. But if read correctly, the realization of the power of the pause to contribute to both rhythm and meaning, will come as a birthday of surprisal. (IV, 36) Here are the lines:

III, 683

> and (wonder beyond wonder) here was harbour'd safe,
> flourishing and multiplying, thatt sect of all sects [?]
> abominable, persecuted and defamed,
> who with their Eastern chaffering and insidious talk [?]
> had ferreted thru' Europe to find peace on earth [?]
> with Raymond of Toulouse,—those ancient Manichees.

Taking the passage as a whole, the end-pause is marked by punctuation in three of the six lines; there is a semicolon stopping the preceding line, 682. Line 686 might easily have carried a comma after *who,* in which case the whole clause in apposition "with their Eastern chaffering and insidious talk" would have been set off by commas, providing for the end-marker in that line. This leaves lines 684 and 687 to be queried. Purely in the matter of literation in the last word of 684 and the first of 685, it is easy to say *sects abominable* without any pause, but reading on, both rhythm and sense are improved if the next line, "abominable, persecuted and defamed," are phrased separately. Further, with the pause, the phrase *sect of all sects* can be spat out with scorn, preparatory to delivering the three adjectives in the next line.

Line 687 proceeds by a quite different and interestingly contrasted movement, slower and smoother as befits the sense. There is no reason in meaning for a pause at the end, rather the contrary, but the wholeness of the phrase "peace on earth," its familiarity in quotation, asks for a pause. In these lines, then, we may hold up the line-ends by fractions of indecision, contrasting with the well-established rhythm.

Among the most flowing parts of *The Testament of Beauty* are the lyric passages, and they will be discussed in a moment. But the following lyric passage shows the prevalence and the essential rightness of the end-pause in a particular way. The passage is a long one, but it will be useful to quote it:

IV, 1218

> But if he join the folk, when at the cloze of Lent
> they kneel in the vast dimness of a city church,
> while on the dense silence the lector's chant treadeth
> from cadence to cadence the long dolorous way
> of the great passion of Christ,—or anon when they rise
> to free their mortal craving in the exultant hymn
> that ringeth with far promise of eternal peace . . .
> or should it happen to him, in strange lands far from home,
> to watch the Moslem host, when at their hour of prayer
> they troop in wild accoutrement their long-drill'd line
> motionless neath the sun upon the Arabian sands,
> hush'd to th' Imám's solemnel invocation of God,
> as their proud tribal faith savagely draweth strength
> from the well-spring of life,—then at the full Amen
> of their deep-throated respond he wil feel his spirit
> drawn into kinship and their exaltation his own. . . .

The reader in finding the rhythms, will be satisfied that he has done so, either by achieving some regularity of accent or some regularity of line length other than accent. Let him experiment by reading the passage aloud, first giving value to the end-pause, without drop in pitch, and slurring any accentual regularity he may be tempted to find. This reading will make sense, and a metrical regularity and beauty will be felt. Now let him read it, trying to establish six accents (varying a bit to five if he wishes) running on the lines as the sense dictates, as he might in reading a good blank verse; experience shows that this method creates major difficulties. Read a third time, the passage should come through with all its variations, and with its dominant musical tone expressive of the emotional value of the meaning.

What comes of these analyses? The end-pause, as fast a rule as the twelve syllables, with a greater metrical effect, is marked in such varied and constant gradations that one really cannot measure them. These gradations are produced by changes rung on words in their combinations, from meaning combinations to the combinations of letters; they produce and enforce the subtleties of tempo and phrasing which are the mark of the best poetry. Any sound metre, well handled, can produce these effects to these purposes. The long line in itself allows flexible and muscular thought to find its channel, the emphasis on the line as a unit, permits the speech-rhythms apparently to dominate, as they must appear to do in dramatic writing.[22] But this particular metre has certain particular values for the kind of poem Bridges wished to write. The regularity which is established so firmly by rhythmic units shorter than those of speech-rhythms, in reality tempers the tyranny of the speech- or meaning-stress it liberates from the accentual pattern. The twelve-syllable line permits the inclusion of Greek, Latin, Italian, and French quotation, with no wrenching of their essentially quantitative movement. The relinquishment of accentual pattern keeps the inclusion of commonplace words and realistic statement from becoming doggerel. On the whole, although criticism should rather claim that a metre is well used for its purpose than that it is the only conceivable metre for that purpose, Bridges' invention emerges as fitted almost exactly to his task, rather better than any of the traditional ones he might have used.

[22] Noted by Stauffer, *The Nature of Poetry*, p. 221.

It is in the permission of all kinds of speech-rhythms that we find the particular virtue of the metre of this poem; Bridges has made use of his freedom to combine the most recalcitrant material, the most various emotional tones. But it is also in the self-discipline of the equalized line that the harmony among the different kinds of passages is achieved. For instance, there is a range of length and importance of end-pause from the full-stop to the almost imperceptible, but further than this, there is a pattern of emphasis upon the pause which draws together the most unlike of the sections. The lightest, least emphasized pauses occur at opposite ends of metrical effect, in the sheerly lyrical passages, which one might call billowy, if one did not care for them, and also in the most scientifically factual or hypothetical; if one likes, crabbed, prosaic. This fact, which at first seems odd, can be thus explained. In the lyrical passages, Bridges has so used other poetic resources, alliteration, assonance, rhyme, familiar accent (with familiar lyrical material), that there is no questioning the poetic movement. Also in the fire and excitement of his feeling, the measured pauses tend to be left behind, as in Hopkins the regular accents are dropped. In the harder passages the tone aims to be free of artifice, to be that of the teacher trying above all things to be clear. Bridges' metre, with its steady pace and varying expression, has harmonized the extremes of material in the poem.

It is only if one has already sensed the unity given to the poem by the factor of oral exposition, that this can be seen as a poetic device in itself. Everything that Bridges has said in his "Letter to a Musician" about the counterpoint of speech-rhythms over the base of strict unaccented time applies to his poem. There is in it the constant tension of the end-pause with the human voice; the voice is thereby molded as the human voice is never molded in conversation or even in written prose. This is a very great metrical accomplishment, comparable to that of Shakespeare and Donne, not less diffi-cult than their creation of voice tones in blank verse and stanzaic forms, because his material contains so much that can only be associated with the human voice by the determined effort to allow nothing to conceal it.

This poem is almost entirely spoken; the effect of *The Testament of Beauty* is gained by changes of tone, sometimes subtle and sometimes in sharp and sudden contrast, always following the kind of feeling, thinking, or explanation expressed by each section. The peculiar part of this is that unlike the purely contemplative poem, the dialogue of the mind with itself (Arnold's *The Future*, or *The Buried Life*) the voice is not just or quite that of the poet himself. It is not on the other hand, of course, that of a fictional, limited individual, like Fra Lippo or Rabbi Ben Ezra, although the affinities of this poem are with the dramatic monologue, not with the contemplative lyric. The subject matter, also, is much more than the experience of an individual man. It is not exclusively the life of Robert Bridges, nor of any specific historical figure, as *Fra Lippo Lippi* attempts to be. It is life atomic, organic, sensuous, as well as self-conscient (I, 428), presented, contemplated, and speculated upon in tones of voice which are modulated as the experience of life unfolds. This is the feat achieved by the loose Alexandrines, and it is its accomplishment in part which dramatizes the philosophy rather than emotionalizing it.[23] The sound of the poem, giving the impression of voices, creates the unity which more than the details of the philosophy itself expresses Bridges' monism. The next chapter will try to reveal these voices.

[23] "George Santayana," *Collected Essays*, Vol. 8, No. xix, p. 162.

CHAPTER FIVE

THE VOICES REVEALED

If the major accomplishment of the metre of *The Testament of Beauty* is its creation of a variously expressive voice which unifies all the material of the poem, it is time to give a clearer and fuller idea of its diversity. The heart of the problem is the disparate nature of the material. Any reading brings out the major differences in effect between one kind of passage and another; all readers can pick out the superb lyric passages from the scientific data, by sound as well as by subject matter. Even experienced critics, however, have usually treated the former as the most "poetic," or indeed sometimes, the only really poetic parts of the poem. They say that the beauty of the whole is marred by the interpolation of the passages of scientific exposition and philosophic reasoning, where the verse becomes prose.

The poem can indeed be broken up and discussed as a loosely knit collection of lyric, narrative, descriptive, and expository passages if the voices are not heard. It will be useful to give examples of all these kinds.

First the lyrical: there are probably a half-dozen or so long passages marked in every reader's copy of *The Testament of Beauty*. These passages have a free, rapid, run-on, musical quality comparable in their effect on the emotions to Keats's *Ode to the Nightingale*, and many of Shakespeare's bursts of lyricism. The tragic note is not to be found in Bridges in these more released passages, but in his profounder, meditative lines. These are more rarely marked except by the true lover of *The Testament of Beauty*, but they are to be grouped in kind with that graver poetry one finds in Wordsworth at his very greatest, and in Hamlet's and Macbeth's more important

utterances. But it is by the lyrical nature passages that
Bridges has been most appreciated, and their quality is un-
deniable. "The sky's unresting cloudland" is probably the
best known of these, but each reader will have his own favo-
rite. This passage is too long to quote in full, but the dominant tone will be clear after the first ten lines or so:

I, 277

> The sky's unresting cloudland, that with varying play
> sifteth the sunlight thru' its figured shades, that now
> stand in massiv range, cumulated stupendous
> mountainous snowbillowy up-piled in dazzling sheen,
> Now like sailing ships on a calm ocean drifting,
> Now scatter'd wispy waifs, that neath the eager blaze
> disperse in air; Or now parcelling the icy inane
> highspredd in fine diaper of silver and mother-of-pearl
> freaking the intense azure. . . .

It is of course very difficult in writing about this passage
not to comment on its images as well as its sound, but a detail
or two can be singled out. Any poetic ear will hear the rush
of force in

I, 278

> that now
> stand in massiv range, cumulated stupendous
> mountainous snowbillowy up-piled in dazzling sheen. . . .

And will feel it subside into the quiet of

I, 281

> Now like sailing ships on a calm ocean drifting . . .

There is a parallel *crescendo-diminuendo* movement in a
later passage:

I, 289

> and gathering as they climb
> deep-freighted with live lightning, thunder and drenching
>   flood
> rebuff the winds, and with black-purpling terror impend
> til they be driven away, when grave Night peacefully

clearing her heav'nly rondure of its turbid veils
layeth bare the playthings of Creation's babyhood. . . .

Next after the lyric in the scale of popularity, is the descriptive verse in *The Testament of Beauty*. Some of the lyric
passages most generally picked out, are of course also descriptive in an elaborate degree, of nature's grandeur or loveliness. But of the descriptive passages which do not really
fall into the character of lyric, one may single out the account
of the digging of the old city of Ur as the one most mentioned:

IV, 292

                         and there,
happening on the king's tomb, they shovel'd from the dust
the relics of thatt old monarch's magnificence—
Drinking vessels of beaten silver or of clean gold,
vases of alabaster, obsidian chalices,
cylinder seals of empire and delicat gems
of personal adornment, ear-rings and finger-rings,
craftsmen's tools copper and golden, and for music a harp. . . .

If the whole passage be read (lines 276-337) it will be clear
that here the effect is gained by the richness of the pictorial
details. In sound the poetic effect is almost entirely that of
smoothness, regulated by the end-pause. However, all but
the most sensitive readers will render this like good rhythmical prose, a bit more steadily and evenly, but still without
the cadences always attendant on the best accentual verse,
as it is found for instance in a somewhat reminiscent passage
descriptive of Cleopatra's barge in *Antony and Cleopatra*.
All will admit this to be excellent writing and will admit, too,
that there is a place for such writing in a poem if the imaginative value of poetry is there in some other way, as it is in the
visual and tactile imagery.

When we come to those passages that have been labeled
narrative poetry, there is an embarrassment twofold; in the
first place, there is a good deal of it, and in the second it is
inevitably shot through with interpretation, sometimes emo-

tional and sometimes intellectual. However, one may choose
without too great difficulty, the passage about the lemmings
of Norway.

I, 501

> THER is no tradition among the lemmings of Norway
> how their progenitors, when their offspring increased,
> bravely forsook their crowded nestes in the snow,
> swarming upon the plains to ravage field and farm,
> and in unswerving course ate their way to the coast,
> where plunging down the rocks they swam in the salt sea
> to drowning death; nor hav they in acting thus today
> any plan for their journey or prospect in the event.

It is clear that this passage is written with a regular metre,
but equally clear that no attempt is made to achieve a particularly lyric affect by sound or imagery. The narrative is
excellent, clear-cut, direct, and sinewy. The lines which
follow it, possibly equally narrative in kind, carry more
connotation:

I, 509

> But clerks and chroniclers wer many in Christendom,
> when France and Germany pour'd out the rabblement
> of the second Crusade, and its record is writ;
> its leaders' titles, kings and knights of fair renown,
> their resolve and design: and yet for all their vows
> their consecrating crosses and embroider'd flags,
> the eloquent preaching of Saint Bernard, and the wiles
> of thatt young amorous amazon, Queen Eleanor,
> they wer impell'd as madly, journey'd as blindly
> and perish'd as miserably as the thoughtless voles. . . .

The factual character of this material is disguised by our
romantic feeling about feudalism and crusading generally,
but the values attendant on more intense and emotional
poetry are conspicuously not there.

When we come to the fourth grouping, we find that
Bridges' exposition ranges in its expression from passages
that carry emotional connotations created by sound in regu-

lar rhythms, as well as imagery, to a few short passages of almost pure scientific observation or philosophical analysis. The following is a middle choice:

III, 335

> And here we are driv'n to enquire of Reason how it came
> that bodily beauty is deem'd a feminin attribute,
> since not by science nor aesthetick coud we arrive
> at such a judgment. But not triflingly to trench
> on prehistoric problems, 'twil be enough to say
> that from the first it may not always hav been so,
> and primacy of beauty may hav once lain with the male,
> in days of pagan savagery, afore men left
> their hunting and took tillage of the fields in hand,
> superseding the women and all their moon-magic. . . .

Properly read with its end-pauses honored, even the first lines of this passage are regularly rhythmical beyond the rhythms of prose, but the most striking quality of course is its completely non-lyrical movement. Even when one continues into the next few lines

III, 346

> whether in remotest orient lands
> whose cockcrow is our curfew, where Chineses swarm
> teasing their narrow plots with hand and hoe . . .

this is clear.

There is then an obvious range of effect in the quoted passages from sound creating a sense of excitement and joy, to simple, direct, and very slightly modulated explanation. That is, when we take these four kinds of passages in the order given above, we feel a sliding scale downward in what is traditionally believed to constitute poetic excellence. By some, the scale is felt to tilt at a very steep angle, shooting the last group out of the range of art entirely. The means may be admitted as appropriate to the material being expressed, but not very readily, as a poetic device in itself. We are all incorrigibly inclined to use the word "poetic" as

synonymous with lyric and to deny therefore the poetic quality to any but lyrical expression. Poe is the most famous
member of this company.

But is this natural and general inclination a useful one in
trying to understand and to enjoy *The Testament of Beauty?*
Under its influence the quality of this poem is thought to
range from great poetry to prose, the prose unnecessarily
composed to twelve-syllable lines. This is the feeling, apparently, of many readers of *The Testament of Beauty* who have
been introduced to it by their eyes in silent reading. If it is
a true indication of the final achievement of Bridges' style,
on its metrical side, then indeed Thompson is right: "It is by
individual passages that Bridges's poem will live."[1] Then
"the harder passages," so-named by Elton[2] will be read only
for their thought, with the reader deprecating their necessity,
even though he admires perhaps Bridges' skill in choosing a
verse form which admits lines like

I, 195
>   and sickening thought itself engendereth corporal pain . . .

I, 209
>   But the sensuous intuition in them is steril . . .

I, 361
>   Man's mind, ...
>   cannot bë isolated from her other works
>   by self-abstraction of its unique fecundity. . . .

And even if he admires, his admiration may be tinged with
Johnson's scoff about the dancing dog. To separate the dis-
tinctive passages into categories of the lyric, descriptive,
narrative, and expository, suggests inevitably that in this
ordering, there is the order of poetic excellence. Just as in
analyzing a symphony by abstracting and grouping all the
themes, this collection would be chosen by the unwary as the
most beautiful or even the greatest passages in the composi-

---

[1] Thompson. *Robert Bridges*, p. 111.
[2] Elton. *Robert Bridges and The Testament of Beauty*, p. 4.

tion, the rest of it in descending scale of excellence. The musician would scoff at this procedure, because in that art the relationships create the beauty. Such a procedure leads to the great weakness of Bridges criticism to date.

It is a mistake, of course, to hold any long poem up to the standard of the concentrated lyric, and that it is a mistake was recognized by Coleridge and more recently by the most skillful of the critics. In fact readers generally know enough not to do this for the great traditional long poems, although it is hard for the unsophisticated reader not to skip the theology in *Paradise Lost* and the associationist psychology in *The Prelude*. But these well-known poems exist within the framework of a narrative, either the kind which has the added aesthetic assistance of myth, or the story of the growth of a poet's mind. And it has been too much for the reader to accept as part of the art, what he of course knows is part of the argument. He has too little recognized that there is another kind of poetry than the clear and transparent lyric, a kind whose total fusion depends on all the resources of the poetic art, but whose connective tissues of exposition have not all been washed away. Ker called attention to this long ago; his words are so apt, he might be imagined to be entering this discussion on purpose, right here: "It does not really matter what you call the poetry so long as you recognize its species. There is a kind of poetry which includes Virgil and Lucretius and *Paradise Lost* and the *Seasons* and the *Essay on Man,* viz. a kind of poetry which explains, puts argument without drama or the heightened form of expression which goes along with music and which we call lyric."[3] To satisfy those writers, however, who, having objected to the argument, would say merely that Ker is widening the scope of the word "poetry" further than they believe proper, his later comment on the poetic intensity of just such writing should follow. The passage opens up and settles many of the confusions that have gathered around *The Testament of Beauty:*

[3] *Form and Style in Poetry,* pp. 151-52.

Some critics . . . may be led to the opinion of E. A. Poe, that there is no such thing as a long poem: that a long poem, the *Iliad* or *Odyssey*, carries too much prose lumber, only partially and occasionally fused into poetry: that a perfect poem is one that burns all through, to apply the well-known phrase of Pater, with a clear and gemlike flame, and it is only to this quintessential sort of verse that the name poetry belongs. . . . The modes of thought in poetry are various. There is the reasoning poem like Dryden's *Religio Laici* or Pope's *Essay on Man,* which is a versification of a prose argument. But this order has in itself many varieties—perhaps as many varieties as there are poems—varieties according to the greater or less degree in which prosaic argument is heated up for poetry. The greatest triumph in this kind is the poem of Lucretius. There the fire of the poet is so strong that it is felt not only in the splendid imaginative passages, but in the most dry and technical exposition of the atomic theory. Dante is not far off; he is a poet when he is discussing scientifically the nature of the spots on the moon. Lucretius and Dante in their dry and technical passages seem to show that the reasoning poet is most successful as a poet when he is most taken up with his unpoetical argument. . . . Lucretius and Dante show what poetic genius can do in overcoming impossibilities, turning the merest slag and clinker of prose into pure flame.[4]

This is an impassioned defense of the presence in a long poem of technical exposition; it gives no clear idea how the poet actually overcomes impossibilities. Eliot, who earlier supported and even propagandized the abolition of prosaic argument from a poem, has later said:

In a poem of any length, there must be transitions between passages of greater or less intensity, to give a rhythm of fluctuating emotion essential to the musical structure of the whole; and the passages of less intensity will be, in relation to the level on which the whole poem operates, prosaic—so that, in the sense implied by that context, it may be said that no poet can write a poem of amplitude unless he is a master of the prosaic.

In the note to this he adds: "this test of the greatness of a poet is the way he writes his less intense, but structurally

4 *Form and Style in Poetry,* pp. 111 and 114-15.

vital, matter."[5] Bridges is explicit as to the necessary means, although he would have had no truck with the idea that the poet in any way proved himself "a master of the prosaic." He writes, "Almost all the power that great poets like Homer and Dante have of poetizing whatever they may handle is due to their fixed prosodies. [Eliot would have no truck with the word *poetizing*.] If this should be doubted, suppose the experiment of rewriting their poems so that they did not scan. It would of course be mere destruction, and observe, destruction not only of the great immortal lines . . . but the mortar also between the stones, which is now hardly distinguishable from them, would perish and rot away, and would no longer serve to hold the fabric together."[6] He illustrates by comparing a passage from *The Divine Comedy* with its translation by Carey, who he says had no metrical skill.

Because of Bridges' metrical skill, the great immortal lines of his poem are brought into relationship with each other by the mortar between the stones. The so-called loose Alexandrines have been used to produce the sound of the human voice in the most extraordinary variety of tone, and flexibility from one tone to another. This is more than a device, more than the suiting of the sound of one part or another to its content or emotion. It is a part of the large unifying concept of the poem, its central monistic philosophy, its principle of organization, and its dominant and recurring image, a concept of the evolution of life from elemental force through organic life, man's emotions and reason, back to elemental force expressed as idea. The tale of this evolution comes through the lips of a man who has understood it, told with the many voices of his shifting experience. Man, not Robert Bridges, is giving utterance to all he knows; image and voice are alike metaphor to make this utterance a work of art, a poem.

[5] Eliot. *The Music of Poetry,* p. 18 and note 1.
[6] "Humdrum and Harum Scarum," *Collected Essays,* Vol. 2, No. ii, p. 48.

The key to the whole matter of voice tones lies in Elton's perception that Bridges has found and used a prosody (Elton misleadingly calls it a form) "that would give voice to all the moods, passions, whims, dreams, exaltations, prejudices, memories, of the natural man."[7] But more significant still is the fact that really turns the key in the lock, the fact that explanation and argument and speculation, the ways of thought of thinking man, have likewise found their proper mode of expression, and appear with their proper voices. In no poetry outside of Shakespearean drama and a few of Donne's poems, where one hears men think and speculate as well as express their emotions, does one hear such variety of compelling voice tones as play behind and through *The Testament of Beauty*. It is the tone of voice in speaking, but of a voice so far from the usual monotony of human talk that art beyond mere use is achieved. It is a voice trained by music study, by the teaching of a boy choir to sing the greatest church music, and by the reading and practice of all kinds of verbal expression. Any reader who listens will hear the range, the tones of wonder, of scorn, of doubt and sadness and pity, the voice of reminiscence, of storytelling and explaining, of speculation, of contemplation, and of mystic vision. Following the changes of voice from the passages of pictorial and emotional beauty recognized by all readers, through the tougher, non-lyric argument, is an experience charged with an excitement that is comparable to the excitement that comes in reading a lyric. And the factual content, or the abstractness of diction, or whatever may have been felt to choke the verse previously, is nothing less than an indispensable part of it.

There are several steps to showing that the voices behind this poem are essential to its aesthetic unity. First, the different tones that give interest and life to important passages must be separated and characterized. The more subtle the reader, the greater the variety that will be heard; only the

[7] Elton. *op. cit.*, p. 13.

more obvious can be demonstrated. Second, some account must be given of the exciting effect of the modulations of one tone to another, and of the function of this excitement in creating the necessary suspension of disbelief, here the disbelief that factual data concerning our biological make-up can ever be poetry. Such an account will explain the aesthetic use of the voice-changes in carrying the factual material along with the more emotional parts of the poem and giving them aesthetic value without the usual values of rich imagery and fluent movement. Later in the book, a pattern in larger outlines created by the voices will appear molding the poem into a whole, an organism whose parts all contribute to its unity.

Coming to the task of documenting one's perceptions of these constant and dramatic variations, one finds a discrepancy between one's recognition of the almost infinite and unanalyzable gradations and the possibility of illustrating each one. It is in the elusiveness of the changes of voice as well as in their arresting differences that the poetic effect lies. The best one can do is to distinguish three personalities, the lecturer, the thinker, and the seer, who make up the personality of man remembering and interpreting "the obliterating aeons of man's ordeal." (II, 674) It is a little artificial, but not fanciful, to distinguish these. But the reader himself must catch the variations of tone which play over the illustrations gathered in these groups. The passages are not chosen to emphasize the dividing lines but rather to show the merging of one tone into another.

Of these personalities, the seer has been greeted as the familiar figure, and he has been called the poet without much cavil; but the utterances of the thinker and the lecturer have often been denied the name of poetry. No mistake has been made about the seer and prophet, except that of sometimes limiting his passages to the more obvious nature lyrics. The thinker, too, has usually been accorded the name of poet, when his thought has taken on spiritual overtones, which it does not always do. But all three really are human and vigorous and what each says has been lifted from statement, or prose, to poetry. The problem of animating the material used by the lecturer was the greatest task Bridges faced; he solved it by giving the greatest range of all to the voice which recounts the details of man's evolutionary course. For this reason the lecturer's voice must be illustrated in considerable detail.

The word "lecturer" was not a very happy choice, perhaps. This learned man did not keep by him a shabby file of long-used notes, with illustration and joke carefully inserted, to be brought out with their edges blurred by custom. To him the accumulated knowledge of eighty years was the basis of his joy, his sorrow, and his hope. This knowledge came from his reading, his medical studies and practice, his observation of the phenomena of human behavior; his hope was his faith.

IV, 1062

> Reason herself here questioneth me how I trust
> her mere ordering of life to make for happiness—
> whereto my answer is my good faith in what I hav writ.

This poem is the testimony of a student of science, the science of physical and biological forces, the science of psychology, history and art. But he is the lecturer in love with his material, relishing the exact and multifarious details of his professional knowledge.

From the beginning, we may hear the teacher taking his listeners into his confidence as he pursues his ideas:

IV, 412

> Now in my thought the manner of it was on this wise—
> As Pleasure came in man to the conscience of self,
> his Reason abstracted it as an idea. . . .

He poses question and answer:

II, 541

> Why should this thing so hold me? and why do I welcome
> now

the tiny beast, that hath come running up to me
as if here in my cantos he had spied a crevice,
and counting on my friendship would make it his home?

He protests to his listeners:

I, 129

Wisdom wil repudiate thee, if thou think to enquire
WHY things are as they are or whence they came: thy task
is first to learn WHAT IS . . .

I, 411

Nor coud it ever dwell in my possible thought
that whatsoever grew and groweth can be unlike
in cause and substance to the thing it groweth on. . . .

He comes smack down to earth when it suits him:

III, 883

Truly myths so ancient and examples of life,
fish'd-up out of the old jumble-box of history,
can find but little credit with this generation . . .

III, 71

yet this amenity of Mammon is to the epicure
mere disgust, a farrago of incongruous kickshaws,
a hazardous pampering, as barbarously remote
from pleasure's goal as pothouse cheese and ale.

IV, 138

and wer I to ask for-why
she is making such pother with thatt rubbishy straw,
her answer would be surely: 'I know not, but I MUST.'

He can be scornful, indignant, and skeptical, with humor
exasperated or sly:

II, 248

For surely (said he) a bastard nursed in a bureau
must love and reverence all women for its mothers. . . .

The whole passage (II, 235-58) should be read to get the
full flavor of this comment on Plato, and it must be said,
socialism. He here aims at analytic psychology with an ironical twist:

III, 949

> [some]   impute precocious puberty
> to new-born babes, and all their after trouble in life
> to shamefast thwarting of inveterat lust.

Here at the epicure, although he himself was one:

III, 117

> In such fine artistry of his putrefying pleasures
> he indulgeth richly his time untill the sad day come
> when he retireth with stomach Emeritus
> to ruminate the best devour'd moments of life. . . .

As we come nearer to the heart of Bridges' thought, we find the lecturer's tone gaining in depth. He glories in the beauty of fine-measured fact:

III, 764

> Many shy at such doctrin: Science they wil say,
> knoweth nought of this beauty. But what kenneth she
> of color or sound? Nothing: tho' science measure true
> every wave-length of ether or air that reacheth sense,
> there the hunt checketh, and her keen hounds are at fault;
> for when the waves hav pass'd the gates of ear and eye
> all scent is lost: suddenly escaped the visibles
> are changed to invisible; the fine-measured motions
> to immeasurable emotion; the cypher'd fractions
> to a living joy that man feeleth to shrive his soul.

He becomes fascinated by the exactness and beauty of the scientific details he is recounting:

II, 267

> Consider the tiny egg-cell whence the man groweth,
> how it proliferateth freely, as a queen-bee doth . . .

II, 275

> Consider then their task, those unimaginable
> infinit co-adaptations of function'd tissue
> correlated delicately in a ravel'd web
> of unknown sensibilities . . .

I, 145

> And science vindicateth the appeal to Reason
> which is no less Nature's prescriptiv oracle
> for being in all her plan so small and tickle a thing:
> How small a thing! if things immeasurable allow
> a greater and less (and thought wil reckon some thoughts
> great,
>
> prolific, everlasting; other some again
> small and contemptible) say then, How small a part
> of Universal Mind can conscient Reason claim!
> 'Tis to the unconscious mind as the habitable crust
> is to the mass of the earth; this crust whereon we dwell
> whereon our loves and shames are begotten and buried,
> our first slime and ancestral dust: 'Tis, to compare,
> thinner than o'er a luscious peach the velvet skin
> that we rip off to engorge the rich succulent pulp:
> Wer but our planet's sphere so peel'd, flay'd of the rind
> that wraps its lava and rock, the solar satellite
> would keep its motions in God's orrery undisturb'd.
> Yea: and how delicat! Life's mighty mystery
> sprang from eternal seeds in the elemental fire,
> self-animat in forms that fire annihilates. . . .

He retells the significant facts of epochs with imaginative
delight:

I, 534

> Follow the path of those fair warriors, the tall Goths,
> from the day when they led their blue-eyed families
> off Vistula's cold pasture-lands, their murky home
> by the amber-strewen foreshore of the Baltic sea,
> and in the incontaminat vigor of manliness
> feeling their rumour'd way to an unknown promised land,
> tore at the ravel'd fringes of the purple power,
> and trampling its wide skirts, defeating its armies,
> slaying its Emperor, and burning his cities,
> sack'd Athens and Rome; untill supplanting Caesar
> they ruled the world where Romans reign'd before. . . .

He gives full value to man's "spiritual elation and response to
Nature" (I, 318), his "generic mark" (319), in the lyric

passages already illustrated with "the sky's unresting cloud-land," passages which must be read not only as lyric poems, but as part of the lecturer's argument. The variety of these lyric parts must impress even casual reading, and their beauty no one will deny. But looked at from this point of view, their especial values are enhanced very greatly by their tones being set against the other passages as their accompaniment.

We are now in the range of tone which will seem more appropriate to the thinker and seer than to the lecturer, but since these speakers are really one, a few examples of a more personal emotion, or a deeper, more prophetic note, are taken from sections where on the whole the intent of the poem seems most explanatory. Reading them in their context is essential to understanding this fully. First, as the lecturer proceeds, he will occasionally bring in a touch or two of personal history, but not often, for this poem rigorously avoids the confessional; and the tone is always unassuming and usually questioning. Such is his recounting of a boyhood visit to a textile mill, an experience which gave him happy confidence in the great but quiet driving power of natural energy. (I, 44-52) Such also is the early memory of hearing great music, "when all thought fled scared from me in my bewilderment." (IV, 38) The concluding lines of Book II echo with the fear of a war-haunted future, even in the armistice days of 1918. (II, 998) In this longer passage the same sense of the tragic potentiality still remaining in our health and our successes sounds through its rhythms and tones:

II, 661

> Yet since of all, whatever hath once been, evil or good,
> tho' we can think not of it and remember it not,
> nothing can wholly perish; so ther is no birthright
> so noble or stock so clean, but it transmitteth dregs,
> contamination at core of old brutality;
> inchoate lobes, dumb shapes of ancient terror abide:

tho' fading still in the ocëanic deeps of mind
their eyeless sorrows haunt the unfathom'd density,
dulling the crystal lens of prophetic vision,
crippling the nerve that ministereth to trembling strength,
distorting the features of our nobility. . . .

And finally this telling voice, modulated by the feeling behind it to these ranges of sound, sinks to profound contemplation; and from contemplation comes the voice of prayer. The way is through thought, not reason alone, for all the resources of the conscient mind must be used and the limitations of this mind have the power to chasten and subdue. The music of these lines is remote from common speech:

IV, 761

AND here my thought plungeth into the darksome grove
and secret penetralia of ethic lore, wherein
I hav wander'd often and long and thought to know my way,
and now shall go retracing my remember'd paths,
tho' no lute ever sounded there nor Muse hath sung,
deviously in the obscure shadows. . . .

But thought is the Prometheus of this drama and its abstract clarity sounds also in Book IV. The philosophical core of the poem, the summary of its metaphysical elements, strikes a different chord:

IV, 112

Reality appeareth in forms to man's thought
as several links interdependent of a chain
that circling returneth upon itself, as doth
the coil'd snake that in art figureth eternity.
From Universal Mind the first-born atoms draw
their function, whose rich chemistry the plants transmute
to make organic life, whereon animals feed
to fashion sight and sense and give service to man,
who sprung from them is conscient in his last degree
of ministry unto God, the Universal Mind,
whither all effect returneth whence it first began.

In these eleven lines, Bridges has given the utmost of smooth regularity (the end-pause must be acknowledged) to an idea that had to be expressed with the polysyllables that are so hard to fit into accentual metre without a Gilbertian echo. There is the clarity of fine prose but to the ear now accustomed to hearing the human voice, these lines in their metrical simplicity are a cornerstone where form and idea meet. They are an integral part of the whole fabric, which has included all kinds of poetic discourse. The poem ends with the poet's full realization of the implications for man of this supreme unity; one hears through the broken phrases and the steady rhythm of the line unit the final and almost inarticulate expression of the deepest religious feeling:

IV, 1436

> Truly the Soul returneth the body's loving
> where it hath won it . . . and God so loveth the world . . .
> and in the fellowship of the friendship of Christ
> God is seen as the very self-essence of love,
> Creator and mover of all as activ Lover of all,
> self-express'd in not-self, without which no self were.
> In thought whereof is neither beginning nor end
> nor space nor time; nor any fault nor gap therein
> 'twixt self and not-self, mind and body, mother and child,
> 'twixt lover and loved, God and man: but ONE ETERNAL
> in the love of Beauty and in the selfhood of Love.

If the reader will turn back to examples previously cited of scientific statement, he will be struck with the distance covered in a roughly ascending scale toward the poetry of vision. The admission that the hardest core of the lecturer's material is but spoken in its peculiar voice may be wrung from Bridges' critics without forcing them to like these parts of the poem. It may be felt that the lecturer is in fact hard to listen to, although many do not find this true. But once the tones of this poem are really heard as inflections of the human voice, the skill with which Bridges has floated the lecturer's factual parts by this oral technique will be recognized and enjoyed. The experienced student and lover of poetry sees gradually, if not at once, that such writing will

III, 493
>   come in the end
>   to its own, from being a tolerated discordancy
>   to be an accepted harmony. . . .

These passages make up just another voice, one which takes its part in the rich background of tonal intricacies against which those passages already admitted to the great anthology of art are set. These last gain their brilliance and their eminence from the chiaroscuro and the perspective.

By the technique of his versification, its temporal regularity, and its accentual freedom, both controlling and permitting the voice tones, Bridges has used an appropriate means of bringing to unity all the unlikely variety of his material. It was impossible and surely it would have been undesirable, for him to "liquefy" the scientific knowledge basic to his vision by a poetic diction and a more familiar metre. Because the experience of knowledge and the experience of vision are different, in appearance, although with Bridges fundamentally the latter "is but a differentiation of the infertile leaf" (I, 420), he heightened instead of lessening the difference in tone between

IV, 806
>   Thus the digestiv kind is stirr'd by touch of food
>   within the body, or by the sight or sound or smell
>   of the object, or ev'n by the unconscious thought thereof . . .

and the conclusion of the thought he is developing:

IV, 825
>   Thus must all kind of stimulus hav come some way
>   across the misty march-land, whereon men would fix
>   their disputable boundary between Matter and Mind. . . .

And later in the same passage he has led up gradually to the intricate music of

IV, 854
>   nay, see the starry atoms in the seed-plot of heav'n
>   stripp'd to their nakedness are nothing but Number . . .

IV, 865

> and 'twas thus Socrates
> coud evoke Reason to order and disciplin the mind—
> the divine Logos that should shine in the darkness,—
> a good physician who must heal himself withal.

These differences, implying the existence of the harder passages which no more choke the work of art than does the dissonance of music, make up the total effect

IV, 952

> like as in music, when true voices blend in song,
> the perfect intonation of the major triad
> is sweetest of all sounds; its inviting embrace
> resolveth all discords; and all the ambitious flights
> of turbulent harmony come in the end to rest
> with the fulfilment of its liquidating cloze.

The problem of unity in a work of art involves both the steady organic progress of the material (in spatial art, the relation of the parts within each section), and the interlocking of these parts in a pattern for the whole (in spatial art the all-over composition). That *The Testament of Beauty* has the unity of both organic progress and organic completeness is felt if the voices are heard. A line by line rendering of the poem shows purpose (or at least such an effect, since it never can be demonstrated how much of an artist's creation of form is spontaneous and how much planned) it shows the effect, then, of purpose, in its shifts of voice from explanation to perplexity to reasonableness, from reasonableness to conviction of hope or fear or mystery. The thought progresses through these echoes of the experience of the mind questioning and thinking. And further there is a change in all-over tone from book to book which links the subject matter of the individual books together, helping to create an organic unity to the sections of the thought which is always denied the poem as a whole, when it is treated as philosophy, not art. We must see how the tones of voice just enumerated have been made active agents in fusing the different kinds of material together.

Bridges' method may be illustrated by a discussion of the first eighty lines or so of the poem. The introductory passage is serene and impersonal, sonorous with its own sonority, but restrained to the tone of thought.

I, 1

> MORTAL Prudence, handmaid of divine Providence,
> hath inscrutable reckoning with Fate and Fortune:
> We sail a changeful sea through halcyon days and storm,
> and when the ship laboureth, our stedfast purpose
> trembles like as the compass in a binnacle.
> Our stability is but balance, and conduct lies
> in masterful administration of the unforeseen.

There is profound feeling behind this tentative expression of the nature of spiritual order, "our stability is but balance," but the expression is one of muted vibrations. It goes on with a more fully emotional note, that of nostalgia, gradually becoming descriptive and then explanatory of the state of mind which produced the poem. "Twas late in my long journey" (I, 8), "Or as I well remember" (19), suggest the reminiscence, both by content and sound. The flow of the lines containing the details of lying down on the fine grass, and breathing in the beauty both of the mapped out landscape and the individual common flowers which were as significant as the gems of painting or music created by master minds (I, 8-36), expresses happy serenity. There has been full critical approval of the lyric tone of this opening section; its feeling, as expressed in rhythms and cadences, is apparently readily felt. It should be noticed specifically, however, that the lyric movement is not traditionally accentual. Its unaccented temper, as contrasted with its measured temporal regularity, makes it possible to shift when needed from lyric values in imagery to the explanatory character of what is being led up to. The details of the section are recounted with an increasingly compelling sound until we are ready for the first complete generalization: "Man's Reason is in such deep insolvency to sense." (I, 57) Without the accentual pattern, the change in emotional character is inconspicuous, yet fully expressed.

It is even more difficult to introduce the first biological facts used as confirmation of the monism, or vision of unity, of the opening lines. For this reason, the joyous passage descriptive of bird-song at dawn, breaks in:

I, 63

> Lov'st thou in the blithe hour
> of April dawns—nay marvelest thou not—to hear
> the ravishing music that the small birdës make
> in garden or woodland, rapturously heralding
> the break of day. . . .

Its intervention raises the pitch of the poem to where it can carry the biological facts of Reason's insolvency to sense:

I, 74

> Hast thou then thought that all this ravishing music,
> that stirreth so thy heart, making thee dream of things
> illimitable unsearchable and of heavenly import,
> is but a light disturbance of the atoms of air,
> whose jostling ripples gather'd within the ear, are tuned
> to resonant scale, and thence by the enthron'd mind received
> on the spiral stairway of her audience chamber
> as heralds of high spiritual significance?
> and that without thine ear, sound would hav no report,
> Nature hav no music. . . .

Explanatory of physical process as it is, the re-created chorus of birdsongs sings resonantly through this section.

It is impossible here as elsewhere really to keep separate the question of voice tones and the larger subject of all the sound effects and the imaginative connotations of the verse, and it is important to stress that in reading the poem one is affected by everything simultaneously, to make the reading a whole experience. The reader as he reads from passage to passage should recognize at the same time the tones of voice and the character of the diction and thought. Of course so minute a sampling from this long poem is no proof that the

same process of changing tone can be detected throughout.
But any eighty or a hundred lines will yield similar conclusions; a more difficult passage, but a very interesting one,
occurs in II, 693-773. Lines 751-73 should be especially considered.

Perception of the organic nature of these changes leads to
this conclusion. The shifts from one voice to another (not
this alone of course, it is only one factor) are a part of the
"corporat alchemy" (IV, 822) of Bridges' creative power. He
has by this means brought to bear on the resisting mind of
the unsympathetic reader, all the resources of a clever,
vivid, and hopeful personality. He has indicated that the
process of the human mind in formulating truth is a com-
posite experience, satisfying and convincing in its variety,
made up of logical reasoning, observation of fact, and experience in the realm of the instincts and emotions. He has suggested to the reader by these persuasive means the truth of
what as scientist, philosopher, and artist, he is presenting in
this poem: that

I, 427
> we observe in all existence four stages—
> Atomic, Organic, Sensuous, and Selfconscient—
> and must conceive these in gradation . . .

and

I, 365
> Not emotion or imagination ethick or art
>
> .   .   .
>
> hath any other foundation than the common base
> of Nature's building:—not even his independence
> of will, his range of knowledge, and spiritual aim,
> can separate him off from the impercipient. . . .

The monism expressed here is given emotional expression
and carries emotional conviction through the dramatic creation of a personality who speaks his understanding of it and
his faith in it.

Part II

THE IMAGERY

CHAPTER SIX

THE PROPERTIES AND THE KEEPING

In his essay "Poetic Diction," Bridges disengages two aspects of the diction of a poem, labeling them the "properties" and the "keeping." "Properties," he says, "is a term borrowed from the stage. The mixture of Greek and Christian types in *Lycidas* and *Adonais* is a good example of Properties. The term Keeping is taken from Painting and has no convenient synonym, but it may be explained as the harmonizing of the artistic medium, and since Diction is the chief means in the harmonizing of Properties, it would seem that any restriction or limitation of the Diction must tend to limit the Properties, since without artistic keeping their absurdities would be exposed."[1] The word *imagery* is generally used to cover most of the ideas behind both *properties* and *keeping*, but it raises questions concerning the shades of difference between sensory details and metaphorical implications that must be left until later. For the moment, the subject of this section will be made clearer if Bridges' terms are used.

Several writers have spoken of a tone or coloring to *The Testament of Beauty* which they might have called its "keeping." Most general is the angry or apologetic notice taken of the aristocratic tone of the whole. Conrad Aiken has spoken of the poem's almost medieval simplicity and old-fashionedness.[2] Elton finds the poem's naturalness "qualified by that continual slight strangeness which lifts it into poetry."[3] But more readers notice the disparity of the properties, feeling strongly that some of them are not in keeping

[1] "Poetic Diction," *Collected Essays*, Vol. 2, No. iii, p. 65.
[2] *New Republic*, LXII (1930), p. 164. Cited by Guérard, *Robert Bridges*, p. 178, with other extracts from the reviews of the poem.
[3] *Robert Bridges and The Testament of Beauty*, p. 14.

with the whole. The problem is really parallel to that noticed
in the sound of the poem. There the passages of musical
lyricism or of tonal grandeur are in marked, and to some
readers, incongruous, contrast with the so-called prosaic sections. Similarly, when the diction of the poem is considered,
readers are struck with the difference in poetical effect between the "great" passages of nature description or historical
re-creation, and the sections arguing a point philosophically
or presenting facts of physical and biological science.

No writer has been a more sympathetic and understanding
critic of this poem than Elton, and in his essay are the clues
to nearly all the means that Bridges used to fuse and give life
to his poem; however, it is he who has given the fullest
critical analysis of this position. "The poem aims at, and often
though not always attains," he says, "the realization of
beauty, both outward and spiritual, in words; and I shall
quote from the passages that do this most conspicuously,
rather than from the harder and more rugged ones. . . . The
critical question, it will appear, is when and how far these
harder passages can be considered poetry; for there is no
doubt about the others."[4] Elton continues about the passages
he calls the harder ones: "The difficulty of a philosophical
poet, as we know, is how to get over stony ground. . . . Every
reader of Milton or *De Rerum Natura* feels this check; and
in the *Testament* the problem is the same . . . (but) where
the reasoning is rooted in some personal experience, and is so
colored and presented, it is more likely to be poetry than
when it comes as bare impersonal argument. For this touch
of nature we can put up with a few technicalities and hard
words. There is a sprinkling of them in the *Testament* and
doubtless they choke the verse."[5] Here is no clear distinction
between subject matter and diction; in this question of properties and keeping perhaps none can be made. However,

[4] *Op. cit.*, p. 4.
[5] *Ibid.*, pp. 13-14.

there is a difference between the effect of the so-called awkwardness of the words in a poetic pattern, and the awkwardness of talking about the proliferation of cells or the onset of periodic appetite at puberty. (II, 268; III, 197) Biological facts seem to be especially "choking," whereas facts about Titian's *Sacred and Profane Love* or even about new agricultural methods, apparently flow more easily. The vocabulary for the latter is undoubtedly more traditional; the words *engin, beam, bolted shares* (III, 360-61), have the connotations of long and respectable use; the invented words like *genes* have none.

But the careful and sensitive readers who object to the bare impersonal argument, the technicalities, and the hard words, and there are many who object more fundamentally than Elton, are not subscribing to the theory that some subjects and some diction are unsuitable to poetry in themselves. It is that they do not believe that these parts of the poem have been made "in keeping" by aesthetic means. In Eliot's words, the disparate experiences have not been sufficiently amalgamated. In his extension of Eliot's distinction between the intellectual and the reflective poet, Matthiessen lists *The Testament of Beauty* as one of those poems whose dramatic quality is lost because the poet "instead of thinking in images and thus giving a living body to his ideas, tends to put his images aside and to fall back on abstract rhetoric when he comes to deliver his statements."[6] Guérard has well pointed out that a poet need not "sensualize thought completely" but agrees that "a poet should not be satisfied with something similar to Bridges' intellectual paraphrase."[7]

The preceding study of the prosodic values of *The Testament of Beauty* has shown the many ways Bridges has used his metre to lift his material to poetry. This way of sound is a generally acceptable one, Guérard having admirably shown

[6] *The Achievement of T. S. Eliot*, p. 68, and note, p. 80.
[7] *Robert Bridges*, p. 102.

that sound and structure may make a fine poem out of almost completely abstract words,[8] and Housman admitting simile and metaphor, if not dramatization, inessential to poetry, provided the movement of the lines be sufficiently fine.[9] Elton, entirely aware of the special quality of the voice tones of the poem permitted by the metre, says specifically: "Only the loose Alexandrines would admit terms like 'supersensuous sublimation,' 'individuality,' and 'euristic.' But they do not bulk large in the 4300 and more lines of the poem."[10] That they also have their place as uttered in the voice of the lecturer has been shown, but it was admitted that perhaps readers may still not like that voice when the material is that of scientific fact or philosophic argument.

Bridges himself has given the perfect words to describe what readers have felt about these parts, using his metaphor for another purpose. He says that the faculty of wonder in a child

IV, 59

> being a superlativ brief moment of glory,
> is too little to leaven the inveterate lump of life. . . .

Certainly there is the problem, in maintaining that this poem has unarrested life throughout its 4,374 lines, of those lines which seem to many to be inveterate lumps lacking even a brief moment of glory. It will be well to look at those harder passages to see how much space is given to them, and how really separable they are from the more imaginative parts of the poem. They do not indeed bulk large, but more than this, they are interwoven with metaphorical values, suspended by the threads of plainly poetic elements. In Bridges' words from still another context, they resolve "melting as icebergs launch'd on the warm ocean-stream." (IV, 821) Once this is sensed, and the lines thereafter carefully read, they take their

[8] *Robert Bridges,* p. 98.
[9] *The Name and Nature of Poetry,* pp. 10, 11, and *passim.* At least so I interpret his essay as a whole.
[10] *Op. cit.,* p. 14.

places without need of apology; they belong, as part of the expression, fortified by association, imagery, and modulated sound and rhythm, as all poetry is.

There are lines in *The Testament of Beauty* composed of words whose purpose is to be analytical of a thought, expository of a system, or descriptive of the evolution and function of an animal organism. Out of the poem's 4,374 lines there are 266 with no leaven of sensory or figurative language, most of them with no hint of traditional, accentual music. This is a rough proportion of about sixteen to one.

Anyone will know, of course, that this numerical proportion does not really correspond to the amount of life and death in the poem, although the proportion of sixteen to one is a very convincing one, if one were to be convinced by figures. Certainly, a reader determined not to be led by the nose with a method he does not approve of, will still feel this poem prosaic in parts, and abstract. But under examination, even these lines come to be touched by faint suggestion of sensation, figure of speech, poetic connotation, or linguistic device such as alliteration. As familiarity with the text grows and the mental eye is sharpened to detect the faintest gleam, lines come to life that were dormant before. The composing of these lines for balance, contrast, and progression of idea, is a further and different value, and accounts for the quality of the whole. The kind of life they finally are given will be shown by considerable illustration.

This poem is no mosaic of sixteen bright pieces of stone to every uncolored one; although even if it were, the analogy of the mosaic might immediately suggest the place of the uncolored lines to offset and emphasize their opposites, to frame the picture, to connect its parts, and so on. But beyond this, the following figures will show how effectively the "corporat alchemy" (IV, 822) is used to melt the hard core. Or rather they will show how small and scattered and surrounded by the warm ocean stream they are, and the rereading of the whole will give the impression of a fluid sea of

poetry. (IV, 818) In the first place, Bridges has infused life
into most of these "dead" lines by extra meanings and connotative value that approach in kind the life given to poetry
by clearly sensory and figurative language. Indeed he draws
them so close to imagery in effect that as one subjects them
to scrutiny, one is likely to remove them one by one from the
original group of two hundred and sixty-six. But there was
sense in this original grouping and the number is so much
smaller already than anyone would predict on first reading
that they must all be analyzed candidly. This analysis shows
that Bridges has handled his problem in two ways. The first
may be understood arithmetically and disposed of very
quickly, although its discovery took rather longer. It is the
grouping of the "dead" lines in relation to the sensory and
figurative material. This is much more important, as will
readily be admitted, than the number of such lines, however
few or many. It is this grouping which really causes the
dominant tone of a passage, along with the quality of the
surrounding passages. When the unleavened line occurs in
a vivid and elaborate metaphor it is only detected by careful
scrutiny, whereas when it occurs in a passage of only faint
sensory or vague figurative quality it stands out, and no
doubt convinces the unsympathetic critic as would a blow on
the head. However, many of even these abstract lines are
syntactically and philosophically so tied into their context
that they are given sensory or figurative value by their bond.

The effectiveness of the association of the two kinds of
lines depends, as is clear, on the grouping of the dead lines
among the live ones. In the first place, throughout the entire
poem, no more than four lines together are without any trace
of sensory or figurative life, and groups of as many as four
lines occur only three times. Groups of three lines also occur
only three times. Pairs of such lines occur twenty-five times.
This means that 198 of the 266 are merely single lines surrounded by sensory or figurative material, imbedded in long
passages whose poetic character is achieved both by connota-

tion and the movement of the lines. Two hundred and fifty-seven of these lines are parts of sentences which contain other lines with some leavening of the sensory or the figurative; ninety-seven of them have leavening within the same clause, in preceding or following lines, and more significant still, forty-five are parts of actual similes, metaphors or personifications, although in themselves composed of abstract words. These forty-five might even have been considered live, not dead, but for the fact that sometimes the personification they help to make up is so vague that some would be loth to admit it as a figure of speech. However, it is in these personifications that we touch upon one of the most interesting and significant matters in the whole study of Bridges' imagery, his permeating metaphor of the human physical organism, a metaphor carried out with completeness and subtlety, as a keynote for the poem as a whole. Discussion of this belongs elsewhere, but its discovery is, in a way, the justification for this laborious and mechanical counting of lines.

In attempting to look at this poem with the eyes of dissent, one should include longer passages, from six lines to a page, where sensory or figurative connotation, and the tones of voice which are here claimed as poetic method, may be missed by the unappreciative. The selection of these passages is impossible except by personal response, but the dozen considered are a maximum. Most of these are considerably less than a page in length and none of them, as noted before, has more than four consecutive lines selected as "inveterate lumps." When read sympathetically, even these melt back into the whole poem and are completely lost to arithmetic. A discussion of a few of these passages will show the rich and varied methods of dramatization Bridges had at his command for the leavening of the lumps. The following is not intended to be exhaustive; other minds will find other poetic significance. The methods of leavening are of at least four kinds; (1) connotative value which is not that of

figure or sense, but of some other kind given to whole lines;
(2) stylistic tricks of repetition, contrast, or radical word-
meaning which light up the abstraction; (3) close and intricate association with vividly concrete, active, or figurative
material which gathers them up completely in the web interwoven of meaning and figure of speech; (4) constant variation in the tone of voice, which has already been sufficiently
discussed. The effects produced by these means are real
effects and will be sensed when the passages are reread.

In the first group there are lines thoroughly abstract and
also dogmatic, which illustrate one of the devices used by
Bridges to give much of the tone to the whole poem, and is
a part of his way of showing indirectly the basic thought as
well. This is his habit of quoting from other poets not just
because they said what he wants to say, but to give richness
to his effects and temporal continuity in the realm of philosophy and art to his poem. In the form of quotation of course,
the echoed lines are usually highly sensory or figurative. But
in two, at least, Bridges has enlivened an idea he has preferred to express abstractly, by making it not so much an
echo of the words as of the thought of other writers. His line
"Corruption of best is ever the worst corruption" (I, 186)
will remind some readers of the Latin tag *Corruptio optimi
pessima,* and others of Shakespeare's "Lilies that fester do
smell far worse than weeds." Both poets are speaking of lust
and wrecked lives. The unadorned line "So that unless itself
it be a thing of Beauty" (IV, 1197) inevitably recalls Keats's
"A thing of beauty is a joy forever."

Similarly, by giving the tone of epigram to several of his
abstract lines, Bridges has mitigated the effect of their abstraction, although here the imaginative connotation is less:

IV, 1369
    Friendship is in loving rather than in being lov'd,

and

IV, 1423
This Individualism is man's true Socialism.

Other lines are so central as expression of the truth explicit or implicit of the poem as a whole that they bear abstract statement lightly:

II, 204
Not knowing the high goal of our great endeavour
is spiritual attainment, individual worth. . . .

If Keats's "Beauty is Truth, Truth Beauty" may be allowed in a short lyric, then such an abstract line as "spiritual attainment, individual worth" may be admitted in a fully philosophical poem.[11]

In the second kind of life-leavening, we run into the main stream of Bridges' style, his virtuosity in the handling of words to give variety and life. Repetition in reversal sometimes enlivens the abstractions:

III, 1051
an everlasting hope not everlastingly

or

I, 596
for all things in their day
may hav opinion of glory: Glory is opinion. . . .[12]

Many, indeed most by a very wide margin, of the verbs Bridges uses in his philosophical abstractions of thought, may be read, and should be so read at first, not as sensory or figurative at all. However, consultation with the dictionary shows them to be active, often violent, at their root. At first reading, the following lines are indeed abstract:

[11] There has been disagreement as to whether Keats's line may be allowed in his ode. I agree with Cleanth Brooks, *The Well-Wrought Urn* (New York, 1947), Chap. viii, that it may.

[12] Smith points out an added interest here in a pun involving the Greek word for both *glory* and *opinion*. *Notes* . . . p. 10.

I, 675

> nor is discerptible in logic, but is itself
> an absolute piece of Being. . . .

But when the root of the meaning in *discerptible* as "torn
in pieces, torn off in chunks, that can be rent asunder"
(Webster) is allowed to spread in the mind, the line takes
on an agitated life. So also

I, 432

> a contradiction in terms; as if the embranglements
> of logic wer the prime condition of all Being . . .

with *brangle*, a Scotch verb meaning to shake or tangle.
Sometimes there is a succession of words with no determinable sensory or figurative connotation that produce the
sharp shock rarely associated with the abstract; the sense of
Duty is a voice

IV, 100

> of horror, maleficent, inescapable. . . .

All of these are characteristic of Bridges' style, whether an
isolated line is abstract or not; opinion and feeling will vary
as to their actual effectiveness. But really significant and
compelling is the close and intricate association of all Bridges'
abstractions with vividly concrete and active lines, and the
interweaving of everything he has to say with images that
carry the difficult burden of his hidden truth.

Since what follows will merely be illustrative of these
ideas, not quantitative proof, the objection may be made
that the illustrations are chosen from those lines which the
more readily make the point. To some degree this was done
for clarity. However, they are all well toward the difficult
end of the scale, most of them passages from Book IV, where
the poem is most metaphysical. But under scrutiny, even
Bridges' theory of mind is found to be expressed poetically,
higher in the scale of art than the "emotionalized philosophy"

Santayana asked of poetry.[13] Abstract lines are chosen at random from this book, as illustration of various kinds of "leavening." The "harder" line will be quoted first, then the lines which surround it:

IV, 21

    than any other after-attainment of the understanding . . . .

And now the passage:

IV, 16

    when yet infant Desire . . . . (the omitted lines are figurative)
                        dieth
    out of remembrance, 'tis in its earnest of life
    and dawn of bliss purer and hath less of earthly tinge
    than any other after-attainment of the understanding:
    for all man's knowledge kenneth also of toil and flaw,
    and even his noblest works, tho' they illume the dark
    with individual consummation, are cast upon
    by the irrelevant black shadows of time and fate.

The personification, the metaphorical "dieth out of remembrance," the sensory suggestion of "earthly tinge," "illume the dark," and "black shadows," are effective in themselves, but the suggestion of an underlying life which moves with physical, bodily movement, and is a part of man's aspirations and achievement through time, is the most significant part of the life of the passage.

    In further illustration, the relation of the abstraction and the concrete and figurative will be made clear by italics. A characteristic short passage:

IV, 35

    nor longest familiarity can ever efface
    its birthday of surprisal. . . .

A longer one:

[13] "George Santayana," *Collected Essays,* Vol. 8, No. xix, p. 162.

IV, 66

>   as in the end of his book
> that maketh *the old school-benches yet to sprout in green,*
> *Aristotle confesseth:* where the *teacher saith*
> virtue cannot *be taught to a mind* not well disposed
> by natur, and he that hath thatt rarest excelence,
> διά τινας Θείας αἰτίας, may be above all men
> styled truly fortunat; and with those *four Greek words*
> *hath proudly prick'd to virtue many a sluggard soul.*

Here the vividness of the old school-benches sprouting their green, Aristotle confessing, the teacher saying, the mind as a pupil, the four Greek words pricking to virtue, is added to the literary connotation of the Aristotelian quotation. And one more:

IV, 240

> and with inspiration of their ampler air we see
> our Ethick *split up shear and sharply atwain;* two kinds
> diverse in kind ther be; the one of social need,
> lower, *stil holding backward in the clutch of earth.* . . .

Here the "split up shear and sharply atwain" has the clear edge of steel, with further, the use of alliteration to contribute to the sudden sharpness of the image. In the "holding backward in the clutch of earth," the pull of the muscle is added to the physical force of gravity, and the touch of personification in the word *clutch.*

In place of bringing forward, in their concrete and lively context, a host of other examples (according to count there are 266), I will cite merely the following, which is different from the preceding in that it follows up its idea with a more elaborate figure of speech:

I, 461

> and tho' common opinion may be assent in error
> ther is little or none accord in philosophic thought:
> *this picklock Reason is still a-fumbling at the wards,*
> *bragging to unlock the door of stern Reality.*

The words "fumbling at the wards" give Reason clumsy

fingers, and a clumsy personality, like the usual braggart. The "common opinion" of the first line has already been presented to us as

I, 459
—that untouch'd photograph of external Nature
self-pictur'd for us nakedly on her own mirror. . . .

Most of these passages do more than inextricably mingle the grain of the abstract in the whole; they are part of the most significant means Bridges has found to fuse his meaning and his material. By emphasis on physical organism in terms ranging from kinaesthetic suggestion to personification, he brings out the full implication of his monism. Instead of a mere verbal trick, this emphasis is one end of the scale of complete objectification of his monistic view. By means of it, he underlines his belief that all life (atomic, organic, sensuous, conscient, and finally, spiritual) is one. The abstract terms, which do not bulk large, are never far removed in space or logic from some aspect of this imagery; that they cannot be isolated from it seems clear enough. The complexity of the relationship in any passage chosen at random is astonishing.

But the problem of the unity of this poem goes beyond the negative technique for preventing the harder passages from choking the verse. Bridges' achievement in making a poem which is indeed one poem out of his great assortment of knowledge and feeling is based on his skill in bringing into "keeping" all his various properties and expressing by them his monistic philosophy, or faith. First it is clear that Bridges presents his view of Being and Becoming as a gradation of consciousness (he always uses the word *conscience*, it must be remembered) and as an evolution in time. This idea is stated in many different ways, illustrated from all kinds of experience, and implied throughout. Near the beginning of Book IV Bridges brings together the strands of his thought in the symbol of the Ring of Being. (IV, 112-30)

Reality, he has shown, appears to man as several interdependent links. Touching Universal Mind, the atoms connect
by chemical law with the organic life of plants upon which
animals feed. Man, sprung from them, when fully conscient
is linked in turn back to Universal Mind. Throughout runs
Duty, the Law of Necessity in inconscient forms, the creative
faculty as it escapes toward Universal Mind. It reënters
eternity by the vision of God. Such a monism philosophers
and scientists alike divide on; Bridges has no clearer logic
and no further facts to settle the problem. He does, however,
subscribe to this monism in specific, as well as general and
mystic terms:

I, 365

> Not emotion or imagination ethick or art
> logic of science nor dialectic discourse,
> not ev'n thatt supersensuous sublimation of thought,
> the euristic vision of mathematical trance,
> hath any other foundation than the common base
> of Nature's building:—not even his independence
> of will, his range of knowledge, and spiritual aim,
> can separate him off from the impercipient. . . .

His poem is the expression, not the proof, of this belief.

The homogeneity of the poem is of the same order as
Bridges' conception of the homogeneity of life. At the centre
of the poem is the mind of the poet; at the unifying link of
the Ring of Being is Universal Mind. Bridges' mind is not
the subject of the poem, as Wordsworth declared his mind to
be the subject of *The Prelude,* but rather the instrument by
which the homogeneity and the unity of the design has been
detected. The particularity of the instrument is never lost:
the coloring, or key, of the poem has been caused by it;
everything which has come within its range has been placed
in a perspective that has a meaning. This kind of unity can
be sensed immediately in a short poem; its effect is powerful
on the sensitive mind. The kind of unity imposed on a poem
by its sound may often be made clear by sympathetic read-

ing aloud; it was fully appreciated, although not demonstrated, by Elton. But the homogeneity of coloring created by the imagery of a long poem is matter for careful study, and is only recognized as an important aesthetic value when discovered by analysis, or pointed out in detail.

The study of imagery as a clue to the particular kind of unity achieved in literature, and to individual characteristics of style, has come to be associated with the names of Rickert and Spurgeon.[14] They first boldly applied the card-catalogue method to this formal aspect of literature. Before them, however, Bradley had brilliantly presented the relationship of the grand metaphors of sky and earth in *Antony and Cleopatra* as the essential element of style revealing the true significance of that play.[15] His success points up perhaps unfairly the claims of too great accuracy and too personal interpretation that keep Spurgeon's *Shakespeare's Imagery* from general acceptance, but her method is widely recognized, if not yet widely used, as potential of significant use in criticism. In a play, or a series of plays, in a novel, or in a long poem, the scope is too great, and the mind too limited, for the full importance of the character of the imagery to be grasped at once. In a long poem, before its details are clear in memory from long familiarity, the paraphernalia of index boxes is the surest evidence of the homogeneity of coloring. We learn from the careful collection on cards of sensory, metaphorical, and symbolical images in *The Testament of Beauty* the precise kind of homogeneity their creation and use has cast over this poem to harmonize its divergent matters. It turns out to be one of the chief mechanisms in the devouring of all the disparate experience.

Such use of the classification and counting of images is clearly very different from the attempt to track down the

[14] Rickert, Edith. *New Methods for the Study of Literature* (Chicago, 1927) and Spurgeon, Caroline. *Shakespeare's Imagery and What It Tells Us* (New York, 1935).

[15] Bradley, A. C. "Shakespeare's *Antony and Cleopatra*," *Oxford Lectures on Poetry* (London, 1909), p. 279.

personality and life of an unknown writer. By such use, no more than a clear and detailed knowledge of the surface of the poem is at first attempted: all the properties of the poem, the sensory details, the matters of fact, the metaphors referring to human concerns, for instance, bankruptcy, or war, or daily life, the objects of whatever sort used as symbols, are collected and shown in their variety, their relative numbers, and their perspective. For the time being, the distinction between figurative and descriptive material, all reference to the deeper imaginative significance of the use of metaphor or symbolism, and all inferences as to ethical or philosophical values are avoided. So, in a rough and ready way, one may see what the poem "looks like," as one might say of a painting; on the cards is captured the surface of the poem, the properties, and by their classification, their particular keeping may be detected.

The method, as may be found in detail in Rickert and Spurgeon, is the collection on separate cards of all the concrete material of the text, and their arrangement with constant cross reference in groupings that seem reasonable. This arrangement must have something of the automatic about it, and should be permitted to grow under the hands. It may finally be partly described numerically, but certainly figures are best used as approximations, not as exact statistics. From such a study of *The Testament of Beauty*, there emerged a pattern, or series of related patterns, of the very greatest interest, by which the material seemed fused and amalgamated from the variety of Being and Becoming into one work of art. Once detected, they became clues to meaning, although great care was taken at first to avoid interpretation. By the first arrangement, the concrete material of the poem gradually accumulated and settled in three separate groups. Each one has special individual character, although they overlap and are not strictly parallel either in composition, or aesthetic use, or significance. These three groups contain the following material: first, reference to the physical world, ranging from detailed sensory description of flowers, birds, sky, weather, and so on, to the larger outlines of physical geography; second, reference to the historical world, with the course of human history associated with place, a kind of cultural history; third, the building up of the nature of man as he is biologically in evolution and character, and psychologically as he has developed and as he is potentially, *homo sapiens.* The next three chapters will present the material as it looks from this perspective. By another system of organization a distinction may be made between the "properties" of the poem as the sum of the concrete references, and the recurrent metaphors. The unifying power of these metaphors will be discussed in Chapter x.

CHAPTER SEVEN

THE WORLD IN SPACE

What is the physical geography of Bridges' world? Is it the planet Earth as Satan saw it, for instance, from his first vantage point on the outermost shell of the universe, or as he saw it when he circled it seven times after his first rebuff by Gabriel at the boundaries of Eden? Is it a limited portion of the world we know, specified as the portion experienced by the poet, as we find it in *The Prelude*? It is neither of these, but in fact, more like the world of *The Dynasts*, although different from it in marked ways appropriate to the kind of poem it is. Bridges' physical world is more detailed than Hardy's at many points, less mapped out from the aerial view, more complete in that he gives account of sailing around it. His world is also perceived mentally and emotionally as existing in the dimension of long extended time; Hardy of course gives this sense of time, but time viewed as the timeless spirits view it. The physical world of *The Testament of Beauty* is colored by what has happened to man and by what man has done; to use these confusing words worse to confound them, the effect is a humanistic and romantic coloring of geography. Man, especially man's aspirations and passions, are seen to have affected his knowledge of what the world is like; this is the way most people think of the globe, although we pretend to think of it as the geographer should. Hardy's imaginative grasp of the actual geography of Europe is comparable to the visual memory of a circling tour by plane from southern England down the Channel, out into the Atlantic, the Bay of Biscay, Spain, the Pyrenees, Paris, Northern Italy merging into Switzerland, Germany, Austria, Russia, and around again to London over the Baltic

shores. Days and nights following one another, light up and
darken the land and water below, and the seasons pass their
different shadows across the earth. On the other hand, one
remembers the details of Bridges' physical world as one
remembers one's own experience of life at home and traveling; a rainstorm here, a glass of wine there, a fragment of
archeological knowledge told by a friend and associated with
the river Nile, one's own association of a poem with a place,
a queer distorted mental map of the distance between places
and their relation to one another put askew by a train journey
by night, or a week's eventless sea voyage.

Most of Bridges' details of the world are scattered asso-
ciatively in this way; his mental voyaging is wide, but his
stand is a fixed one. With a few exceptions, the most detailed
descriptions of natural scene might have been taken from
one garden with surrounding woods and farms. We know he
wrote in his Oxfordshire garden:

I, 114
    and now, disturbing me as I write, I hear on high
    his roaring airplanes, and idly raising my head
    see them there . . .

IV, 134
    Ther is a young black ouzel, now building her nest
    under the Rosemary on the wall, suspiciously
    shunning my observation as I sit in the porch,
    intentiv with my pencil as she with her beak . . .

IV, 466
              The imponderable fragrance
    of my window-jasmin, that from her starry cup
    of red-stemm'd ivory invadeth my being,
    as she floateth it forth . . .

IV, 471
            checquering the grey wall
    with shadow-tracery of her shapely fronds. . . .

It matters no whit from how many gardens his memories
have come, the effect of this centre of the world is of one

centre, and the most detailed account of Earth concerns this centre, giving a unity to the poem as a kind of gravity point around which the far parts of the earth are attracted. There are surrounding woods and fields:

I, 299

> The dance of young trees that in a wild birch-spinney
> toss to and fro the cluster of their flickering crests,
> as rye curtseying in array to the breeze of May;
> The ancestral trunks that mightily in the forest choirs
> rear stedfast colonnade, or imperceptibly
>   sway in tall pinewoods to their whispering spires;
> The woodland's alternating hues, the vaporous bloom
> of the first blushings and tender flushings of spring;
> The slumbrous foliage of high midsummer's wealth;
> Rich Autumn's golden quittance to the bankruptcy
> of the black shapely skeletons standing in snow . . .

IV, 482

> Lily-of-the-vale, Violet, Verbena, Mignonette,
> Hyacinth, Heliotrope, Sweet-briar, Pinks and Peas,
> Lilac and Wallflower, . . .

IV, 492

>   —I know
> that if odour wer visible as color is, I'd see
> the summer garden aureoled in rainbow clouds,
> with such warfare of hues as a painter might choose
> to show his sunset sky or a forest aflame;
> while o'er the country-side the wide clover-pastures
> and the beanfields of June would wear a mantle, thick
> as when in late October, at the drooping of day
> the dark grey mist arising blotteth out the land
> with ghostly shroud.

But diligent tidying up and close cultivation make almost a garden of pine woods and beanfields.

We are raised from this lowland loveliness to the uplands at the beginning of the poem:

I, 19

    Or as I well remember one highday in June
    bright on the seaward South-downs, where I had come
        afar . . .

but there is a garden even there:

I, 20

               where I had come afar
    on a wild garden planted years agone, and fenced
    thickly within live-beechen walls: the season it was
    of prodigal gay blossom, and man's skill had made
    a fair-order'd husbandry of thatt nativ pleasaunce. . . .

The only other reference to an upland region comes with the
account of the change in ploughing from ox-teams to the
tractor:

III, 354

    How was November's melancholy endear'd to me
    in the effigy of plowteams following and recrossing
    patiently the desolat landscape from dawn to dusk . . .
                . . . .
    They are fled, those gracious teams; high on the headland now
    squatted, a roaring engin toweth to itself
    a beam of bolted shares. . . .

    In the long and sympathetic section concerning the life of
bees, we have another one of those detailed pictures of the
centre of the world of this poem:

II, 345

    Nay, whether it be in the gay apple-orchards of May,
    when the pink bunches spread their gold hearts to the sun,
    nor yet rude winds hav snow'd their petals to the ground;
    or when a dizzy bourdon haunteth the sweet cymes
    that droop at Lammas-tide the queenly foliage
    of a tall linden tree, where yearly by the wall
    of some long-ruin'd Abbey she remembereth her
    of glad thanksgivings and the gay choral Sabbaths,
    while in her leafy tower the languorous murmur
    floateth off heav'nward in a mellow dome of shade;—

or when, tho' *summer hath o'erbrim'd their clammy cells*
the shorten'd days are shadow'd with dark fears of dearth,
bees ply the more, issuing on sultry noons to throng
in the ivy-blooms—what time October's flaming hues
surcharge the brooding hours, till passionat soul and sense
blend in a rich reverie with the dying year;—
when and wherever bees are busy, it is the flowers
dispense their daily task and determin its field. . . .

II, 396

Thus passeth summer, and with her draggled pageantry
they too giv o'er, and stay all business in the hive,
and huddling upon the foodstore in their dark den
by numb stagnation husband the low flicker of life,
sustain'd by the unheard promise that their prison again
shall feel the sun, and they with the brave buds of March
shall drink the valiance of his steepening rays, they too
be hearten'd to revive, and venturing forth renew
the well-worn round of toil . . .
                    the sweet honeycomb
for which man thanketh them, is but their furnishment . . .

            .   .   .

wherein their forlorn hope, their last shift may hold out
thru' the long sleepless night of winter's starving gloom.

Here, we may feel, is the summing up of nearly all the details
of the poem's central world.

Strengthening, deepening, and confirming the effectiveness of these longer passages is the constant use, both as
factual data and as figure of speech, of the words and ideas
of blossom, flower, bud, fruit, seed, leaf, foliage, root, and
so on. The surface of the poem is filled in by these whether
they are a part of the botanical information or a part of the
language as metaphor. The numerical weight of these details
is very great.[1]

This demi-Eden observed and described by Bridges was
the spot from which his thought ranged in memory and
speculation. The accent of its nearness is unmistakable in
these longer passages and strengthened by the incidental

[1] There are about one hundred and fifty of them.

references. In them, too, we can find details of daytime and nighttime, the seasons and the fluctuations of weather, without which any known landscape would have no expression. All passages which might have been quoted to illustrate the above idea include these changes; sun, wind, mist, spring, high midsummer, autumn, winter, daybreak, noon, and twilight are all present in them. Reaching out into the next circle of details of the physical world, treated less completely, or less locally, we find many more lines descriptive of these diurnal, seasonal, and weather changes, lines which may be fitted to the garden and its surroundings with no distortion of verisimilitude; we find also that this aspect of physical life is used heavily for figurative purpose. All of them collected give life to that garden and its surroundings. Their effect spreads over the more remote world, too, of course, and so becomes a pivot on which to turn away from this England.

The epitome of the diurnal and weather changes lies in the storm lyric which has had such praise. (I, 277-98) Here night and day, as well as sun, wind, and rain, are given prominence to touch the surface of the poem with chiaroscuro.

The same kind of material (rain, sun, shadow, wind), is scattered throughout, with day and night, darkness and gloom, used descriptively, suggestively, or figuratively impressively often.[2] Some of these are as follows:

I, 589
> Our fathers travel'd Eastward to revel in wonders
> where pyramid pagoda and picturesque attire
> glow in the fading sunset of antiquity . . .

II, 146
> and watching o'er the charm of a soul's wondering dawn . . .

II, 150
> In the sunshine of her devotion . . .

[2] About thirty times.

III, 232
> at the still hour of dawn which is holier than day . . .

IV, 499
> at the drooping of day . . .

IV, 971
> the heart-blaze of heaven . . .

III, 187
> thatt darkness
> where all origins are . . .

Storms blow through these pages about ten times, chiefly in
connection with shipwreck, but we have also

I, 681
> phantasies intangible investing us closely,
> hid only from our eyes by skies that wil not clear . . .

I, 696
> scatter'd its pregnant seeds unto all the winds of heav'n . . .

II, 166
> As when a high moon thru' the rifted wrack
> gleameth upon the random of the windswept night . . .

II, 518
> no storm
> blind as the fury of Man's self-destructiv passions. . . .

The seasons are mentioned about fifteen times:

III, 604
> Full Springtime was not yet surely . . . (of lyric poetry)

IV, 5
> ev'n as in a plant
> when the sap mounteth secretly and its wintry stalk
> breaketh out in the prolific miracle of Spring . . .

IV, 1320
> this springtide miracle of the soul's nativity. . . .

Dawn and spring hold more emphasis in the day and season
references, although the cold dark is used as effectively when

symbolic. The dark of the night sky, with the starry firmament, combine these influences of a more etherial kind. In the unresting cloudland passage the full power of beauty informs this theme; there are a dozen or so other references. One of the most beautiful metaphors follows:

IV, 1314

> For not the Muse herself can tell of Goddes love;
> which cometh to the child from the Mother's embrace,
> an Idea spacious as the starry firmament's
> inescapable infinity of radiant gaze,
> that fadeth only as it outpasseth mortal sight. . . .

All these extracts add up to a very particular kind of landscape. We have been given by them a vivid and loving presentation of the outdoor world from which this poem was produced; when we think of the poem, if we have noted the effect of these details, we think of this garden world, surrounded by woods and farms, covered by the canopy of sky, passed over by the seasons, day and night, stimulated and stirred by sun, wind, rain, and hail. Although this canopy of atmosphere covers also the larger world, and has been captured from the poem throughout, whether it was picturing an English or a wider-spread world, the tone, the coloring, the key, of the foreground view is homogeneous, and so far outweighs in quantity, brilliance, and loving care in detail, the physical description of other lands, that it is a major factor in the unification of the poem, being its geographical focal point.

Beyond this immediate well-known foreground, urgent with detailed life, stretches the world as known by the comfortable traveler alert to the earth and to art, and known further to the reader of anthropology and travel, history and poetry. Great plains stretch to the horizon of space and the horizon of time:

II, 97

> Even among beasts of prey the bloody wolves, who found
> some selfish betterment from their hunting in packs,

had thereby learn'd submission to a controlling will,
their leader being so far charioteer of their rage;
while pastoral animals, or ever a drover came
to pen them for his profit, had in self-defence
herded together; and on the wild prairies are seen
when threaten'd by attack, congregating their young
within their midst for safety, and then serrying their ranks
in a front line compact to face the dreaded foe.

The wild beasts of the world are the beasts as much of
legend as of every day encounter:

I, 180

                    the brutes
.... love life and enjoy
existence without care ...

Methusalah sat

II, 631

watching the whelm of water on topmost Everest,

II, 630

... with the last wild beasts tamed in their fear. ...

It is, of course, here only the spelling which suggests Blake
instead of actuality, but suggest him it does:

III, 35

for a Tyger, when once he hath tasted human flesh,
in pursuit of his prey is more dangerous to men
and chooseth daintily among them. ...

He seems first cousin, too, to

III, 37

                    those cannibals
who yet, for all their courtesy (so travelers tell)
and Spartan stoicism, gaily devour their kind.

There are about forty references to wild beasts, sometimes
as part of comments on primitive impulse, sometimes suggesting the wide and dangerous corners of the world one
thinks of when safe at home. These last belong with

I, 326

    the unseen unicorn reposed in burning lair—

in association with which even the

I, 319

              wolf that all his life
    had hunted after nightfall neath the starlit skies

and the wild antelope (I, 325) seem somehow fabulous, like the Dragon with whom Michael and his Angels fought. (II, 623) It may be a matter for concern, as Thompson thinks,[3] that Bridges knew so little of the Orient, but in the perspective of this idea concerning adjustment of foreign lands to the focal point of the garden, in the interests of aesthetic unity in the poem as a work of art rather than a treatise, the references to the Chinese are perfect:

I, 588

    The best part of our lives we are wanderers in Romance:
    Our fathers travel'd Eastward to revel in wonders
    where pyramid pagoda and picturesque attire
    glow in the fading sunset of antiquity;
    and now wil the Orientals make hither in return
    outlandish pilgrimage: their wiseacres hav seen
    the electric light i' the West, and come to worship;
    tasting romance in our unsightly novelties . . .

and

III, 346

              —whether in remotest orient lands
    whose cockcrow is our curfew, where Chineses swarm
    teasing their narrow plots with hand and hoe, càrrying
    their own dung on their heads obsequiously as ants. . . .

This last passage switches directly to the Far West:

III, 350

    or on our western farms where now machines usurp
    such manual labor, and hav with their strange forms
        dethroned

[3] *Robert Bridges,* p. 111.

the heraldry of the seasons, fair emblems of eld
that seem'd the inalienable imagery of mankinde . . .

and with it we are introduced to a round-the-world journey.
Some would choose to dwell in Provence (III, 659) where

III, 671

I long'd but to be
i' the sunshine with my history . . .

III, 674

Avignon, Belcaire, Montélimar, Narbonne,
Béziers, Castelnaudary, Béarn and Carcasonne . . .

III, 660

tho' some would rather praise the green languorous isles,
Hawaii or Samoa, and some the bright Azores,
Kashmire the garden of Ind, or Syrian Lebanon
and flowery Carmel; or wil vaunt the unstoried names
of African Nairobi, where by Nyanza's lakes
Nile hid his flooding fountain, or in the New World
far Pasadena's roseland, whence who saileth home
westward wil in his kalendar find a twin day.

And in this Western world, Bridges finds material for his
discussion of the bees, but it is very different in treatment
and effect from the English passage descriptive of the life
of the bee. The weight of the interest lies in the exotic names,
Antilles, Ohio, Java, Demerara (II, 332), the honey is not
gathered by gardeners but by an old black bear in the
American Adirondacks or the Asian Himalya (II, 442). In
fact, with little or no exception, the natural world beyond
the English garden and its immediate surroundings are
"strange lands far from home" (IV, 1225) " 'neath the sun
upon the Arabian sands" (IV, 1228) or in Eden's paradise,
to which there are about twelve references.

These lands of far away are also long ago, stretching
north, south, east, and west likewise into the aeons of time
and the leagues of distance that separate the world of actuality from the world of imagination. Egypt, the Near East,
Greece, Italy, and France, however, have a greater exactness

of meaning as places than these so far talked of, but their significance is rather more cultural than geographical. There is little if any of the precise and careful delineation of a locality such as we had for the English garden and its surroundings.

Those regions of the world where we come to rest, so to speak, after our flight from Kashmir to Carmel on the wings of alliteration, are regions associated strongly with literature, indeed are put exclusively to the use of explaining and emphasizing the arts, religions, and history. The origin and growth of lyric poetry is introduced with this geographically located simile:

III, 617

    As well might be with one who wendeth lone his way
    beside the watchful dykes of the flat Frisian shore,
    what hour the wading tribes, that make their home and breed
    numberless on the marshy polders, creep unseen
    widely dispersed at feed, and silent neath the sun
    the low unfeatured landscape seemeth void of life—
    when without warning suddenly all the legion'd fowl
    rise from their beauties' ambush in the reedy beds,
        and on spredd wings with clamorous ecstasy
    carillioning in the air manoeuvre, and where they wheel
    transport the broken sunlight, shoaling in the sky—
    with like sudden animation the fair fields of France
    gave birth to myriad poets and singers unknown,
    who in a main flight gathering their playful flock
    settled in Languedoc, on either side the Rhone
    within the court and county of Raymond of Toulouse.

The evolution of architecture and sculpture calls up the following *ad hoc* description of the Nile Valley:

I, 632

    Yet not to those colossal temples where old Nile
    guideth a ribbon oasis thru' Libyan sands,
    depositing a kingdom from his fabled fount
    —like thatt twin-sister stream of slothful thought, whose flood
    fertilized the rude mind of Egypt—not to these,
    nor those Cyclopean tombs, which hieroglyphic kings

uprear'd to hide their mummies from the common death,
whereto their folk dragging the slow burdensome stones
wer driven and fed like beasts, untill the pyramid
in geometrical enormity peak'd true—
'Tis not to these—nay nor in Gizeh to thatt Sphinx,
grand solitary symbol of man's double nature,
with lion body couchant and with human head
gazing out vainly from the desert—not to these
look we with grateful pleasur or satisfaction of soul,
wonderfine tho' they be, and indestructible
against sandblast of time and spoliation of man—
nor tho' with sixty centuries of knowledge pass'd
still those primeval sculptors shame our paltry style. . . .

The detailed and imaginative account of the contents of a
long-buried tomb (IV, 277-338) brings with it what we are
to know of Mesopotamia, on whose desert

IV, 282

poor nomads, with their sparse flotilla of swarthy tents
and slow sand-faring camels, cruise listlessly o'erhead,
warreners of the waste. . . .

Armenia is called to witness of a curious Christian heresy
and scarcely warrants its place here in geography:

IV, 930

Nay, see the Armenian folk in their snow-burrows,
as if distrustful of their high mountainous plateau
between the seas, hav riveted their patriotism
by stubborn adherence to an ancient heresy,
a paradoxy anent the two natures of Christ,
which some theologic bishop, peering in the fog
of his own exhalations, thought pleasing to God;
altho' no creature might possibly understand it.

After these moderately long passages, which should be put
alongside the detailed descriptions of the English neighborhood for full contrast, all other geographical reference occurs
only to give local habitation to the long course of cultural history. These habitations have their names on our maps, but the
coloring is not the coloring of geography; it is the coloring of

an English mind, with a particular education, contemplating them. As might be expected from this fact, Greece, Palestine, and western Europe take precedence over other parts of the world.

This Greece is the land of Plato, sitting with Socrates on the banks of the Ilissus, under the plane trees (II, 7) and of Sappho on her Lesbian isle condemned by Apollo as well as Aristotle (III, 398-470), of Aphroditè (III, 248) and Zeus (II, 617), the temples and the sacrifices, of Zeno (II, 766), Heraclitus (I, 422), Pythagoras (I, 742), Homer (I, 745), Olympic games (I, 757), sea pirates (I, 759), Marathon, Issus and Xerxes (I, 763-64), to the beginning of the end with Alexander (I, 766). This Greece exists geographically for the pretty fancy:

I, 653
> Long had the homing bees plunder'd the thymy flanks
> of famed Hymettus harvesting their sweet honey:
> agelong the dancing waves had lapp'd the Aegean isles
> and promontories of the blue Ionian shore
> —where in her Mediterranean mirror gazing
> old Asia's dreamy face wrinkleth to a westward smile . . .

and

II, 335
> A jar of Hymettan from a scholar in Athens
> regaled our English laurel above all gifts to me. . . .

The references number about one hundred.

Palestine is the habitation of that other great tradition of the Western world, and the concluding lines of Book I show how place and idea are interwoven almost inextricably:

I, 771
> So it was when Jesus came in his gentleness
>   .   .   .
> men hail'd him WORD OF GOD, and in the title of Christ
> crown'd him with love beyond all earth-names of renown.
> For He, wandering unarm'd save by the Spirit's flame,

in few years with few friends founded a world-empire
wider than Alexander's and more enduring;

.   .   .

HIS kingdom is God's kingdom, and his holy temple
not in Athens or Rome but in the heart of man.

Many are the references to Palestine, but the promised land,
the rocky soil, the tares in the wheat, the eternal mansions,
the Assyrian feast (II, 610), the garden of Eden, Zion's hill-
top and the Dead-Sea shore (IV, 744), and the pastures of
eternal life are more the loving recollections of religious
reading than geographical locations. They also number about
one hundred. Naples exists for Saint Thomas where "he fell
suddenly in trance." (I, 486) Umbria is where Saint Francis
walked as Jesus walked in Galilee (I, 246) and Italy was
visited by the Muse

III, 99

to prepare
a voice of beauty for the joy of her children,

to be sung by the voices of the violins of Stradivari and
Amati. Italy, too, is constantly in the poem as the home of
the great painters Raphael, Giorgione, Titian, and the remembered color of their paintings hangs in the mind. Paris
is a part of the teeming intellectual life of the late Middle
Ages and early Renaissance, with reference to

III, 599

passionat Abelard, who . . .
was heralding in Paris the full Renaissance
which should illumin Europe, and plant her cities
with Universities of learning. . . .

Spain comes in with Cervantes (I, 574), France with the
Crusades (I, 509), Norway with the analogy of the lemmings
and the second Crusade (I, 501), and the Baltic shores and
northern Europe are laid in as an imaginative background
for the wanderings of the Northern peoples:

I, 535

> Follow the path of those fair warriors, the tall Goths,
> from the day when they led their blue-eyed families
> off Vistula's cold pasture-lands, their murky home
> by the amber-strewen foreshore of the Baltic sea. . . .

Altogether such references number up to about two hundred, fairly equal in number to those which captured the material of the focal garden, but treated with the effect of haze, of fancy, of historical association. They provide a graded perspective, focussing back to this garden spot, this England. The world of this poem is one world, because of its arrangement, to express it fancifully as Browning speaks of the angels in the Botticelli picture, "rang'd orb on orb."

There is one further idea to be presented regarding this physical world speaking in geographical terms: that the waters of the earth surround it. By specific statement, by isolated figure of speech, and by sustained metaphor, we find that in our view of the physical globe of which the English garden is the focal point, we have the flowing sea around it, just as we found the stars and air above it: these two factors are united by storms. Something will be said later of the navigation metaphor which is introduced in the first lines of the poem:

I, 3

> We sail a changeful sea through halcyon days and storm,
> and when the ship laboureth, our stedfast purpose
> trembles like as the compass in a binnacle.

It will do here as the first of the sea suggestions. We have already had the part about sailing around the world and finding the dates mixed in the middle of the Pacific, and mention of the Baltic and the Mediterranean. Methusalah, too, has appeared with the beasts in the flood, but the fact that he was overlooking the Indian Ocean was not stressed before, lest it confuse the mind. Here we have him moving on after his temporary rest, apparently stimulated to further

travels after seeing Noah ride safely by in his crowded ark
(II, 632):

II, 633

>   and sailors caught by storm
> on the wide Indian Ocean at shift of the monsoon,
> hav seen in the dark night a giant swimmer's head
> that on the sequent billows trailing silvery hair
> at every lightning flash reappeareth in place,
> out-riding the tempest, as a weather-bound barque
> anchor'd in open roadstead lifteth at the seas.

There are about twenty-five references to ocean and ships,
with about ten more suggesting floods of waters, excluding
the flooding of rivers and rain. The following relates this
suggestion of surrounding seas to history, toward which we
are moving in this study:

III, 589

>   the gracious emblems
> of Hellenic humanity, that long had drown'd
> where they had sunk o'erwhelm'd in the wreckage of Rome,
> undersuck'd in the wallow, when Caesar's great ship
> founder'd with all its toys decadent in the deep,
> now freshly of their buoyancy up-struggling here and there
> to ride in sparkling dance on the desolat sea. . . .

CHAPTER EIGHT

THE WORLD IN TIME

The material descriptive of the geographical world, when examined in the previous section, was found to be saturated with legend, existing for the exposition of man's activities in each locality and colored by the residues of his activities, especially those in the mental realm. It was viewed from, and in a sense arranged around, the fixed point of an English garden, the perspective on the far away being both physical and mental. "The Chineses swarming in remotest orient lands whose cock-crow is our curfew" (III, 346-47) recalls Milton as well as geography. Turning now to the world in time, as given by the poem's surface, can we find an analogous arrangement and coloring of the historical material? The question is, not what is Bridges' philosophy of history, but what is the picture of man's past as it creeps toward his present and suggests his future, which this poem creates by its properties and their keeping?

First, no more complete or comprehensive account of man's story is attempted than of the geographical world, no more dispassionate presentation of the details. Although time moves in waves, no genuine chronologies emerge. The record of man's past lies not in events but in what we know of his living conditions, his methods of providing food, clothing, and shelter for himself, in his institutions, private and public, his relations with his immediate neighbors and the relations of tribal or national groups, and finally in his hopes, fears, and accomplishments in the realms of science, philosophy, art, and religion. The record we have here is sharply focussed, as was the description of the physical world, and the perspective is peculiar to the poem, its coloring an important

unifying factor. The fixed stand from which the mental
voyaging goes out into the past, is like the garden, English.
It is one man's experience, widened and deepened by acquired knowledge of past times and alien ways of life. This
man knows of dark terrors in primitive times, as he knows
the plains and the jungles, as a safe traveler; in this realm,
too, he is the careful and imaginative amateur. But the focal
point is very real; it is precise in detail and faithful to fact.
It is a pinpoint in all man's experience, but the character and
temperament and social environment are unmistakable.
Circling out from this point, man's experience is arranged in
shades of light and dark, the aeons of his ordeal explored
(II, 674), but by one mind. Thus the perspective; the coloring is as artfully contrived. This coloring is that of a kind of
medievalism, an unmistakable aura achieved in several different ways, and quite consonant in itself with the treatment
of geography and with the particularized individual mind
of the poem.

Much of the unity of *The Testament of Beauty* comes from
the straining of the known facts of man's history through this
particularized mind. Before characterizing this mind with
specific details, I must return for a moment to the kind of
investigation that discovered them. At least one reader has
felt the poem to be "the expression of not one mind but
several."[1] When the concrete material of the poem, or, in
Spurgeon's terms, its imagery, was skimmed off and given
what seemed a reasonable arrangement, three large groups
of cards emerged. The material in each of these groups
showed the same gradation of character from the clear factual details of a limited and particularized centre, with concentric circles outward toward an idealized periphery. The
centre of the poem's geographical world was found to be
the English garden, although no claim was made that a
specific garden contained all the flowers and birds and

[1] Boas, George. *Philosophy and Poetry* (Wheaton College, Mass., 1932),
p. 35.

weather of the poem. It would have been foolish to ignore
the known facts of Yattendon and Chilswell, but only the
poem, not extraneous material, was allowed to re-create this
garden. It would be foolish to deny also that the personality
standing out from the material of the poem with realistic
and immediate effect is very like what even strangers may
learn of Robert Bridges' life and character. But the picture,
as will be seen, is very incomplete, whether viewed as a
representation of a typical man, or of the poet himself. The
central figure seems largely unconcerned with the bread and
cheese question, or the working of social or political organization: there is no mention of the twelve-year medical experience of the student and hospital physician in the three
great London hospitals, St. Bartholomew's, the Hospital for
Sick Children, and the Great Northern.[2] There is mention
vaguely of but one mortal distress (IV, 1280). The omission
of any specific reference to personal tragedy, or difficulty,
even, was possibly a matter of taste, possibly a limitation of
view; however that may be, the history of mankind appears
in the poem, not without its terrible side, but unmistakably
colored by a happy experience and a faith in the preponder-
ant significance of the intellect and the spirit.

Here are the important details concerning this central
figure. He is born into a babyhood of "muffling wraps," a
"frill'd and closely curtain'd cot" and "silken apparel of
wealth." (II, 323-24) Almost immediately "his eyes and skin
welcome the sun." (II, 321) "With his first life-breath he
clarioneth for food!" (II, 69) His childhood games are in
mimicry of tales read of wild Indians, dressed in "the feathery
tinsel and warpaint of the Cherokees." (II, 575) He remembers the cake "sliced for grabbing school-boys at a teaparty."
(II, 597) His experience widens: he visits "the rattling work-
shops of a great factory." (I, 45) He goes to football games

[2] Thompson. *Robert Bridges*, p. 6. Bridges' report on the activities of the
Casualty Department of St. Bartholomew's can be read in *Collected Essays*,
Vol. 10, No. xxx, p. 265.

"where tens of thousands flock throttling the entrance-gates."
(IV, 1204) He knows good food and good wine (III, 40-
116), plucks a peach in a walled garden (IV, 434), is familiar
with garden fêtes in a politician's park (II, 882), walks on
the South-downs. (I, 20) His mature life brings him knowledge of the London slums, close and filthy. (IV, 360) He
comments on the little choir-boy reading his Bible for its
gory savagery (II, 576), and Oxford youths forgetting their
brothers' deaths in war. (II, 967) He is clearly, however, a
man wrapped up in art and spiritual contemplation. He is
a working poet:

III, 668

> But I in England starving neath the unbroken glooms
> of thatt dreariest November which wrapping the sun,
> damping all life, had robb'd my poem of the rays
> whose wealth so far had sped it, I long'd but to be
> i' the sunshine with my history. . . .

He looks from afar at agricultural processes, concerned with
their poetic values: November's melancholy was endeared
to him by the plow-teams crossing and recrossing the deso-
late landscape of the headlands; when tractor and threshing
machine take the place of these old ways, he feels great loss,
but comes to find a new poetry of toil as he listens to the
warm industrious boom of the thresher spreading far afield
with throbbing power. (III, 354-84) He has learned to
understand the depths of music:

IV, 36

> and great music to me
> is glorify'd by memory of one timeless hour
> when all thought fled scared from me in my bewilderment.

He joins the folk in city churches:

IV, 1220

> while on the dense silence the lector's chant treadeth
> from cadence to cadence the long dolorous way
> of the great passion of Christ . . .

and can compare the experience "in strange lands far from home," where he has watched the Moslem host

IV, 1230
> as their proud tribal faith savagely draweth strength
> from the well-spring of life. . . .

And finally, with what seems to be the unhurried evaluation of old age, he gives two sides of the phenomenon of war. The first side is the recognition of the virtues of great soldiers, typified by Plutarch's Brasidas, who let go the mouse that bit him:

II, 541
> Why should this thing so hold me? and why do I welcome
> now
>
> the tiny beast, that hath come running up to me
> as if here in my cantos he had spied a crevice,
> and counting on my friendship would make it his home?

The second side is the frightening prognosis of the future of man on a war-ridden earth, even on the day of armistice.

Such is the central figure of the poem; what is the larger view of man's experience shown by the properties of the poem which deal with facts of history? Is there no further consideration of social frustration or tragedy than the pitying and apprehensive attitudes toward urban poverty and war included above? Such considerations are not given as relating to the central personality, but they exist clearly and powerfully amongst the details of the poem which are arranged in the outer circles of the material and they are unified by the coloring of the central mind. Government and taxes, church organization and civil duties, frustration and annihilation by the great forces of historical movements have a significant place, although the main interest of the historical material lies in the cultural and the religious activities of man.

The material which deals with the life of mankind as recorded in his history appears as nearly a third of the poem's properties, only slightly less than the geographical material.

It can be filed under the customary headings of the history books: government, law, social organization, war; commerce, business, and manufacture; the production of food and clothing; other aspects of daily life, such as sports; religion, the arts, philosophy, education, the sciences. The relative proportions of these items broadens the conception of the life of man considerably from the base of the central figure. The world of man with its history is preponderatingly a world of the spirit, to be sure, but it is also suprisingly copious in its details of earning a livelihood, suffering from disease and the dislocation of war; government and social organization are of great importance to the total picture. The proportionate amount of emphasis as shown in the analysis of the imagery is as follows: Man's activities as a part of society include government, about 55 references; law and crime, about 45; social classes, about 55; and war, about 75; the total, about 230. His economic activities and daily living include commerce, business, and so on, about 60; production of food and clothing, about 75; the total, about 135. The activities of the mind and spirit divide roughly into religion, about 200; philosophy, about 40; education, about 20; science, with medicine and biology predominating, about 75; the arts, especially architecture and building, well over 100; the total, about 435. The properties are thus seen to be as varied as life itself, with attention to the social and economic far beyond the limits of the central figure. The coloring is, however, clearly toward the mind and spirit, with art and religion especially emphasized. The large figure describing the emphasis on war shows that the effort involved in living is seen to be very much a matter of strife; man's history and the surface of this poem resound to the cries of battle.

Although the life of mankind as recorded in his history is not given any consecutive narrative in this poem, there are materials to build up a steady chronology. The story of man shows us a few details of the primitive savage, the companion in spirit of the Wolf and the Tyger. We learn of the head-hunters (IV, 163), women at their tillage with their moon-magic (III, 343), the "obliterated aeons of man's ordeal" (II, 674). We stop for the myth-making days of the early Hebrews, the Paradise (III, 855), the flood (II, 628). We hear of the luxuries and brutalities of buried Assyrian civili-zations (IV, 277), the slow and inarticulate life of the flooded Nile Valley (I, 632), hieroglyphic kings and Great Sphinx. Early argricultural methods are evidenced in the primitive ways of the Chinese (III, 346), and continued in the descrip-tion of the oxteams on the headlands (III, 354). Much is made of the glorious flowering of Greek accomplishment, the coming of Christ and his walking in Galilee, to found an empire "wider than Alexander's and more enduring." (I, 777) Of Rome, the poem is concerned mainly with the wreckage of Caesar's great ship (III, 591), the sack of Athens and Rome by the Goths until finally "they ruled the world where Romans reign'd before." (I, 545) We hear of the settling of the Troubadours and the development of their poetry, and then the bloody wrath of the Albigensian War in the county of Raymond of Toulouse (III, 630, 723); fur-ther horror, "disease, starvation and massacre," follows the blind course of the second Crusade. (I, 519) The scholarship and art of the early and later Renaissance, and the closely related philosophy and science of the astronomers and Spinoza and Leibnitz touch the horizon of the modern period. (*passim*, and III, 163, III, 774, and I, 430.) Brief reference to the lax imperial rule that allowed Suttee in India (IV, 346), to the crusade against Nigerian slavery, "while the London poor in their Victorian slums lodged closer and filthier than the outraged alien" (IV, 357), leads directly to our present period. It is the era of the tractor and the thresh-ing machine (III, 360, 376), and the great driving power in the engine room of the factory visited in boyhood (I, 48). The crowded treadmills of modern industry (II, 211), the people starved and shut out from the sun (IV, 360), the airplanes overhead (I, 115), the ocean ships fed and sped with fire (I, 113), and the smoke and gas of war's new armory (II, 876), bring man's life in society up to date.

This story of man in his toilsome journey "from conscience of nothing to conscient ignorance" (I, 435), does not give either the proper proportion of emphasis on the various aspects of the record of man, nor much idea of the tone of the whole. Both the bulk of the factual material and the atmospheric tone created by stylistic techniques are medieval; the medievalism is of a highly idealized sort, it is true, but it is a dominant factor in the homogeneity of the poem.

A preponderance of the historical fact of the poem deals with philosophy, religion, and art, as has been suggested by the proportionate figures, and now we find that most of this is devoted to the medieval period in its longest span, from the fall of Rome, perhaps, to the full Renaissance. The proportion is nearly two to one. Under each of the headings of man's activities may be found material from earlier and later periods, of course. Particularly in the field of philosophy, Greek writers are given first place, Plato's myth of the charioteer has inescapable importance in the idea and structure of the poem, and *The Republic* provides opportunity for some jesting as well as serious consideration. Aristotle's *Ethics* underlies much of Book IV. Besides the Greeks, modern philosophers take their places: Spinoza, shaping his lenses to make a tool for science to discover the laws of heredity (III, 163), Leibnitz

III, 778
> imagining two independent worlds that move
> in pre-establish'd harmony twixt matter and mind. . . .

Santayana, unnamed, yet casts a constantly impressive shadow on the properties of the poem. But Saint Thomas appears full length in his conversion from logic to vision, when he fell suddenly in trance.

I, 492
> when Reynaldus, with all the importunity of zeal
> and intimacy of friendship, would hav recall'd him
> to his incompleted SUMMA; and sighing he reply'd
> > *I wil tell thee a secret, my son, constraining thee*
> > *lest thou dare impart it to any man while I liv.*
> > *My writing is at an end. I hav seen such things reveal'd*
> > *that what I hav written and taught seemeth to me a small*
> > *worth.*

In the field of religion, some reference is made to primitive cultures. We find account of the fire worshippers

I, 424
> > who, seeing the Sun
> to be the efficient cause of all life upon earth,
> welcomed his full effulgence for their symbol of God ...

and of "those colossal temples" of old Nile (I, 632), of auguries (II, 232), of primitive ghastly creeds of sorrow (II, 521), and even of Atlantëan adoration (II, 658), of the naked Goddess of man's breed, Aphroditè. (III, 248) Equally primitive,

III, 893
> Vestiges of his stony asceticism imbue
> all time, thick as the strewage of his flinty tools,
> disseminat whereso'er he hath dwelt. ...

But the bulk of the material dealing with religion has to do with the traditions and sacraments and spiritual joys of the Christian church, presented in the garb of medieval church organization, medieval personages, medieval pageantry. The clerks and chroniclers, with their consecrating crosses and embroider'd flags (I, 509-14), and good Saint Andrew in plate-mail (III, 581), are only a small part of the pictorial richness presenting the more worldly Christianity; the following passage more fully expresses the theme:

III, 534
> Now when Rome's mitred prelates ambled o'er the Alps
> to hold the Gallic provinces, whose overlords

> their missioners had won to the confession of Christ,
> the pagan folk submissiv to constraint wer driv'n
> in flocks to th' font, but got little washing therein. . . .

On the other hand, the reality of spiritual ideas and vision to men is made clear and full in the fifty-line section about Saint Francis, who, espousing Poverty

I, 246

> would walk in Umbria as He walk'd in Galilee

.   .   .

I, 253

> no purse nor scrip for his journey, and but one garment—
> and scorning intellect and pursuit of knowledge
> liv'd as a bare spirit in its low prison of flesh. . . .

In these quotations there is a suggestion of the constant echo of the phrases and rhythms of Coverdale (II, 585 and IV, 654, and *passim*), directly and through their reincarnation in the King James translation. And visually, most of this material suggests vignettes from early Italian paintings, confirming the impression of Western European medieval culture.

Medieval poetry and Renaissance art do far more than share the space with Greek and modern art. Dante and his *La Vita Nuova* almost take over the argument when first love, "which is to many a man his only miracle" (III, 225), is discussed as a manifestation of Breed:

III, 220

> In higher natures, poetic or mystical,
> sense is transfigur'd quite; as once with Dante it was
> who saw the grace of a fair Florentine damsel
> as WISDOM UNCREATE. . . .

The dark ages pass with the outburst of Troubadour poetry,

III, 613

> thatt first impetuous raid that storm'd
> the rear of the dark ages prematurely; and yet
> the singers wer so many that man marveleth stil
> whence they came, or by what spontaneous impulse sang.

Renaissance painting especially is used to objectify and develop two dominant ideas of the poem, the first that mother-love is the ideal flowering of Selfhood, and the second that spiritual vision springs from intellectual wonder. The evidence here is scattered widely through Books II and III, with these passages as especially suggestive:

II, 154
> and for a generation needing an outward sign
> of this transcendent mystery, 'twas well when Art
> fashioning a domestic symbol in worship of Christ
> pictured him as an infant in his Mother's arms,

and

I, 328
> but the true intellectual wonder is first reveal'd
> in children and savages and 'tis there the footing
> of all our temples and of all science and art.
>   Thus Rafaël once venturing to show God in Man
> gave a child's eyes of wonder to the baby Christ;
> and his Mantuan brother coud he hav seen that picture
> would more truly hav foreshadow'd the incarnation of God.

Finally, a detailed description and interpretation of Titian's picture of the two women at the well closes Book III, for the reason that "Thus Titian hath pictured the main sense of my text." (III, 1118)

The above material gives the limits of the chronological and "subject matter" aspects of the historical properties of *The Testament of Beauty*. But the historical, to be specific, the medieval, details which create the tone of the poem, are not exhausted by these items. The next circle outward consists chiefly of figurative material, used in discussing a great variety of the poem's ideas; the properties in this group are more widely spread over all of man's activities than in the factual group. They include man's daily social and economic activities, and the institutions by which he has expressed his concern with them; there is here a special emphasis on war, and there is throughout again the strong tincture of medievalism.

Strong as this tincture is, however, it comes from the world of the imagination, not the world of fact. It is a rather peculiar aura that suggests the Middle Ages, perhaps, but one which is hard to pin to exact knowledge and certainly eludes classification according to any school of medieval historians. Anyone trained in medieval history finds himself rather skeptical of the interpretation of facts and when he begins to search, rather desperate really to find any facts at all. The explanation of this is that the tone is not really medieval in the historical sense; it is the tone of medieval romance, as it is found in the old folk and fairy tales, as it has influenced our literature and painting. There is more than a suggestion of *Morte d'Arthur,* and even of *The Lady of Shalott.* It has, however, more passion than Pre-Raphaelite painting. This characteristic is less a presentation of facts than a way of expressing ideas concerning the nature of man. Underlying the poem is Bridges' concept of a universe based on atomic structure, rising to transcendence of spirit with no essential change in its nature, as Catholic theology underlies *The Divine Comedy;* the aura of idealized medievalism expresses both the unity and the ideality of that universe.

There are about five hundred references responsible for this effect, but even the pseudo-medieval tone is not always clear in the examples out of context. We are, however, led to interpret some material which is not colored by such suggestion, as "romantic" in the eighteenth-century sense of "medieval." In the first place, there is enough reference to "story" of this sort, to establish the note very firmly. The look of wonder, which grows in man to vision is

I, 325
                              by fable assign'd
        to the unseen unicorn reposed in burning lair. . . .

Bees have

II, 370
> won immortal place
> in divine story and in poetic fable and rhyme. . . .

History has been romanticized into "old tales of far-off things" (II, 652):

II, 598
> and in [historians'] exaltation of dread and derringdo,
> prowess is magnified and cruelty condoned. . . .

and

I, 533
> the wrongs and sufferings
> alike of kings and clowns are a pitiful tale.

Much is made of the re-dressing of old myths and stories. So Churchmen have taken the old theme of mythological warfare

II, 620
> and pass'd it on the folk
> who, shadow'd in the murk of vulgar vainglories,
> wil prick their ears to hear how "Ther was war in Heav'n,
> and Michael and his Angels (like knights of romance)
> fought with the Dragon" . . .

III, 565
> while with their clerkly skill they sat fast to transcribe
> the old pagan tales. . . .
> . . . with what other numberless
> wonder-lives of the Saints they wrote. . . .

III, 581
> time was when good St. Andrew strode forth in plate-mail.

In the second place, the vague and story-booky medieval tone pervades much of *The Testament of Beauty* by reason of its diction, spelling, and grammar, which frequently have been noticed for their archaism, much as in Spenser and even Chatterton. References to hunting, for instance, seem to contribute to the medieval atmosphere, though there are rarely actual details that are not equally descriptive of modern riding to hounds. The following, to be sure, has the castle to suggest the fairy tale:

I, 390

But from his sleepy castle he wil be tempted forth
if ever a hunting-horn echo in the woods around,
for he loveth the chase, and, like a good sportsman,
his hounds and his weapons as he loveth the prey.

But these next lines carry that suggestion only by a possible linking in the memory with the earlier one; the real strength of the link lies in the archaic *-eth* suffix, and possibly the odd, or quaint, spelling of *wil* and *hav:*

III, 766

tho' science measure true
every wave-length of ether or air that reacheth sense,
there the hunt checketh and her keen hounds are at fault;
for when the waves hav pass'd the gates of ear and eye
all scent is lost. . . .

The quest for truth is not discussed in an historical context at all, but diction, spelling, and grammar are at work in the following passage, where the suggestion of the Old French in the word *mappemond,* joins with the idea of quest and *sweareth fealty:*

III, 689

Restless and impatient man's mind is ever in quest
of some system or mappemond or safeguard of soul,
and coming not at Truth . . .

.   .   .

he espouseth delusion and sweareth fealty thereto. . . .

In Book I the style sets this tone unmistakably, and the opening lines, which cannot be quoted in full, should be read with the point in mind. Here is the first firm chord (the first three lines having the tone more faintly)

I, 4

and when the ship laboureth, our stedfast purpose
trembles like as the compass in a binnacle.

And here are the miscellaneous but close-packed phrases: *when I had clomb, outspredd, mapp'd at his feet, he scarce wil ken familiar haunts, planted years agone, pleasaunce, flowersprent, lain me down and long'd, that drinketh, nor kenneth, small birdes, tickle, monarch beam, hustled sieve,* all in the first two hundred lines. There are other archaic words in the poem, *abredged, unworth, rangled, eterne, intrinse, sithence, solemnel,* for instance. Several with an archaic ring were invented by Bridges, *rangle* being perhaps one of these. Other peculiarities are *wonderfine,* the using of *Breed* for sex, the spelling of *Ethick,* unusual usages that sound out of date, like *vaunt* and *retent. Methought* and *meseems* are used occasionally, and the suffix *-eth* is ubiquitous. Philologically, these and a few others do not add up to much; but Bridges' style is saturated by them, making "the gloss of the lye" unmistakable. Their use is extremely skillful; although one is tempted to think of Chatterton's spurious fifteenth-century imitations when one is considering the quality abstractly, it is obvious how considerable a factor it is in bringing the properties of the poem into its keeping. One may enjoy more a sparse, clean diction and syntax, or a truly nervous, intense one, but here, in use, the effect is important.

To return, then, to the figurative material of the poem which helps to create this effect. The properties in this group, as has been noted, include man's daily social and economic activities, and the institutions by which he has expressed his concern with them. Whether war is an activity or an institution, its prevalence in this material is so noticeable that we may well start with it. Its idiom is used in a great variety of ways, to describe the natural world, for instance, to present events of literary history, as metaphor for philosophical, historical, or poetic concepts. Over all, combat is used as the essential metaphor of the upward striving of the emergent spirit from the atoms, and of the struggle of man to attain his highest nature.

Here are a few examples of the first three groups. Birds fly in ordered phalanx (I, 118), pastoral animals serry their ranks (II, 105),

III, 623

> the legion'd fowl
> rise from their beauties' ambush in the reedy beds . . .

and the summer garden is

IV, 494

> aureoled in rainbow clouds,
> with such warfare of hues as a painter might choose. . . .

In the history of poetry, "with the sword follow'd the song" (III, 513), and after the emergence of Troubadour poetry,

III, 613

> thatt first impetuous raid that storm'd
> the rear of the dark ages prematurely . . .

"the Muse hath doff'd her armour for a silken robe." (II, 645) To Lucretius, Aphroditè comes

III, 249

> waving the oriflamme of her divinity
> above the march of his slow-trooping argument. . . .

Historians all are

II, 593

> as children in this,
> and eagerly from battlefield to battlefield
> jaunt on their prancing pens after their man of war. . . .

And in philosophy, Plato's delicate doctrine of Ideas "held no shield to Zeno's lancing logic." (II, 765)

From the twenty or more passages developing the theme of man's struggle upward to spiritual attainment in metaphors of combat, the following give the bare outline. First, as the youth goes forth:

II, 480
>   all the hope of mankind
> is sharpen'd to a spearpoint in his bright confidence,
> as he rideth forth to do battle, a Chevalier
> in the joyous travail of the everlasting dawn. . . .

Then, as

II, 514
>   the enemy appeareth
> waving triumphant banners on the strongholds of ill,

II, 501
>   good warriorship welcometh his challenge of death.

During the course of the individual life and of the life of man,

IV, 1060
>   all human activities
> may be order'd equally for ravage or defence. . . .

In moments of complete spiritual conquest,

IV, 1357
>   by near approach to an eternal presence
> man's heart with divine furor kindled and possess'd
> falleth in blind surrender. . . .

There is also abundant use of the trappings of war to express the emergence of conscience (consciousness) from the blind habit of atoms, the effect of an idealized struggle to victory being equally impressive in the physical realm.

The institution of feudalism by which medieval society was chiefly organized, appears in a large group of details, next to warfare in importance. We have here the trappings of feudalism, rather than the hard facts of the institution itself, the banners, the castles, the jousts, and the courts of love. The knight appears

I, 233
>   standing forth, as chivalrous knight and champion
> of holiness, in his devotion of heart to God. . . .

In the "faint dream of chivalry" (III, 653) "he espouseth delusion and sweareth fealty thereto." (III, 693) Pleasure is "the champïon of our integrity." (IV, 408) Heraldry and heralds with their banners and oriflammes are used as constant metaphors:

IV, 378

    it is the lordly heraldry of the banner'd flower . . .

I, 65

    the ravishing music . . .

                       . . . rapturously heralding
    the break of day. . . .

The "heraldry of the seasons" (III, 352) is in keeping with all the other pageantry, that of summer, for instance (II, 396), and the "consecrating crosses and embroider'd flags" (I, 514), and "true Wisdom's panoply" (I, 562). The castle:

II, 308

        because the slumbering guards
    In Memory's Castle hav lagg'd at his summons
    for to let down the drawbridge and uplift the gate. . . .

The court of love:

III, 394

    But howso in patriarchal times our code upgrew,
    it hath decretals honour'd in the courts of Love. . . .

The central government of this society is clearly monarchical, the kings are "of fair renown." (I, 512) This monarchy, and the formalities of court procedure are nearly always of a storybook character. The diction of the poem shows constant use of the words *majesty, monarch, crown, sceptre, throne, realm, kingdom, empire, rule,* and *power,* in an imaginative, idealized sense, building up, with the diction and spelling, to the same medievalism of romance. Here are some of the fullest metaphors drawn from court life: the jostling ripples of the atoms of air are

I, 79

> by the enthron'd mind received
> on the spiral stairway of her audience chamber
> as heralds of high spiritual significance. . . .

IV, 388

> So, flaunting their motto
> "Pleasure for pleasure's sake," these doughty Hedonists,
> having got rid of whatsoever oldfashion'd king
> had ruled by right divine, chose out for his good looks
> and crown'd this gay pretender, against whose privilege
> men in the street and schoolmen are for once agreed. . . .

IV, 812

> For never can those privy-councilors in the brain
> withhold official knowledge from the corporat mind;
> ther is no deliberation or whisper'd thought, not ev'n
> unspoken intention among them, but it wil leak out
> to thatt swarming intelligence where life began. . . .

With this last quotation comes the suggestion of the swarming crowds of the governed. The distinction of class is constantly made in the double reference to "kings and clowns" (I, 534), "the diffidence of the ruler and conceit of the crowd" (IV, 254), and the unnamed many, usually that of mediocrity rather than class in a sociological sense, appear as "the herd," or "the crowd" (*passim*).

The many references to the law and the semi-institutional life of commerce have less of this atmosphere of the medieval, but still some. Isolated on cards, they may be modern or medieval; in context, from time to time, and with the quaintness of spelling, comes the storytelling connotation. For instance, "this Autarchy of Selfhood . . . outlaw'd from the noble temper of man" (II, 84) a plant "thrusting its roots downward . . . taketh tenure of the soil" (II, 47) and man's soul "searching for tenement" (III, 230) suggest the wording of the medieval legal records. The champions and ordeals of the feudal system are, of course, really medieval. There is emphasis on gold, riches, and treasure, rather than money, the word "inventory" is spelled "inventary" (II, 467), we hear of piecemeal reckoning (II, 682), weighing "our gold by single grains" (III, 483), finding a "true tally" (III, 864), and measuring the peace of the world in sacks. (III, 484)

There is much among these details concerning the activities of man recorded as history that deals with private life, and it is given very consistently the tone of a storied past. Hunting, among the sports exclusive of the jousts already accounted for, is suggested in the frequent use of the word "lure"; God hounded Adam and Eve (IV, 101), as science measures the wave-lengths of sound as they approach the inner ear, the hunt checketh (III, 768), the hunter for ethical right is "on fuller cry after true happiness than after mental truth" (IV, 194), the Arabs are the warreners of the waste (IV, 284). Another fuller passage, straight from the pages of romance, has already been quoted (I, 390).

Faint but unmistakable, the tone of the Middle Ages runs through the constant references to food and clothing, and small items of domestic life. Here the cataloguing method seems the only one to use. The crafts of weaving and dyeing are suggested in many ways. Much use is made of the word *fabric;* the fabric of art (III, 652), the fabric of mind (III, 941), nature's fabric (III, 987). It is extended to textiles, their weaving and dyeing and making up into clothes: velvet (I, 157), "the ravel'd fringes" and the "wide skirts" of purple power (I, 541), the "seamless web of invisible strands" woven by radio (I, 727), the reins of Reason woven of unknown intangible stuff (II, 26), with a number of other such examples. All the *blend, merge, absorb* verbs, of which there are a great many, have some suggestion of the dyeing of textiles; in the following the relation is explicit:

IV, 720

> the soul wash'd pure
> of absorb'd taint may take a strange gloss of the lye.

III, 570

> So all these divers stuffs thru' the dark centuries
> lay quietly a-soak together in the dye-vats, wherein
> our British Arthur was clandestinly christen'd
> and crown'd, and all his knights cleansed and respirited,
> reclothed as might be. . . .

There is considerable reference to clothes, if not medieval, at least not of our era: Earth's green robe (I, 298), Beauty's Adoration robes (I, 624), the silken robe (II, 645), the high-kilted gossips (III, 887), *mantle* as a verb, very frequently. Eating (except in the verbs to gnaw, etc.) is always feasting. We have a golden cup (IV, 1199), friendly rushlights (I, 296), a servant and drudge (II, 736), a housecarl in Loyola's menie (IV, 436), wild bubbles in a pot with the red fire underneath (II, 746), pothouse cheese and ale (III, 74), the leavening of the lump of life (IV, 60), the clock called a dial for measuring the day (II, 777), and honest pots and pans (IV, 949). Not that all these details are specifically medieval, but they are references to habits and customs and tools developed by man over aeons of time, and remaining almost changeless until our modern era of industrialization. We tend to think of such developed but changeless, and now outmoded, things or customs as medieval.

No one who knows *The Testament of Beauty* at all well will be surprised to hear of this tone, although its consistency and permeating effect may not have been sufficiently noticed or correctly interpreted. For one thing, the peculiarities of diction and syntax, not seen in relation to the historical properties, may be thought of merely as old-fashioned, that is, as unwisely ornamented with outworn beauties. There is some justification for this; the diction considered historically has eighteenth-century echoes. To balance *mappemond, clomb,* and *solemnel,* are *gloom, enamour, o'erblown.* However, the real effect is, as has been shown, that of a romanticized Middle Ages, with the emphasis not on the mere picturesqueness of eighteenth-century medievalism, but on intense spiritual vision.

Had this effect been merely that of the charm of old-fashioned things and the mistaken idea that the past is always beautiful, the power of the medieval keeping of the historical properties of the poem would not be what it is. No aesthetic effect in art is isolable from the communication of significance. This particular effect creates a focal point of time when changes seem to us now to be least rapid; it helps our minds to find a stand in history that will stabilize our concept of man's place in the order of things. No period is of course really static; Bridges was intelligent enough to have known this elementary historical fact. The fusion of centuries with each other is deliberately achieved by blurring their outlines; by weaving back and forth from style to style, partly by quotation and veiled quotation, partly by a return to older tones and appearances of diction. Thus *The Testament of Beauty* is an expression of a unity in thought and feeling among men in all ages, a unity which is as fundamental, in Bridges' view, as is the indivisibility of physical, biological, emotional, rational, and spiritual life. By this device, all knowledge is contemplated from a vantage point well-removed from present-day attitudes, in so far as they are limited by our day; if one may say so, from a kind of eternity where change is unimportant, and the continuing values of religion and art are the only essential ones. Quite aside from the actual facts of science and history concerning the becoming of man, there is what one may call a metaphorical veiling of permanent and idealized cultural far away and long ago. In the full exploitation of metaphors drawn from painting, architecture, poetry, and above all, music, the web of unity is drawn even closer. In Chapter X the idea will be developed.

CHAPTER NINE

THE WORLD OF MAN

The third division into which the properties of *The Testament of Beauty* fall may be called the nature of man. The nature of the geographical world is shown to be a far away and man-endowed and man-illumined world, stretching out orb on orb from the realistically portrayed beauty spot of the garden. The course of history, man's activities and institutions, is concentrated in his spiritual achievements, the central seed, so to speak, of the harvest of ideas about it being that of the experience of a particular personality. This kind of arrangement continues with the material dealing with man as *homo sapiens:* the matrix can be identified as the biological organism, and the surrounding matter seen to deal with its potentiality for evolution in man to the highest intellectual and spiritual life. All readers know that much of the material of *The Testament of Beauty* concerns the biological and psychological evolution of man; indeed, it is felt that the poem is really made up of the combined romantic beauty of the lyric parts and undigested awkwardness of the scientific. One of the usually quoted examples of this kind of undigested lump is

III, 198
                    next in higher animals
        an early differentiation, and at puberty
        periodic appetite with mutual attraction . . .

and out of context it is indeed at least stylistically surprising to the sensibilities. There is, however, only a minimum of this kind of biological information; of the approximately 1,500 items of this division less than a fifth are used in a directly scientific way. The rest either appear as metaphors or are presented with unmistakable imaginative coloring to a spiritual end.

The central information is given in consecutive passages, not more than four to a book, with the last book *Ethick*, containing only one of consequence. Their special character will be understood only by reading in full, but there is no need for long quotation here. No comprehensive outline of the strictly biological nature of man can be arranged from them; the passages refer to those aspects of our biological knowledge which contribute to our understanding of the whole nature of man. Arranging the material in a rough evolutionary chronology for the sake of clarity, we begin with the secret miracle of chemistry by which we hold internal poise between the unimagined heat from which all life has sprung and measured zero (I, 162-73). Through the riddle of the hiving bees, we learn of the proliferation of cells and the relation of the individual cell to the whole organism (II, 259-304). The blind and preying search of the seed and then the plant for sustenance provides the pattern for the habit of all life toward self-preservation (II, 44-83). The stages in the differentiation of sex and the variation of offspring in character by interchange of transmitted genes are carefully presented in the terms used by the geneticist (III, 151-204). The growth of conscience (consciousness) is shown as analogous to the evolution of the flower from the infertile leaf. (I, 414-21) And finally the subtle and infinite coördinations between the senses and resultant meaningful response are traced across the misty marchland between Matter and Mind (IV, 781-833). In these passages the facts are packed closely, and this concentration is part of their quality. They are the centre of the explicit, scientific, material from which the emotionally colored biological references spread out.

Before proceeding to the more idealized material, however, we can find that there are many items of strictly biological suggestion that greatly strengthen the impression created by these longer passages. The analogy here to such strengthening of the impression of the central garden point by the words *blossom, bud, fruit,* and so on in the geographical section, is clear. Whatever their context, about a third of the properties of this poem relate to a living, moving, biological organism, even though the longer biological sections are not of great extent. This organism is clearly a physical body, rising, turning, stretching, pushing upward. Even where the professed subject is the "secret penetralia of ethic lore" (IV, 762), there is this activity. It is illustrated admirably by the lines from which these words were taken:

IV, 761
    AND here my thought plungeth into the darksome grove
    and secret penetralia of ethic lore, wherein
    I hav wander'd often and long. . . .

The words *plungeth* and *wander'd* give physical motion to the process of thought.

Once detected, this sense of bodily presence is very clear, and it comes from several different sources, one of the most important of course being the sensory images. It is not just that there is an abundance of sensory imagery. There is not, for instance, a great amount of actual color, like red or blue. It is that the more "physical" or bodily sensory words predominate. It is generally felt, in both psychology and literary criticism, that in the different classifications of sensory imagery, as visual, auditory, olfactory, gustatory, tactile, and kinaesthetic, those creating images of objects in motion, of smells, tastes, touch (including hot and cold and pain), and of muscular tension, are of the more physical sorts, and it is these that are a part of the creation of the effect of biological organism in the poem. Because it is doubtful, however, whether the smell and taste images have had very much to do with the impression, they are not included among the effective group. There are about 60 of them, about 60 color words, about 200 objects seen as unmoving pictures, and about 120 sound images, making about 440 sensory references giving their own kind of richness to the poem, but not contributing to the effect of biological life. There are, on the other hand, about 500 images suggesting motion, most of them evoking a muscular or kinaesthetic response, and there are, in addition, about 150 tactile images. Whether this is unique in *The Testament of Beauty* one may doubt, and just how unusual will remain a question until more analyses of imagery are published. The final judgment as to the effect in the poem of such proportionate quantities will always be a matter of debate. However, the surface of this poem is what it is at least partly because it presents kinaesthetic images and visual pictures in motion more often than images involving all the other senses combined. The central matrix from which the biological material spreads out in rings of greater and greater idealization has thereby been confirmed.

In the next circle beyond the centre there are twenty-five or so shorter groups of lines containing scientific matter. They are almost all of slightly more figurative character; it would be noticed by any biologist, if not by the ordinary reader of poetry, that much of what has been given is expressed in a rather fancy way, but as we proceed from these matrix passages, the expression becomes a bit fancier, and the coloring of ideality a bit deeper. The following example concerns the biological drive for self-preservation automatically producing its own curbs:

II, 94

> Selfhood had of itself begotten its own restraint—
> like as small plague-microbes generate their own toxin
> in antidote of their own mischief (so 'tis said) . . .

Sex likewise develops from the foundation:

III, 325

> The allure of bodily beauty is mutual in mankind
> as is the instinct of breed, which tho' it seem i' the male

more activ, is i' the female more predominant,
more deeply engaging life, grave and responsible.

The relation of sense and ideality:

II, 784

Nor hath man ever a doubt that mere objects of sense
affect his mental states. . . .

II, 787

The Greek astronomer,
gazing with naked eye into the starry night,
forgat his science and, in transport of spirit,
his mortal lot.

These are among the closest to scientific information of the
peripheral passages. Thus one sees that the poem swings
immediately from its factual centre as soon as that is established, at whatever point in the poem one may find an
example of this centre. That there is a naturalistic base for
all man's life is its main intellectual concept (I, 365); however, the emphasis is always on the elements built up from
that base.

Most of the discussion of these matters is in the tone of
romantic idealism. Here the growth of the embryo is used
as an analogy with mental evolution.

III, 1005

As with the embryo which in normal growth passeth
thru' evolutionary stages, at each stage
consisting with itself agreeably, so Mind
may be by observation in young changes waylaid,
agreeable all, tho' no more congruous with themselves
than what a baby thinketh of its naked feet,
when first it is aware of them, is like the thought
of piteous sympathy with which when an old man
he wil come to regard them.

The following is perhaps one of the most elaborately disguised references to the physiology of sex. The fully-clothed
figure of Titian's *L'Amor Sacro e Profano*

III, 1115

> hath the arm bent down
> and oppositely nerved, and clencheth with gloved hand
> closely the cover'd vessel of her secret fire.

Selfhood, far removed now from the low organisms like pythons "gliding to seize and devour some weaker Self" (II, 78), has developed into Motherhood, and may be left

II, 164

> in her fond sanctuary awhile
> with the unseen universe communing and entranced
> strangely. . . .

The potentiality of sex in adolescence is thus described:

III, 224

> in thatt awakening miracle of Love at first sight,
>
> .　　.　　.
>
> his one divine Vision, his one remember'd dream. . . .

This is certainly biology at many removes, indeed quite lost in idealized interpretation.

Beyond this kind of material, of which there is much, lies more with a strongly symbolical cast, increasing the tone of idealization to a marked degree. It is concerned in a way with biological matters, that is, with the life cycle of man, his birth, growth, sickness, and death. Frequently there are times in this life course when

I, 528

> honest hope turneth away repell'd
> by the terror and superstition of savagery. . . .

But our living, growing, and searching is predominantly upward and into vision:

IV, 660

> Delicat and subtle are the dealings of nature,
> whereby the emotionable sense secretly is touch'd
> to awareness and by glimpse of heav'nly vision drawn
> within the attraction of the creativ energy
> that is the ultimate life of all being soe'er. . . .

At each stage of growth, man may have his spiritual revelation, as child, boy, or adult. All this material is highly generalized, not including any activities which are not common to all men; all men, from birth through childhood to manhood, may have glimpses of heavenly vision.

No completely logical ordering of this material is possible, although the main groupings around birth, childhood, manhood, and death, are clear enough. As in all poetry, these subjects are in constant metaphorical use, although here there is also some of the authenticity of detail that owes a great deal to Bridges' training and practice as a physician.

There are some fifty references to birth, the word, or synonyms of it, being used more or less literally and in increasing degrees of metaphorical meaning. First, of course, there is birth as a physical, though never obstetrical, fact, as we find it in the following:

III, 739

the second Essene War
brought the New Life in which full soon Dante was born. . . .

or

II, 67

Look now upon a child of man when born to light. . . .

There are many miscellaneous, vaguely figurative examples such as we find in frequent use, as in "or ever a man was born to rob their honeypots" (II, 191), "inborn love of Beauty" (IV, 621), "the look of it is born already of fear and gentleness" (I, 323), "the fair fields of France gave birth to myriad poets" (III, 628), and in the idea of birth behind the word *nascent (passim)*. Most important numerically is the constant use of the metaphor for the idea of the emergence in evolution of mental and spiritual activity, as in the lines, "But any man may picture how Duty was born" (IV, 132), "thatt firstborn pleasur of animal conscience" (IV, 676), and "the first-born intimations of spiritual life." (IV, 1096)

Then, to express the idea of Essences:

I, 670

> As some perfected flower, Iris or Lily, is born
> patterning heav'nly beauty . . .

and

I, 683

> activ presences . . .
> like bodiless exiled souls in dumb urgence pleading
> to be brought to birth in our conscient existence. . . .

Finally, the important idea of new birth at the moment of vision, with its resultant purification and joy, is a thread of technique and meaning throughout the poem. Its use runs from the "birthday of surprisal" when music first stirred the poet deeply (IV, 36), to the formulation of the idea of the whole poem when in the opening vision of familiar haunts estranged by beauty,

I, 10

> a glow of childlike wonder enthral'd me, as if my sense
> had come to a new birth purified. . . .

Using roughly the same order of illustration, we find childhood as a stage of growth:

II, 464

> 'tis a delight to look on him in tireless play
> attentivly occupied with a world of wonders,
> so rich in toys and playthings that naked Nature
> wer enough without the marvellous inventary of man . . .

III, 191

> a child thinketh
> he is nearer to the Pole-star when he is put to bed. . . .

And relating that stage to historical development:

III, 40

> From the terrifying jungle of his haunted childhood
> where prehistoric horror stil lurketh untamed,
> man by slow steps withdrew. . . .

As a state of being, that of wonder, which is "divinest child-hood's incomparable bloom" (I, 335), or to characterize Reason, for instance, as "a helpless nursling" (II, 727), or nations which

III, 695
> lie fascinated in their swaddling clothes
> crampt, and atrophied with their infantile suctions. . . .

And finally to describe a quality of the moment of vision, when "this glimpse or touch of immanence" is "a superlativ brief moment of glory" (IV, 59), the child is shown as the recipient of God's love:

IV, 1314
> For not the Muse herself can tell of Goddes love;
> which cometh to the child from the Mother's embrace,
> an Idea spacious as the starry firmament's
> inescapable infinity of radiant gaze. . . .

There has been a hint of the growth of childhood into youth, both the process of growth and the changing charac-teristics of the later stage of life, in these quotations, and they need not be extended. But a different kind of material comes in the presentation of adolescence and the emergence into manhood. There are fewer scattered examples, but the stage itself is discussed quite fully. Here are two examples of the idealization of the state of manhood:

I, 539
> in the incontaminat vigor of manliness . . .

I, 713
> true beauty of manhood
> outfeatureth childish charm, and whether in men or things
> Best is mature. . . .

Growth to maturity is revealed in many direct statements and many figures of speech; the effect of adolescent expan-sion is presented almost entirely with that coloring of ideality

which has been seen to be spread throughout the poem. The
following passage shows how rich this coloring can be:

II, 472

    and as he ever drinketh of the living waters
    his spirit is drawn into the stream and, as a drop
    commingled therewith, taketh of birthright therein
    as vast an heritage as his young body hath
    in the immemorial riches of mortality.
      And now full light of heart he hath willingly pass'd out
    thru' the sword-gates of Eden into the world beyond:
    He wil be child no more: in his revel of knowledge
    all the world is his own: all the hope of mankind
    is sharpen'd to a spearpoint in his bright confidence,
    as he rideth forth to do battle, a Chevalier
    in the joyous travail of the everlasting dawn:
    Ther is nought to compare then, truly nought to compare:
    and wer not Fortune fickle in her lovingkindness,
    all wer well with a man—for his life is at flower,
    nor hath he any fear. . . .

This passage deals with the expansion of self at the time
when childhood turns into manhood; its relation to first love
is described in Book III:

III, 795

               as wonder to intellect,
    so for the soul desire of beauty is mover and spring;
    whence, in whatever his spirit is most moved, a man
    wil most be engaged with beauty; and thus in his "first love"
    physical beauty and spiritual are both present
    mingled inseparably in his lure: then is he seen
    in the ecstasy of earthly passion and heav'nly vision
    to fall to idolatry of some specious appearance
    as if 'twer very incarnation of his heart's desire. . . .

This relation of Beauty to desire is expressed in the most
ideal terms at the beginning of Book IV:

IV, 16

    when yet infant Desire hath neither goal nor clue
    to fix the dream . . .
               . . . 'tis in its earnest of life

and dawn of bliss purer and hath less of earthly tinge
than any other after-attainment of the understanding. . . .

The fully productive period of man's life, in his thinking,
in art, in religion, appears throughout the poem as stable
and enduring, as in fact, the long period of his maturity
before disease leads to death. In this period, marriage, sexual
and affectional, is assumed by the poem as the normal relationship, and is explicitly so described:

III, 478

> Now to the most who are like to read my English poem
> christian marriage wil seem a stablish'd ordinance
> as universal, wholesome and needful to man
> as WHEAT is, which, ubiquitous, and sib to a weed
> that yet wil hamper its cultur, overruleth all else,
> weigheth our gold by single grains, and harvested
> measureth in sacks the peace and welfare of the world,
> our BREAD OF LIFE, and symbol of the food of the soul.

In the properties of the poem, the sexual experience, as has
been seen, appears in its biological roots; the effect of the
scientific statements concerning sex is increased by the constant figurative use of the words *engender, generate, progeni-
tor, procreate, propagate, proliferate, prolific, beget, fertilize,
pregnant, barren,* and *sterile.* However, in the fullest passage
concerning the relation of man and woman, the physical act
is shown as the basis of revelation:

III, 421

> true loves are mutual and of equal strength
> and their bodily communion is a sacrament—
> like those irrevocable initiations of yore
> whose occult ritual it was profane to disclose—
> and in its uttermost surrender of secrecies
> hallowing brute instinct, symbolizeth approach
> to satisfaction of unattainable desire. . . .

Frustrations and perversions are not ignored; sex "hath sanctified fools and degraded heroes" (III, 215); but the keeping
of all this material is nevertheless consistently that of the
ideal, not of its unrealization.

It is, finally, in the mystic vision of Beauty that man's life
cycle closes. Any death he may have is transcended by it,
and his immortality is contingent on this transcendence.

IV, 1253

> Nor doubt I that as this thinking machinery
> perisheth with the body, so animal thought
> with all its whimper and giggle must perish therewith,
> with all shames, all vain ostentation and ugliness. . . .

IV, 1262

> This mind perisheth with this body, unless
> the personal co-ordination of its ideas
> hav won to Being higher than animal life,
> at thatt point where the Ring cometh upward to reach
> the original creativ Energy which is God,
> with conscience entering into life everlasting.

Disease and death are treated as unbalance or disharmony,
as deformations and corruptions. As unbalance:

I, 169

> our soft bodies [are] vext and harm'd
> by their own small distemperature, nor could they endure
> wer't not that by a secret miracle of chemistry
> they hold internal poise upon a razor-edge
> that may not ev'n be blunted, lest we sicken and die.

As disharmony:

IV, 1026

> I find
> Reason wil diagnose the common ailment of Mind
> a lack of harmony. . . .

Plague has a bad moral connotation:

II, 985

> when Plague invaded the cities,
> Athens or London, raging with polluted flood
> in every house, and with revolting torture rack'd
> the folk to loathsom deaths . . .

.   .   .

II, 991

>   alas then in what plight are we,
> knowing 'twas mankind's crowded uncleanness of soul
> that brought our plague! [war]

No pestilence is believed so poisonous as man's "hideous sins." (II, 520) As the child may draw good from beauty, deprived of it he will draw "infection and death from evil as quickly as life from good." (IV, 650) Death is also mere oblivion "whereon our loves and shames are begotten and buried" (I, 155) or the negation of life,

I, 192

> for howso deliberatly a man may wish for death
> still wil he instinctivly fight to the last for life.

In the cycle of daily life, sleep has its prominent place, and Bridges' treatment of it follows his pattern for the other material, the emphasis being perhaps especially clear in the realm of metaphor for spiritual discovery. This, of course, is an almost universal poetic, indeed psychological, relationship, and it is furthered by the importance of the dream among the symbols of the poem. The progress of the treatment of the biological state of sleep toward heavenly vision does its part in establishing the keeping of the poem. Sleep is closely associated with joy in the beauty of nature. The blooms "that sleep i' the sun" (IV, 484), "the slumberous air" (III, 96) full of the incense of the pines, "the slumbrous foliage of high midsummer's wealth" (I, 307), are important in what Keats would call the luxury of nature. Sleep and awakening are associated with joy in life in the following:

IV, 1348

> of faintest ecstacies aslumber in Nature's calm . . .

and

II, 144

> The unfathomable mystery of her awaken'd joy
> sendeth her daily to heaven on her knees in prayer. . . .

The emergence of mind from the blind habits of atoms is constantly expressed in the word "awaken." And finally we have the pure example of the symbolic use of sleep:

II, 173

—nay, incommunicable and beyond all compare
are the rich influences of those moments of bliss,
mocking imagination or pictured remembrance,
as a divine dream in the vaulted slumber of life.

It is by the metaphor of sleep rather than death that the immortality of the spirit is expressed.

Quite conclusively, then, the surface of this poem, as gathered by an analysis of its imagery in the widest sense, shows both variety and unity. The physical world, the world of time, and man himself, are of one substance, and implicit and emergent throughout is the vision of significant beauty. The fiction of concentric circles need not be accepted fully for the acceptance of the more important underlying fact. Anyone not keeping in mind the method of a study like this, might well suspect such clear and repeated arrangement to be the inveiglings of Reason, in Bridges' words (IV, 1300). Indeed caution is always well taken in any exact study of a work of art, as of any survey of the nature of things: Bridges says of Plato's myth and his use of it:

III, 3

'twer well here to remember how these pictured steeds
are Ideas construed by the abstract Intellect.

But before refusing attention to the abstract idea because it looks false, one must remember also, that "all altitude expanse or grandeur of building" (III, 10) in any kind of art

III, 11

subsisteth on foundations buried out of sight,
which yet the good architect carrieth ever in mind,
and keepeth the draft by him stored in his folios.

Whether he intended to follow it or not, Bridges' draft exists in a letter written to Bradley in 1901. He said then, "I always seem to see man as the center of concentric spheres, the nearest to him being the 'circle' of common sense and matter of fact, beyond this the circle of science and intellect, & beyond that, stretching out to infinity, the realm of imagination, which imagination, if it be present, radiates from the center and is related to everything, at least if *it be present* at all."[1] Confidence in the plan of what has gone before should be increased by the fact that it was revealed by the mechanical task of sorting the cards on which the concrete material was skimmed off. The unity and homogeneity of the material of the poem has not, it is true, been obvious to readers of *The Testament of Beauty,* but only because the wood has not been seen for the trees. Time alone will determine whether this characteristic ordering of material, intentional on Bridges' part or not, will be effective with readers.

[1] *Correspondence of Robert Bridges with Henry Bradley,* p. 5.

CHAPTER TEN

THE DOMINANT METAPHORS
AND SYMBOLS

That the unity of *The Testament of Beauty* is partly created by the patterning of the world, history, and the individual man, as shown in previous chapters, seems clear and provides a key for the reading of the poem. The sense of a significant order as well as of a general homogeneity grows as one returns to the text. More generally realizable and probably acceptable to most people before they begin to feel these effects themselves, is the seamless web cast over the poem by a few dominant metaphors. When we consider only that part of the imagery of the poem which is figuratively used, we have a new and sharper perspective. The result of such restriction and reorganization is the discovery that there are metaphors recurrent throughout the poem of greater and less preciseness and importance. They are all of course closely related to the subjects just discussed as the properties and keeping of the poem; indeed they make up part of that material looked at from another point of view. There are several of greater importance than the others. The archaisms of diction and the dominant medieval note of the historical material have been already sufficiently discussed. It is not too much to call this tone a kind of permeating metaphor. Equally stylistic, and more clearly figurative, is the use of the terminology of the arts, especially of music, for the expression of all kinds of ideas. The most dominant is the metaphor of the living organism which pervades the poem. Connected with this is the highly dramatic character of the style created by the use of varying degrees of personification. And last, the symbols of dream, journey, search,

174

with related ideas, such as light and dark, origins and the like, both unify the poem and suggest its deeper significance.

In Chapter VIII Bridges' world of history was shown to be largely a medieval world suggestive rather of fairy tale than of government documents. The conclusion was that this atmosphere was a kind of metaphorical veiling of permanent and idealized culture. Here a discussion of the metaphors drawn from the arts will give further detail contributing to the same end.

A poem called *The Testament of Beauty*, and the humanistic world it presents, would naturally have a large place for the arts; the idea of the poem demands this. The opening lines bring the

I, 32

gems
[that] master-minds in painting or music
threw aside once for man's regard or disregard . . .

in line with the "flowers that starr'd the fine grass of the word" (I, 29), as

I, 35

things supreme in themselves, eternal, unnumber'd
in the unexplored necessities of Life and Love.

Terms borrowed from the arts are used constantly, but perhaps need only be mentioned in passing. The word *pictured* appears over and over again; *foundations, builded, dancing, molded,* and especially *harmonized* are key-words, representing Bridges' conception of the nature of things and their evolution and proper relationships. They occur several hundred times, to the extent that they constantly suggest the creative urge and shaping power of art, which Bridges believes to be but Nature herself "who danceth in her garden." (IV, 976)

The function of music as a metaphor needs somewhat more extended illustration. It is admirably adapted to indicate Bridges' final conclusions concerning man's highest conscient development, the power he has through his Reason to harmonize his own impulses and in the highest natures, all possible eternal essences. And poetically speaking, this metaphor is provocative above the other arts, by suggestion of the loveliest harmonies of sound. The philosophical implications can rarely be disentangled from the resonance and melody; in a sense, the musical power of the verse is itself a figurative way of expressing the highest spiritual significance of the intellectual idea of order, or harmony.

The first idea developed in the poem, after the introductory presentation of the vision, is the idea involved in the relation of atomic motion to beauty of sound, and the reference is drawn on to music.

I, 63

> Lov'st thou in the blithe hour
> of April dawns . . . . . to hear
> the ravishing music that the small birdës make

. . .

I, 74

> Hast thou then thought that all this ravishing music,

. . .

I, 77

> is but a light disturbance of the atoms of air. . . .

. . .

I, 99

> see then how deeply seated is the urgence whereto
> Bach and Mozart obey'd. . . .

Poetry is presented largely (aside from the long passages dealing with Dante) in terms of song:

I, 743

> And ev'n to Apollo's choir was a rich voice lacking
> in the great symphonies of the poetic throng. . . .

Of the Troubadours, after the simile of the carolling birds,

III, 615

>the singers wer so many that man marveleth stil
>whence they came, or by what spontaneous impulse sang.

Of love poetry:

IV, 1349

>like thought in a closed book, where some poet long since
>sang his throbbing passion to immortal sleep—. . .

Of the relation of nature's creative powers and the artist's:

IV, 961

>—as when Sebastian preludeth, all her [nature's] voices
>that ever hav reach'd our ears are crest-fal'n and abash'd. . . .

Of the contribution of radio in the realm of music:

I, 724

>   and now above her globe-spredd net
>of speeded intercourse [science] hath outrun all magic,
>and disclosing the secrecy of the reticent air
>hath woven a seamless web of invisible strands
>spiriting the dumb inane with the quick matter of life:
>Now music's prison'd raptur . . .
>mantled in light's velocity, over land and sea
>are omnipresent. . . .

Of the mystic's ecstasy, stimulated by asceticism:

IV, 452

>   Nature ne'ertheless
>singeth loud in her prison, and for all ecstasy
>these mystics find no language but to echo again
>the psalm of her captivity. . . .

Of his major premises, Selfhood and Breed, Bridges speaks metaphorically as his figuration of "the twin persistent semitones of my Grand Chant." (III, 940)

The idea of the necessary and productive harmonies of the parts of man's psychological make-up, may be amply illustrated; most essential in Bridges' idea of the nature of Mind, is the function of Reason:

II, 710

> to comprehend aright and wisely harmonise
> the speechless intuitions of the inconscient mind. . . .

II, 817

> and thus I stand where I conclude
> that man's true wisdom were a reason'd harmony
> and correlation of these divergent faculties. . . .

A proper "will" (IV, 1043), good marriage (III, 495), the best of English motherhood (III, 899), are all presented as harmonies of divergent elements.

When the highest spiritual harmonies lead to the perception of great truth, the metaphor of music produces Bridges' greatest poetry. He believes that "the soul's nobility consisteth" "in harmony of Essences" (IV, 945).

IV, 952

> like as in music, when true voices blend in song,
> the perfect intonation of the major triad
> is sweetest of all sounds; its inviting embrace
> resolveth all discords; and all the ambitious flights
> of turbulent harmony come in the end to rest
> with the fulfilment of its liquidating cloze.

II, 168

> on early worshippers
> at some rich shrine kneeling, stealeth thru' the eastern apse
> and on the clouded incense and the fresco'd walls
> mantleth the hush of prayer with a vaster silence,
> laden as 'twer with the unheard music of the spheres. . . .

In a very strange context, the effect of wine:

III, 97

> to the mind exhilarating, expelling care,
> even as those well-toned viols, matured by time, which once,
> when the Muse visited Italy to prepare
> a voice of beauty for the joy of her children,
> wer fashion'd by Amati and Stradivari and still,
> treasured in their mellow shapeliness, fulfil
> the genius of her omnipotent destiny,—
> speaking with incantation of strange magic to charm

the dreams that yet undreamt lurk in the unfathom'd deep
of mind, unfeatur'd hopes and loves and dim desires,
uttermost forms of all things that shall be.

Perhaps the most aesthetically moving of all the beautiful
lines of *The Testament of Beauty* accompany the introduction to the conclusions concerning Mind:

IV, 765
tho' no lute ever sounded there nor Muse hath sung,
deviously in the obscure shadows. . . .

As a testament to the spiritualizing effects of natural
beauty, and beauty in art, this poem, itself a work of art,
calls on the arts for one of its enveloping metaphors, working as do the others, for the fusing of all the material into an
organic whole.

During the years of its composition, Bridges gave a pro-
visional title to his poem, *De Hominum Natura:*[1] as a physician with a continuous interest in biology, he emphasized
the importance of the body in the nature of man; as a religious man he might have set up a debate in the medieval
manner between the body and the soul. But as a philosopher-
scientist, he believed that man's mind cannot be isolated
from Nature's other works (I, 362) and set up his poem to
express his glad faith that all the miracle of man's spirit is
held in the biological organism "in intrinsic potence." (I, 421)
This is the saturating idea of the poem; the biological material of life is not only shown as producing spirit, but is used
as a metaphor for the development of ideas, a metaphor with
which the style is equally saturated.

To begin with, *The Testament of Beauty,* as has been
shown, has a kind of surface crepitation, an impression of
movement, of activity, constant and keen. Even when ideas,
theories, opinions, and facts are the subject matter, the texture of the lines is so constantly sensory that it is alive, with
a continual stirring and rippling movement. More specifically

[1] Smith. *Notes* . . . , p. ix.

the preponderance of the kinaesthetic among the senses gives the suggestion of a bodily organism. Once detected this sense of bodily presence is very clear. An indication of its ubiquity is that in one arrangement of the images of the poem, we find them about equally divided among the following groups: one part for man's activities in society and mental attainments, one part for symbols of his spiritual evolution, one part for sensory data relating exclusively to bodily action, and one part for all other senses. Out of this organic material comes next an awareness of the presence of living conscious beings that become the subject of small dramatic fictions. These fictions extend finally to narratives of greater or less length.

The first gradation in this development may be seen in a device or mannerism frequently objected to in Bridges as old-fashioned and unrealistic. He infuses his world, his history, and his ideas with the quality of personality, that is, he uses metaphors tending toward the pathetic fallacy, or achieving the pathetic fallacy outright, and he uses personifications much more than the modern mind readily accepts. This *humanizing* is, however, to a great degree what gives the poem its "keeping" of the living, feeling, thinking organism. In a way, nearly all the mixed metaphors are embryo personifications, but there are some that attribute botanical characteristics to zoölogical forms, zoölogical to chemical and mechanical, and so on in any pattern of mixture. There are about a hundred and fifty such that give the feeling of the indivisibility of all life, with the effect of a moving, conscious life throughout. We can see that the following fuses the conscient, the sentient, and the mechanical:

IV, 828
> —as every sensation must suffer translation
> ere it can mediate in the live machinery. . . .

The mental and the biological mingle in the phrase "their eyeless sorrows" (II, 668) and in

I, 194

> Yet with the burden of thought pains are of great moment,
> and sickening thought itself engendereth corporal pain. . . .

Here are the abstract, the physical, and the human:

I, 347

> a structur of blind atoms to their habits enslaved . . .

and

I, 288

> > huge molten glooms
> mount on the horizon stealthily. . . .

The humorous mixture of the following is very complex:

III, 119

> he retireth with stomach Emeritus
> to ruminate the best devour'd moments of life. . . .

The vaguest of the personifications are almost indistinguishable from some of the above; they consist really in
applying adjectives or adverbs of a human connotation to
nonhuman objects, or giving them human activities. For
instance, there are "leisur'd gardens teeming with affection'd
thought" (I, 311); art divines "fresh motiv for skill" (III,
642); equality is

IV, 253

> —a doctrin kindly at heart, that cajoleth alike
> diffidence of the ruler and conceit of the crowd. . . .

This kind of thing is developed many times into little thumb-
nail sketches by personification. These are among the lines
most often quoted by the anthologizing admirer who has
probably missed the extended metaphor of which they are
a part. For instance:

I, 657

> —where in her Mediterranean mirror gazing
> old Asia's dreamy face wrinkleth to a westward smile . . .

III, 1068

> dive down in the mine
> where cold philosophy diggeth her fiery jewels. . . .

The following is more extensive:

IV, 665

> While Science sitteth apart in her exile, attent
> on her other own invisibles; and working back
> to the atoms, she handleth their action to harness
> the gigantic forces of eternal motion . . .

IV, 671

> dreaming, amid the wonders of her sightly works,
> thru' her infinitesimals to arrive at last
> at the unsearchable immensities of Goddes realm.

It is important to recognize that Bridges' use of personification is not the fancy literary device that it is in mediocre verse, and not the decoration used by a formal and anachronistic mind, as some readers have said. The impression of body and personality and mind as all a part of Being is thus built up metaphorically.

An understanding of these personifications leads to one's perceiving the importance of the many dramatic fictions which develop from time to time into full-fledged narrative told with the techniques of a storyteller. Nearly all the illustrations from the natural world and from history are presented in narrative, and even the steps of an argument or the various elements in a conclusion are dramatized by human figures doing and moving. Even in passages of nature description where the lyric effect is especially notable, the verbs are interesting. The much-quoted passage beginning "The sky's unresting cloudland" (I, 277) would seem to be especially dramatic, but its effect is not unique. Here the sky is a moving, mounting mass of cloud and wind. The clouds "stand in massiv range," cumulate, up-pile, sail, scatter, disperse, scurry, fling, laugh, o'er arch, mount, gather, climb, rebuff, are driven away, and cleared. The green robe of earth, imagined to be made from the various wind-blown trees, sways and glows with changing colors. The equally well-known garden passage in Book IV (466) shows the same characteristic; the flowers and their odors invade, float, wanton, chequer, hang, escape, spread, withhold, mingle, and steal forth. In the long Bee section of Book II, usually also classified as lyric, the framework is conspicuously a narrative. The life of the bee is told as a tragic story, beginning in the gay apple orchards of May (II, 345) and continuing into "the shorten'd days" "shadow'd with dark fears of dearth." (356) "Forty days, six unsabbath'd weeks of fever'd toil" (381) "wasteth and wearieth out their little frames." (382) They finally perish and disappear or huddle in their dark den and "by numb stagnation husband the low flicker of life." (399)

The many figures from cultural history introduced by Bridges always act upon the stage he has set for them. Saint Francis, who illustrates the idea that even an ascetic may be a worshipper of nature's loveliness, climbs a ladder (I, 229), learns by taste of vanity, abjures and stands forth. He reshouldered the yoke his Master offered, walked in Umbria, scorned intellect, lived as a bare spirit, and lying sick in Damian, composed his canticle to Nature. (I, 239-76) Saint Thomas, the angelic Doctor, toiled to found an irrefragable system and with open eyes accepted for main premiss the myth of a divine fiasco. He fell suddenly in trance, in Naples, and replied sighing to his friend Reynaldus that his writing was at an end. (I, 470-500) Jesus came in his gentleness and was hailed Word of God, and crowned with love; he wandered unarmed, and founded a great empire. He once preached to the herd, but now to the wise. (I, 771-83) Bees settled on Plato's lips while he lay slumbering in the cradle; he launched his whole Utopia in dreamland. (II, 230-58) Spinoza sat at his bench in his pride intently shaping his lenses, in irksome toil to earn his bread. (III, 163) Innocent III, who held his wide ambition for the will of God, and his fulminating censure for the voice of Christ, was troubled that he could not either cleanse nor cure, persuade nor command. Betrayed by zeal, he preached a crusade within the fold, that bloody wrath, the Albigensian war, becoming a sinking millstone around the neck of the Church. (III, 716f.)

The life of the bee and the activities of Saint Francis seem more likely material for dramatic treatment than the development of ideas, but these too are frequently dramatized in the process of their elucidation. The following is a presentation of the intricacies and delights of a well-planned dinner:

III, 50

> the eye is invited
> by dainty disguises and the nostril with scents,
> nay ev'n the ear is fed, and on the gather'd guests
> a trifling music playeth, dispelling all thought,
> that while they fill the belly, the empty mind may float
> lightly in the full moonshine of o'erblown affluence.

More seriously:

III, 952

> Now Woman took her jointure from the potency
> of spirit stored in flesh . . .

III, 958

> for while man's Reason drew him whither science led
> to walk with downcast eyes fix'd on the ground, and low
> incline his ear to catch the sermon-whisper of stones—
> whence now whole nations, by their treasure-trove enrich'd,
> crawl greedily on their knees nosing the soil like swine,
> and any, if they can twist their stiffen'd necks about,
> see the stars but as stones,—while men thus search'd the earth,
> stooping to pick up wisdom, women stood erect
> in honest human posture, from light's fount to drink
> celestial influences. . . .

Add to these the effect of the constant emerging of little actions such as man's spirit coming more and more out of slumber into vision (III, 976) and the many already cited as carrying with them the flavor of pathetic fallacy or embryo personification, and we find that the world of the poem is crowded with people, a metaphor by which all its material is brought to life.

At first glance, perhaps, the Ring of Being, or the snake with its head in its mouth, or the seamless fabric, would seem to be the better metaphor to have developed throughout the poem. All three are used upon occasion. But the loss to the vitality of the poem would have been irreparable. The power of a metaphor does not lie in the perfection of its analogies, but in the profound emotional conviction aroused and confirmed in the individual. Bridges' ardour is stirred by the idea of the oneness of idea and flesh, pattern and landscape, spiritual beauty and the beauty of the sensuous. The most difficult of these identities for us to capture is that of the idea and the flesh, the one so abstract and remote, the other so particular and urgent. For this reason, he throws the weight of quantity into the body metaphor. The emotion aroused by the conception of the basic ideality of flesh carries over to the other dichotomies.

So far in this study of *The Testament of Beauty* very little has been said of symbolism. The dividing lines, it is well recognized, between the various degrees of indirection in poetic language need not be drawn sharply. In this poem the relationship of the descriptive and the factual with the suggestive is especially close; the simple description or fact comes to suggest metaphorical meaning; the metaphor by recurrence, becomes the symbol. This expanding and contracting of figurative meaning is not so much an ebb and flow as a progressive development, constantly reiterated, from the concrete object (the physical base) to the potentiality of spirit, a course which Bridges saw as the unending activity of Being. In a sense, the handling of all the concrete imagery of the poem is as symbolic of the monism and emergent evolution he was writing about as is the particular symbol of the Ring of Being in its repose and in its motion. (IV, 112) However, in one group of the properties, or rather in three related groups, the symbolism inevitably suggests that universally used in religion and art.

Of the recognized eternal symbols of man, Bridges uses many, although selectively. As is suggested in the concluding chapter, one does not have to subscribe to any particular theory of symbolism to be interested in the recurrence through literature of certain words whose poetic value seems to be that they arouse emotions of a generalized sort (fear, joy, wonder, etc.), and suggest relationships with something greater than the individual human being. Most of these words, which have become the "consecrated images" of poetry,[2] are related in some way to the four medieval elements of air, fire, earth, and water. From them spring such symbols as light and dark, day and night, seed-time and harvest, birth, growth, sleep, dream, source, springs, well, river, sea, and the like. The dominance of one of these symbols has given particular power to many poems: the star, for instance, in *The Ring and the Book*, the river and the sea in *The Buried Life*, or *Four Quartets*. In *The Testament of Beauty* the important symbols relate to the origins of life, the journey of experience, and the goal attained in vision. The full believer in the mystic power and function of the poet to seize upon everlasting and absolute truth by means of universal symbols will recognize at once the ubiquitous metaphors of birth, sleep, flooding waters; he will be surprised, however, to find how little symbolic use Bridges makes of sun, star, seed, the seasons, birds, and so on, although of course those words appear constantly in descriptive passages adding greatly to the decorative beauty of the poem. Bridges' particular and personal slant appears then in the pervading use, not of the life cycle, or the paradox of life and death, for instance, although both occur, but of the journey of life toward discovery, the theme behind the alle-

[2] Day Lewis, Cecil. *The Poetic Image* (London, 1947), p. 40, citing G. H. W. Rylands. Chapters i and vi give an interesting amateur account of the psychological *rationale* of the subject of the symbol.

gory in many medieval poems, conspicuously *The Divine Comedy*.

Almost all the symbolic words gather under the headings (1) Search, (2) Origins, and (3) Vision. Referring to the passages from which these words came, one finds that they usually occur not in isolation, but in the company of several others, often many others, from the same group. And finally, turning to the key passages of the poem, where the main ideas are presented as conclusions, passages which are pivotal in a structural sense, one finds a fusing and intermingling of the three groups, making these passages chords, as one would say in music.

The first of these discoveries came with the selection from the whole list of "properties" of the poem of those words which had some symbolic suggestion, using the word symbolic as described above, and their grouping according to a very definite relationship of idea and tone. By seeing these words together, the relationship becomes striking. In the first group, the important ones are:

(1) Search: seek, quest, goal, find, clue, door, key, unlock, advance, approach, discover, win, arrive, attain, pursuit, lead, hunt, hark back, walk, wend, wander, ramble, waver, mount, climb, stumble, halt, steps, staircase, map, maze, trail, way, by-path, road, journey.

These words are used almost exclusively to describe the journey of the mind and spirit toward truth, and the growth of being from atomic structure to the highest conscience in man.

(2) Origins: origin, dark, gloom, shadow, shade, turbid, smoke, veil, night, dim, dusk, overshadow, murky, darkened, dull, murk, tarnish, grey, darksome, obscure, clouding, adumbration, unsearchable darkness, dark mind, black darkness, unfathom'd density, sunless, sunset, elemental fire, secret flame, nascent flame, kindle, light's fount, begotten, buried, fading in oceanic deeps, night fall, terrifying nightmare, storm, dark fears, black-purpling haunt, spectre, ghost, secret penetralia, unseen powers, fountains, springs, living waters,

source, fount, well, ocean, streams, drown, fluid sea, warm ocean-stream, murky pools, flux, flood, flushings, teeming, fertilize, flooding, surge, whelm, submerge, throng, burst forth, torrent, undersuck'd, flooding fountains, sluices, purify, taint, soil, smirch, contaminate, incontaminate, pollution, dregs, crowded foulness, washing, cleansing, grime, absorb, blend, commingled, fusion, melting.

This second group suggests darkness and fear, but also mystery, and the brightness at the core as well as the dregs; flooding causes pollution and cleansing, drowning and fertilizing.

(3) Vision: dream, sleep, awakening, escape, trance, enthralment, entrance, slumber, dreamland, commune, consummation, secret, marvel, incantation, divination, disenthralment, charm, revelation, spell, wonder-dreams, wonder-gleams, the unseen, delusion, illusion, magician, joy, magic, mystery, glow, wonder, elation, absorb, mystic, inspiration, gleam, transcendence, transport, awe, ecstacy, rapture, secret strength, transfigure, miracle, glimpse, dawn, phantasy, nightmare, touch of immanence, surprize of joy, surprize of magic, light, day, dawn, sun, star, ray, bright, dazzling, blaze, heart-blaze, nimbus, fire, spark, sparkle, crystal, flashing, radiancy, luminous, starry, irradiance, wondering dawn, clearing, everlasting dawn, fire-brand, fire-worshippers, furtive fire, flaming, spirit's flame, glow, kindle, sun-joys, come to life, burst into life, flush, flood, marvel, crowding, thronging, urge, urgence, brought to birth, energy, surge, impulse, soar, driving, craving, spring, bloom, sap mounting, blushing, rose-bud, fertilize, ripen, seeds, budding.

These words in the third group are descriptive of what is understood and felt in vision, the goal of the journey of search into origins; in the moment of vision we feel the domination of nature's secret urge and the prolific miracle of Spring.

All of these groups could be extended by other words whose connections with the three themes might seem to be as clear as many that are included; their symbolic suggestion was slighter, however, and certainly the lists are long enough. The maximum number is roughly equal to all of the purely sensory images, and once noticed, their special effect in the poem is analogous to the key in which a musical composition is written. But more important than the number of such unifying words, is the constant blending and tying together among these images, and their particularly close interweaving whenever a passage is addressed to the central ideas of the poem.

The use of two or more of these words from each of the groups in short passages may be briefly illustrated. From the first group the following:

III, 193

> yet, tracing backwards in the story of sex, the steps
> of our carpeted staircase are familiar and strong . . .

III, 689

> Restless and impatient man's mind is ever in quest
> of some system or mappemond or safeguard of soul . . .

IV, 1394

> Of which living ideas. . . .

> .   .   .

> Reason builded her maze, wherefrom none should escape,
> wandering intent to map and learn her tortuous clews. . . .

In the second group the chief interest lies in the mingling of dark and light, the fire which kindles and the flood which pollutes and their opposites, the fire that destroys and the living waters. It is these dichotomies that are especially effective in connecting this group with the third group, but their connections within group two are illustrated as follows:

I, 635

> [the Nile]—like thatt twin-sister stream of slothful thought,
>   whose flood
> fertilized the rude mind of Egypt . . .

II, 663

>   so ther is no birthright
> so noble or stock so clean, but it transmitteth dregs,
> contamination at core of old brutality;

inchoate lobes, dumb shapes of ancient terror abide:
tho' fading still in the ocëanic deeps of mind
their eyeless sorrows haunt the unfathom'd density,
dulling the crystal lens of prophetic vision . . .

I, 162

Life's mighty mystery
sprang from eternal seeds in the elemental fire . . .

II, 706

Truly inscrutable and dark is the Wisdom of God. . . .

To illustrate the intermingling of the symbols in the third
group, it is almost impossible to find lines that do not also
include words from the other two as well:

I, 683

activ presences, striving to force an entrance,
like bodiless exiled souls in dumb urgence pleading
to be brought to birth . . .

III, 104

speaking with incantation of strange magic to charm
the dreams that yet undreamt lurk in the unfathom'd deep
of mind, unfeatur'd hopes and loves and dim desires,
uttermost forms of all things that shall be.

II, 144

The unfathomable mystery of her awaken'd joy
sendeth her daily to heaven on her knees in prayer:
and watching o'er the charm of a soul's wondering dawn
enamoureth so her spirit, that all her happiness
is in her care for him, all hope in his promise;
and his nobility is the dream-goal of her life.

II, 425

the exhilaration of the voluptuous air
that surgeth in our flesh to flood the soul . . .

III, 810

but Hope
incarnat in the blood kindleth its hue no less
with every breath, to flood all the sluices of life
long as the heart can beat.

To be complete on the final evidence of the unifying power of these symbolic words would be to quote in full the several long passages which are crucial to the development of the thought of the poem and pivotal in other aspects of its structure. Much of this material will be quoted in Part III, where the structure of the poem is analyzed; when these passages are read, the importance of the symbols will be recognized. Three such passages should be illuminating here, however, the final musical metaphor having special significance in a discussion of the harmonizing power of the symbols. A full comment on these passages may be side-stepped; the condition they illustrate is clear. The first concerns the power of human love, a physical force, to transform itself and the person caught up by it to spiritual beauty:

III, 227

it happ'd to Dante, I say, as with no other man
in the height of his vision and for his faith therein:
the starry plenitude of his radiant soul,
searching for tenement in the bounties of life,
encounter'd an aspect of spiritual beauty
at the still hour of dawn which is holier than day:
as when a rose-bud first untrammeleth the shells
of her swathing petals and looseneth their embrace,
so the sunlight may enter to flush the casket
of her virgin promise, fairer than her full bloom
shall ever be, ere its glories lie squander'd in death:—
'Twas of thatt silent meeting his high vision came
rapturous as any vision ever to poet giv'n;
since in thatt Sacrament he rebaptized his soul
and lived thereafter in Love, by the merit of Faith
toiling to endow the world: and on those feather'd wings
his mighty poem mounted panting, and lieth now
with all its earthly tangle by the throne of God.

This passage emphasizes the miracle; the following one, the search:

IV, 761

AND here my thought plungeth into the darksome grove
and secret penetralia of ethic lore, wherein

I hav wander'd often and long and thought to know my way,
and now shall go retracing my remember'd paths. . . .

One cannot possibly remain oblivious to the intermingling
of the repeated symbolic words in *The Testament of Beauty*.
Some passages suggest the earth, and death, with the meaning turned then toward life and heaven; some point rather
more toward the dream and sleep as the entrance to vision,
and others to the flooding waters. It is in the passages dealing with the creative richness of the unconscious mind
("Powers unseen and unknown are the fountains of life" II,
774) that the mystery and the security join, where the heart-
blaze of heaven and the unvisited deep come together. These
last metaphors lie in the final passage which joins many of
these symbols with the musical metaphor:

IV, 961

—as when Sebastian preludeth, all her voices [nature's]
that ever hav reach'd our ears are crest-fal'n and abash'd:
for tho' man cannot wield her infinit resource
of delicacy and strength, yet hath he in lieu thereof
a range triumphant, where his exorbitant thought
defying Space and Time hath power to blend all things
visible and invisible, and freely redispose
every essence that he knoweth, to parcel them at will—
or so he thinketh—, like an occult magician
whose summons all spirits must attend and obey,
from the heart-blaze of heaven to the unvisited deep;
tho' he hav no wizardry to exorcise them withal.

Part III

THE STRUCTURE

CHAPTER ELEVEN

THE STUDY OF STRUCTURE

Critical theory today adds up to the aesthetic demand that a poem have a life of its own created from a fusion of its materials. But today's critics have seen that it is easy to claim qualities of fusion and life for the poem one likes. The generalizations are not touchstones at all, but merely what one says when the poem has succeeded in working its will, or when one has perhaps too generously responded to it. In analyzing the generalizations descriptive of one's feeling of "wholeness" or "rightness," one may never quite get to the bottom of what is after all a metaphor. *Life* is essentially a biological term, and a poem has no life in this sense; *fusion* is a chemical term, and although paint may fuse with oil or one color with another, words do not actually fuse into a poem. However, one may call the kind of homogeneity discovered in the imagery of *The Testament of Beauty* fusion with some justice. But what of the word *life?* We are aware that the kind of life possessed by any particular organism depends more on its composition, or structure, than on its elements. Bridges expresses it this way: there are many organic substances, all combinations of the same simples, which are yet "wholly dissimilar and incomparable in kind" (III, 932)

III, 935
>   so that whether it be starch, oil, sugar, or alcohol
>   'tis ever our old customers, carbon and hydrogen,
>   pirouetting with oxygen in their morris antics. . . .

By analogy, we say then that the life of a poem may be created by its subordinations and coördinations, its progressive unity toward an end, its final shape, or structure.

If this constitutes a leap in logic, it is an idea very preva-
lent just now in literary criticism. Beginning at least as far
back as Beach's quite revolutionary book about the novel,
The Technique of Thomas Hardy, criticism of novels, plays,
and poems has insisted that structure is a vital factor in the
living *whatness* of the work of art. Tillyard's brilliant discussion of Blake's *The Echoing Green* and the comparable village green section of Goldsmith's *The Deserted Village,*
makes it very clear that the bare lines of the structure alone
may be the oblique method by which the words say something in a poem that they could not have said in any other
arrangement. He says that the idea has been "translated into
completely concrete form; it has disappeared into apparently
alien facts."[1] Eliot's convenient, if awkward phrase, the
objective correlative, expresses a related idea: "it is the
formula of the particular emotion of the poem."[2] The frequent use of the metaphor *embody* and *living body* reflect
this prevalence also.

It is of course true that the idea of a living body, or of the
objective correlative, applies to the product of all the techniques by which the miracle of incarnation takes place in
art, not always specifically to structure. Matthiessen is especially referring to imagery: "the merely reflective poet . . .
instead of thinking in images and thus bringing a living
body to his ideas, tends to put his images aside and to fall
back on abstract rhetoric . . ."[3] Eliot, although the word
formula suggests a firm composition (after all, a rearranged
formula is nonsense, or at the most, some other formula)
allows his objective correlative to be "a set of objects" as well
as a chain of events. But Guérard has shown by his convincing discussion that the excellence of Jonson's *Ode to
Heaven* is its structural life, not its imagery.[4] Brooks, demanding metaphor more explicitly if not more insistently

[1] *Poetry Direct and Oblique* (2d ed., 1948), p. 15.
[2] "Hamlet," *Selected Essays,* p. 145.
[3] *The Achievement of T. S. Eliot,* p. 68.
[4] *Robert Bridges,* pp. 98-99.

than Matthiessen, nevertheless is interested in its structural rather than its sensory value.[5]

However different the perspective, and therefore the expression of the above writers, they are all trying to analyze and then reformulate the same idea, that a fine poem is something which is more than the sum of its parts. The new whole created is surely a whole by virtue of its peculiar shape, although the effect of structure is always augmented by other elements. Poetic criticism is tending to fix on structure as the crucial factor in this creation of a new life, a kind of organism, out of the separate pieces.

It is in the long poem that structural unity and progression are the most needed. There is bound to be more complex thought, more diverse material, and a less concentrated emotional impact in four thousand lines than in fourteen; the imagery will be more various, and the sounds of greater range. It is then by the subordinations and coördinations of the material, by the working out of the structural principle, that the long poem must primarily be fused into a whole. The value of narrative for this purpose is obvious. It is conspicuous that through the centuries the great long poems are the poems of epic narrative. There have been long poems without a story, but Lucretius' *De Rerum Natura* is the only one that has universal acclaim. We haggle over Pope's *Essay on Man,* and laugh at Darwin's *The Botanic Garden* even if we have never read it. But story has held old men from the chimney corner, as well probably as the spinsters and the knitters in the sun from their song from time to time. "The facts of life are found in story," a recent book on long poems tells us.[6] But it has been too readily assumed from the successes and failures of the past, that the structure, or formula, of the long poem must be that of narrative. Both *The Prelude* and *Prometheus Unbound* have been inappropriately criticized because of this assumption, although the growth of a

---

[5] In both *Modern Poetry and the Tradition* and *The Well Wrought Urn.*
[6] Van Doren, Mark. *The Noble Voice* (New York, 1946), p. 320.

poet's mind is of course a narrative in a sense, and there is a myth in Shelley's poem bearing some relation to a dramatic sequence.

If a long poem has no story, how may it be organized to give it the progressive unity demanded for what we have called organic life? Historically, we find a few poems that propound a philosophy, the outlines of the discussion being the structure of the poem. With the general approval accorded Lucretius' *De Rerum Natura,* we might conclude that a philosophical framework will be accepted as a possible means of giving a living body to an idea. But criticism of *The Testament of Beauty* has been loth to acknowledge this, and is also rather confused as to just what the issues are.

There are indeed problems. The truth of the particular philosophy is not really in question here; we are considering the value of any philosophy as framework. Chief of the doubts is the suitability of philosophy as material for poetry at all. Smith says, "Philosophical argument—and *The Testament of Beauty* is full of argument—is not, in general, suitable material of poetry."[7] The reason no doubt is the danger that the poet will rely on abstract rhetoric to carry the movement of his poem, without supplying the poetic means as well.[8] The distinction should be made between philosophical logic and poetic logic.[9] It is said that "Logic may be used as a powerful instrument by the poet . . . but the logical unity does not organize the poem."[10] But even what Ker calls the "prose lumber" in narrative[11] is objectionable to some readers. Henry Bradley wrote Bridges that in reading thirteen books of the *Iliad,* he was "bored a good deal with reading how X wounded Y, how Y killed X, and what a lot of blood ran out of X + Y."[12] However, there must indeed be connective

[7] Smith. *Notes on 'The Testament of Beauty,'* p. xii.
[8] Matthiessen. *The Achievement of T. S. Eliot,* p. 68.
[9] Ker. *Form and Style in Poetry,* p. 124.
[10] Brooks. *Modern Poetry and the Tradition,* p. 66.
[11] Ker. *Form and Style,* p. 111.
[12] *Correspondence of Robert Bridges and Henry Bradley,* p. 99.

tissues in any long poem. The important question to decide
is whether the philosophy really does provide a framework,
and then whether other more particularly aesthetic means
are used to augment its effect, means which are in keeping
with the nature of the philosophy of the poem. To provide
a framework, the philosophy must be reasonably enough
presented so that the argument is not logically fallacious;
to be poetically convincing, the connectives must be of
an imaginative kind, and aesthetic patterns must under-
score and support the logical structure. It is not enough
merely to emotionalize the philosophy, in Santayana's
words.[13] Further, when logic fails to solve a problem, it is
by the tensions between the philosophical way and the emotional way, between the argument and the aesthetic patterns,
that the full meaning of the poem is expressed.

Does the structure of *The Testament of Beauty* live up to
these requirements? On what principles is this long poem
constructed?

It is misleading to speak of the poem's formlessness and to
say that it is deliberately loose and disorganized.[14] Although
from the philosophical point of view, the outlines of the
poem's thought do not make up a systematic treatise, yet it
"has an inner logic of its own."[15] However, it is true that this
inner logic runs underneath a surface flux. Perhaps Bridges
could have linked his four books more securely in a chain of
argument had he wanted to; some critics believe he tried and
failed, either because he was no philosopher, or because, like
Santayana's, his philosophy cannot be so developed. His own
lines comparing himself to an old black bear are more truly
representative of his intentions:

II, 442
    Me-seemeth in my poem these poor hive-bees fare
    as with an old black bear that hath climb'd on their tree
    in the American Adirondacks or Asian

[13] Bridges. "George Santayana," *Collected Essays,* Vol. 8, No. xix, p. 162.
[14] Guérard. *Robert Bridges,* pp. 245 and 185.
[15] Smith. *Notes . . . ,* p. xi.

Himalya, and clawing their comb, eateth it in,
grubs, bees, and honey and all: it is all one to him,
for the brute is omnivorous and hath a sweet tooth.

There are reasons in the very nature of Bridges' thought
for calling on other methods of moving from part to part of
his poem than a strict logic. Boas objected to this characteristic of his thought: "Out of hesitancy may come poetry, but
not philosophic poetry, for there is no philosophy in saying,
'The answer is either *yes or no.*' "[16] But this very hesitancy
is a part of the tone of the poem: Bridges admits the open
question. In reviewing Santayana's *Little Essays,* he said:

The philosophy, as I understand it, is very consonant with my
own thought: there is no pretense of hiding the unsolved riddle
of life. The Sphynx lurks in all systems; different schools only
hustle her from pillar to post, and if she is to be driven into any
corner where her presence is obvious, her best refuge is in the
unsearchable atom. And this is an honester method than that of
dismembering her and seeking to hide her mutilated fragments by
dispersal, as a piano-tuner will distribute the error of his wolf all
up and down the scale: . . .[17]

For the poem, as well as the philosophy, this last is a good
figurative way of describing what has happened structurally.
The whole keyboard is sufficiently in tune, because the
philosophy of emergent evolution is scientifically and philosophically defensible in its broad outlines; it is consistent and
coherent within its own bounds. But the riddle of life yet
remains; it may be pushed to the unused keys, that is, it may
take refuge in the atom; it may also be distributed, as it is
when an instrument is tuned on the principle of equal temperament. A keen ear will know where these dissonances are.
In thinking, one should know where lies "the intrinse knot"
and show it rather than cutting it out and proclaiming "no
knot had been." (III, 776-77) In unfigurative terms, Bridges'
scientific and philosophical study and his personal experience
led him to a belief in the philosophy of emergent evolution

[16] *Philosophy and Poetry,* p. 30.
[17] *Collected Essays,* Vol. 8, No. xix, p. 164.

through the early stages to conscious life. The ego drive he saw as potential of motherhood, creative joy, and art; sex is potential of the greatest of spiritual miracles; the sense of Duty (the law of necessity)

IV, 128

closeth the full circle, where the spirit of man

.   .   .

re-entereth eternity by the vision of God.

But the more man studies the earth to pick up wisdom (III, 965) the more he loses heart "at the inhumanity of nature's omnipotence." (III, 978) Faith alone can save man's soul (III, 975), but it must not be confused with philosophy. Where logic breaks, aesthetic means must be used for structural firmness.

The poem, for all its scientific and philosophic reference, is not an argument; it is a vision of truth. It begins and ends with notification of this fact, and the sequence of batches of material seems to be that of a vision, or even a simple dream, where logic and memory and ecstasy and fear follow one another. Its tone fluctuates from emotional certainty and joy to moments of caution and despair and confusion. Its realistic detail accumulates, then breaks up in expression of the invisible and the inaudible. The evidence given is the evidence of an experience which ranges from sensuous perception to pleasure and pain, from consideration of scientific data and the history of philosophic speculation, to the ecstasy of mystic trance. This vision includes much recalcitrant matter: the incompetent disorder and the irredeemable shame of our history and present social condition; the Sphinx in all systems, the relation of atom to spirit. Admitting the recalcitrancy, the poet has used as his guiding coördinating principle the adjustment of feeling to the inexorable facts of man in his world. These facts are presented as experience in the process of being contemplated; they are not rigorously synthesized.

To this end *The Testament of Beauty* is built up carefully and organically, with large groupings of material aesthetically arranged. There are countless interweavings of rational ideas, memories, *cul de sacs* of thought, factual material, feelings communicated by imagery and sound, arranged in various patterns. No doubt many more of these patterns may be detected by future analysis of the poem. The following are clearly consonant with the idea of the poem. According to the best theory, there are shifts and changes of rhythm and tone, essential as Eliot puts it, "to the musical structure of the whole";[18] there is a central metaphor, the evolutionary process;[19] there is a central dramatic figure, the personification of Reason; and finally, there is the progressive repetition of symbols which creates what might be called the myth of the dream-journey in search of truth. The discussion of these means will appear in later chapters of this section on the structure of *The Testament of Beauty*.

However, although its structure is aesthetic in the main, the ideas of *The Testament of Beauty* are not in a muddle, although one's own views may assume some of its views mistaken and one may have thought of other facts and other arguments to discredit them. There is indeed an inner logic of the greatest structural value underneath the surface of this poem. This logic does not follow quite as simply as one may think the titles of the four books of the poem. Book I does not merely introduce the poem in miniature; Books II and III do not proceed like a textbook to a discussion of the two physical bases of man, the drives for self-preservation and for reproduction; and Book IV does not end with the part played by man's ethical sense in developing his spiritual nature. Instead, all four books establish the four gradations of Being as atomic, organic, sensuous, and self-conscient, and consider the question of the dominance in man's knowledge of this, of his Reason and his love of Beauty. The whole poem

---

[18] *The Music of Poetry,* p. 18.
[19] Noticed but not elaborated by Boas, *Philosophy and Poetry,* p. 33.

is threaded through with the belief that ego, sex, and sense of duty all spring from the physical foundations of reality, and all may rise, although they do not always do so, to the highest spiritual reach. The shape of the thought in the poem is a sphere, not a ladder.

Allowing for the unexpressed connections of position (contrasts, for instance), one finds that there is plenty of common sense in the building up of conclusions, considerable knowledge of philosophical method and a minimum of logical fallacy. Contrary to Smith's view, one can "give an intelligible connected analysis of the poem without frequently supplying extraneous matter, suppressing apparent irrelevancies, and in general forcing the interpretation."[20] Although the material has to be rearranged, and the connectives articulated, the thought as framework will be found to meet high standards.

The next chapter will show the course of the inner logic, by going over the ground of paraphrase again in the footsteps of Smith and Guérard, indebted to them at every turn. It is impossible to discard their careful and thoughtful work. But in seizing upon slightly different turning points and guiding clues to this inner logic, the following *précis* sounds different from theirs. The main difference is that the phrases "and the poem turns to," "and then we go on to," or "after a digression, we come back to the argument," are not used. To verbalize the relationships expressed by non-logical juxtapositions, one has to work forward from any point until the development of the idea becomes clear, then by rearrangement, express the meaning. It is of course not easy to avoid supplying and suppressing and forcing the interpretation, but it can be done, and in so doing, several confused points in previous analyses of the content have been cleared up. In only two conspicuous places are there the irrelevancies and confusions we have been asked to accept throughout the poem. They occur where Bridges' thinking, as is always acknowledged, is least informed and judicial, in the section

[20] *Notes* . . . , p. xi.

using the bees as an example of the fallacy of socialism, and that concerning the limitation of woman's creative powers and the idealization of aristocratic motherhood. Bridges' attitude toward war, which is also complained of, emerges in a quite different light, however, under this different kind of analysis. Finally, the metaphysics of the doctrine of Essences, undeveloped here and unacceptable to most schools of philosophy, is probably sufficiently supported by Santayana's *Scepticism and Animal Faith* for poetic treatment.

CHAPTER TWELVE

THE INNER LOGIC[1]

BOOK I.

PART I. *The Vision.* (1-56)

It is vital to see the meaning and importance of the first fifty-six lines of Book I. They have been considered previously as a traditional literary device (as of course they are), a conventional opening for the poem. The convention is that the poet at a particular season of the year or of his life, has a dream, full of wonders, which in some way appears to him as the world of experience brought finally in line with a world of values. Robert Bridges in *The Testament of Beauty* gives a highly detailed, analytical, and well-documented account of the significance of the vision for the modern seeker of truth. In his insistence that the vision must be followed up by scientific and philosophical reasoning and balanced by common sense, as speaking psychologically the content was determined by all of these, Bridges seems to be unique. In his genuine catholicity of approach, he nowhere contradicts the rules of investigation of any method, except those of the narrow mystic who fears the use of the intellect or the experience of the senses, or both.

(1-7) Keeping this idea of the vision steadily in mind, one finds the opening lines taking an integral place, no mere conventional invocation. "Mortal Prudence, handmaid of divine Providence" must be related to the eternal through

[1] This account of the argument of *The Testament of Beauty* is necessarily long and inevitably repetitious of the material though not the ideas of the previous chapters. It may prove useful to students in familiarizing them with the content of the poem, but it can be omitted by the reader who is primarily interested in what the analysis of formal elements contributes to its full understanding.

the Biblical association of Prudence, Wisdom, and God in *Proverbs*. "I wisdom dwell with prudence and find out knowledge of witty inventions . . . The Lord possessed me in the beginning of his way, before his works of old." (*Proverbs*, VIII, 12, 22) The relationship is tightened in a later section:

I, 616

> WISDOM HATH HEWED HER HOUSE: She that dwelleth alway with God in the Evermore, afore any world was,

picks up *Proverbs*, IX, 1, and goes back to VIII, 23: "I was set up from everlasting, from the beginning, or ever the earth was." The epithet "handmaid of divine Providence" is a short cut that fools the unwary. The important idea of these first eight lines is, however, that of Bridges' poem *South Wind*. In that poem he says:

> For me thou seekest ever, me wondering a day
> In the eternal alternations, me
> Free for a stolen moment of chance
> To dream a beautiful dream
> In the everlasting dance
> Of speechless worlds, the unsearchable scheme. . . .[2]

Here he says that Mortal Prudence "hath inscrutable reckoning with Fate and Fortune" (I, 2) and as we sail "a changeful sea through halcyon days and storm" (I, 3) we find that "our stability is but balance." (I, 6) Whatever philosophy we arrive at is a dream of order momentary in the everlasting dance of speechless worlds. The opening lines have also the meaning attributed to them by Smith: "He is conscious of using an opportunity which he neither created nor foresaw, but for which nevertheless the master-purpose of his life, the pursuit of wisdom and beauty, has prepared him."[3] However, this account is not specific enough to show how close the relation of the invocation is to the succeeding section describing the physical surroundings of the vision.

[2] Bridges. *Poetical Works (New Poems)*, p. 337.
[3] *Notes* . . . , p. 1.

(8-56) In a stolen moment of chance, the reckoning inscrutable, unforeseen, the poet had his vision. " 'Twas late in my long journey," "a glow of childlike wonder enthral'd me." Here is the ecstasy of vision, with its psychological effect of new birth. It is followed by a conviction that multifarious experience has a pattern, the landscape is "mapp'd at his feet," and the beauty of the pattern is so great, that his familiar haunts seem estranged by that beauty. But looking at the specific details of his world as well as the pattern, he finds them so beautiful also that he would willingly give up everything merely to enjoy them, the prodigal gay blossom, the blue sky, the soft air. So far, then, we are given the sense that the journeying, with its arrangement from the vantage point of the upland, and the eternity where things are supreme in themselves, works of art and common flowers, are both, and inextricably, a part of the vision. This is the philosopher's becoming and being, the poet's river and sea, time and eternity. But this is the vision of a modern man who does not fear either experiment or reasoning; one who does not immediately commit himself to a divine Being as author of this vision, although the words used to describe it have religious association, "new birth purified," "enrapt," "fresh initiation." What he thinks of in relation to his vision is natural, intellectual, and practical. He sees life vivid, instead of dormant: a winter rose-bed burst into bloom, fossils in a museum come to life; he feels Nature's secret urge, as he had in boyhood when the quiet driving power of machinery in a factory was kin to him. Nature's secret urge may become dominant when one is in contact with the power of the combustion engine as with the vitality of the flower or the masterpiece of art.

This section shows the overwhelming assurance of vision that all reality is one; the reality the poet knows is the reality of ordinary experience, of natural beauty, of practical science, and of study of the documents (from fossils to works of art) left by the course of evolution. For all its emotional connotations, Bridges assumes that he has had a mental experience, that his conscience (consciousness) has been the focal point of it, that he can dissect and evaluate it, and that it came to him because his life had been a life of Reason, in Santayana's sense. There is no claim that this was a visitation of truth coming from on high to fill an unworthy vessel, like the claims of Amos and Joan of Arc. This vision includes all man knows as well as what he is; it does not drown the world of time in the sea of eternity, nor annihilate matter in the realm of spirit. Therefore the instrument of the vision must be considered: man's mind.

Here is the logical link (unexpressed in the poem) between the first section and the succeeding lines beginning, "Man's Reason is in such deep insolvency to sense." The link between the mystically derived and emotionally expressed truths of the first section lies in the line

I, 52
                    the mind
          is indissociable from what it contemplates. . . .

"Man's Reason" is roughly synonymous with "mind" in line 52, and here is related on the one hand, to the world of the senses, and on the other, further along, to the world of consciousness. It must be understood at this point and from now on, that Bridges only loosely defines his terms and frequently uses them with variant meanings. This is not a slipshod practice, but recognition that authorities disagree about these things, especially when their distinctions are sharp. Bridges constantly and consciously makes clear his assumption of a

IV, 826
                    misty march-land, whereon men would fix
          their disputable boundary between Matter and Mind. . . .

With this clear, one may say that Reason here and elsewhere is a part of consciousness, that part which examines the nature and relationships of experience: likenesses, differences, sources, and conclusions. It extends from awareness at one extreme, to logic at the other; cutting through the other direction, like a cross, from factual knowledge to mystical interpretation. The latter is perhaps the same as "Reason in her most exalted mood," which Wordsworth speaks of;[4] it is the spirit which seized Bridges at the beginning and end of his poem when his moment of vision summed up for him the nature of reality.

But because the educated mind is not content with a summary, the vision is also the point of entry into an examination of the external world which seemed to lie before him "so various, so beautiful, so new," and the relation of man's consciousness to it. This relationship has proved to be most difficult for logic to establish. Bridges has a slim feasting smile for Leibnitz

III, 776

>   because he boldly excised the intrinse knot from the rope
>   and, showing both ends free, proclaim'd no knot had been;
>   imagining two independent worlds that move
>   in pre-establish'd harmony twixt matter and mind;
>   —a pleasant freak of man's godlike intelligence. . . .

He himself has to stop for the problem, and therefore he enters upon a meditation concerning the many points of contact of the two worlds. He begins the dissection of his vision with the tools of his knowledge, constantly watching the qualifications of the guide, Reason.

PART II. *What is the nature and origin of life as we know it?* (57-500)

(57-336)   In this section a group of observations and comments suggests the homogeneity and continuity of life, its substance and affects, and shows the unbroken gradations from what may seem only "a structur of blind atoms to their habits enslaved" (347) to "the true intellectual wonder" (328) which is "the footing of all our temples and of all science and art." (329)

---

[4] *The Prelude* (1850), Book XIV, line 192.

The first section (57-119) is from the logical point of view, made up of discursive observations about birds, and from the aesthetic point of view, high in emotional value and exquisite effect. But the residuum of idea, after the accidents of

I, 63

the blithe hour
of April dawns— . . .

I, 65

the ravishing music that the small birdës make

. . .

I, 75

making thee dream of things
illimitable unsearchable and of heavenly import . . .

and of the airplane circling over the poet's head as he writes, is the center of gravity of the thought of Part II. The homogeneity: this music is but jostling ripples of air made by birds whose flight is a symbol of man's soaring thought; the continuity: these birdsongs are the same that woke poetic eloquence in Sophocles and Keats, their urgence the same as that which Bach and Mozart obeyed, their flight now matched by the phalanx of airplanes disturbing him as he writes. The total significance of the structure of the atoms of air includes all experience, human feeling, art, applied science: it is presented here as beautiful.

Can we accept this illustration as full demonstration that we may hunt for the why of the universe in the happiness of man's relationship with the beauty of Nature? (129) Wisdom would have us go cautiously here; there is ugliness in Nature that may not be thought of in the abstractions and simplifications of Reason. Reason is Nature's prescriptive oracle, but even of Universal Mind a very small part. (151)

I, 148

How small a thing! if things immeasurable allow
a greater and less . . .

I, 162
> Yea: and how delicat!

This tiny part of man, this intellect, nascent also in brutes, has, however, the great function of providing man with a sense of values setting him apart from animals who enjoy existence without care. (I, 181) The satisfaction of release from pain and our human sorrow caused by our corruption, alike come from our possession of it.

Thus are human beings linked to the ugliness as well as the beauty of Nature, and this connection lies behind the ascetic's vision of a diviner principle which causes him to loathe even pleasure, as did Saint Francis. But the bond with Nature's beauty is so great that, despite his refusal of all compromise with ease, he praised her in his great hymn. (223-76) For the rest of us, because

I, 260
> from such altitude whatever pictur is drawn
> must be out of focus of our terrestrial senses . . .

the great forces of sun, wind, day, night, the seasons, bring the spiritual elation that is Man's generic mark. (318) The bond between the beauty of Nature and all consciousness is so strong, that even the wolf, pastoral animals, and the antelope and unicorn, feel this Wonder; it is clearly the footing of all our religion, science, and art, as we see it in the child's eyes as Rafael painted them.

I, 335
> 'Tis divinest childhood's incomparable bloom,
> the loss whereof leaveth the man's face shabby and dull.

(337-500) Reason and a sense of Beauty then being linked not only in the indivisible unity of all, but by their relationship in wonder, we can go on to search for a first cause. How close can we come to finding a first cause, now that we see that atoms, sensory perception, art, and spiritual elation are inextricably linked? "Man, in the unsearchable darkness, knoweth one thing" (I, 339) that "our conscient Reason and our desire of knowledge" (I, 342) are essential to the making of man. Can they be said to be a part of nature's plan? The universe "external to our precipient sense" (I, 345) may be only "a structur of blind atoms to their habits enslaved" (347) or else, examining our senses, we may suspect them to be "a dream of empty appearance and vain imagery." (349) The first is the generalization of the limited scientist, the second, that of the limited philosopher. But Science will not allow man's mind to be isolated from her other works. We have already seen that the first description (blind atoms) stops before the triumphant conclusion of birdsong and Mozart; now through the analogy of the window into the darken'd house which reflects back the man's face unless he hoods his eyes, we are told:

I, 358

> See how they hav made o' the window an impermeable wall
> partitioning man off from the rest of nature
> with stronger impertinence than Science can allow.

The foundation of all man's emotional, imaginative and intellectual activity is the common base of Nature. (I, 365)

Man's mind has more individuality within the species than other forms, and amongst the many kinds is the skeptic, who has destroyed the gods, low symbols of the eternal (385), as soon as man has made them. These symbols come naturally and exist side by side, but they grow and change as explanations of the root of all. The idea of God as the root, found in the semitic matrix of Christianity, changes in the individual as it has changed in man's mind by the criticisms of those skeptics and by normal growth. Even the primitive religion of the fireworshippers has justification in the homogeneity and continuity of all: the sun is a cause of life, and Mind exists, if only as a miracle of intrinsic potence, in atoms. The denial of this possibility by the embranglements of logic merely shows that

I, 434

> man in his toilsome journey
> from conscience of nothing to conscient ignorance
> mistook his tottery crutch for the main organ of life.

This last passage is the first important warning by Bridges that, although he is proceeding as reasonably as he can, he has had to fall back on a conviction:

I, 411

> Nor coud it ever dwell in my possible thought
> that whatsoever grew and groweth can be unlike
> in cause and substance to the thing it groweth on. . . .

This conviction is supported by scientific observation, but can be contradicted by the rationalist philosopher. Bridges prefers to follow as far as the scientist will take him; he makes no pretense that he has used logic to get him to philosophic certainties at this point. Both Smith and Guérard slide over the relationships of ideas through here; the thread of logic is indeed broken, but for the reason given. The idea in these lines:

I, 427

> And since we observe in all existence four stages—
> Atomic, Organic, Sensuous, and Selfconscient—
> and must conceive these in gradation,

is so essential to both Bridges' thought and, as will appear later, to his structural scheme, that it was imperative it be stated, even though the argument as such is incomplete.

Brought to this position where conviction confirmed by scientific observation is a better guide than logic, Reason now examines her own limitations, having previously admitted how small and delicate a thing she was. Reason is indeed the exception and the marvel, and instinctive conduct the more usual in life, but she has to rely ultimately on axioms and premises which she can neither question nor resolve. (437-56) These are, however, relevant and of value. (453)

Common opinion, too, may only be assent in error, and it
is wise to use all means toward truth, of course. Of these
means, one is vision, and even Saint Thomas, though honest
and keen in thought, gave up his work on his system of metaphysic. When his friend Reynaldus would have recalled him
to his incompleted *Summa,* he replied that his writing was
at an end, because he had seen such things revealed as made
what he had written seem of little worth. (497-500)

This change took place during his vision at mass: "in
Naples it was when he fell suddenly in trance." (I, 486)
It is in some sense a parallel to Bridges' own vision, the
resemblance and difference suggested by the comment that
it "was some disenthralment of his humanity"; his own was
"an enthralment." Saint Thomas put his writing to an end,
believing that what he had taught was of little worth. But,
seeing that Reason, though how small a thing, and a tottery
crutch, is nevertheless "the characteristic faculty of humanity" (341) and as clearly part of being and becoming as any
other part, Bridges takes up his questioning again. He looks
with Reason to see what the course of human history can
tell him about these things. It is significant that the vision of
Saint Thomas becomes a structural pivot for this part of
Book I, its major turning point.

Part III. *What is our history and our possible future?* (501-
        790)

(501-98) It is inevitable that Reason

I, 524
        would look to find the firstfruits of intelligence
        showing some provident correction of man's estate
        to'ard social order. . . .

But if we consider Europe since the birth of Christ, all is
"a lecture of irredeemable shame." (532) For all their records
and vows and eloquent preaching, the rabblement of the
Second Crusade

I, 517

> wer impell'd as madly, journey'd as blindly
> and perish'd as miserably . . .

as the lemmings of Norway who plunge to drowning death
without "any plan for their journey or prospect in the event."
(I, 508) The tall Goths,

I, 540

> feeling their rumour'd way to an unknown promised land,
> tore at the ravel'd fringes of the purple power,

and

I, 546

> from those three long centuries of rapin and blood,
>
> · · ·
>
> ther is little left. . . .

All that is left is the mingled character of Spanish blood
which in "one grandesque effigy of ennobled folly" (559)
stands forever alive. Although it is "among fair Beauty's fair-
est offspring unreproved" (560), we may not laugh at this
waste. Laughter is good, but it must always be balanced by
faith; there is vary and veer in Reason as elsewhere in the
flux of life; Orientals whom we visited for the sake of their
wonders, now return to us to see the electric light. We should
rejoice in the great abundance,

I, 585

> the indigenous fruitage of our gay Paradise,
> that Persia, China and Babylon put forth their bloom,
> that India and Egypt wer seedplots of wisdom.

However, it is nevertheless mightily

I, 610

> to the reproach of Reason that she cannot save
> nor guide the herd. . . .

I, 600

> with civilization delusions make head;
> the thicket of the people wil take furtiv fire
> from irresponsible catch words of live ideas. . . .

It is not, then, as Reason would expect, that there has been an evolution toward a wise discriminate purpose in history (526). But the truth lies here, that as the energy of the nascent Earth has "come to evolution in the becoming of Man" (619), man has created in his Art, adoration robes for the eternal Wisdom. (616-31) But "wonderfine tho' they be" (647) it is not "those colossal temples" of old Nile, nor the Cyclopean tombs nor the great Sphinx which justify the evolutionary process in the becoming of man. (632-52) It is to Greece that we come to find art like the perfected flower, Iris, or Lily (670). These forms may be perishable, but they are each an absolute piece of being (676), and with other such,

I, 690

> in moments of Vision
> their unseen company is the breath of Life. . . .

The mind of Hellas having blossomed and died (691-704), we might fear that their accomplishment

I, 711

> wer a grace . . . like the grace of childhood
> lost in growth, a glory of the past, not to return.

The history of the accomplishment of Greece is an evidence of those eternal, "mysterious beauties unexpanded, unreveal'd" (680) which insure that "with new attainment new orders of beauty arise" (699) as "knowledge accumulateth slowly and not in vain." (698) It is true that Beauty can hardly live and thrive in our crowded democracy, and yet modern culture has enriched a wasting soil (717-21) and man's animal poverty has been comforted by Science. (722) Science also has come to the service of music, outrunning all magic, and

I, 727

> hath woven a seamless web of invisible strands
> spiriting the dumb inane with the quick matter of life. . . .

However, because "ugliness also groweth proudly and is strong" (716), this same magic is no guarantee for our society. By it, indeed, the drowned voice of truth speaks to every ear the unhindered message of Universal Brotherhood. But men's increased communication only turns War from savagery to fratricide. (734) Whatever the political result of this, however, in music and mathematics and lyric poetry, the becoming of man has created new things. (737-70) The greatest advance of all was prefigured by the coming of Jesus in his gentleness. (771) And yet, here as in all things, there is no final assurance. The light of Jesus' message is surrounded by great darkness, and the dual nature of man as represented by the Sphinx leans toward the lion's part. (I, 786)

BOOK II.

In Book I, then, the vision is analyzed into the various elements of existence which were there revealed as a unity. Amateur observation and science alike, common sense and philosophy, proceeding with varying degrees of accuracy, wisdom, and authority, seem to bear out the vision. But there are grave problems that must have further consideration, problems of analysis and problems of interpretation. Even by the end of Book IV, when he has massed all his pertinent experience, Bridges feels that he lacks the complete demonstration, although Reason has ordered it tellingly. But what he knows and what has been revealed do not contradict each other; he feels or knows that he can trust his vision now, and that it remains for others to fill in the details if they will. At the beginning of Book II, the ultimate justification for attempting these "precise focusings of the unsearchable" (I, 565) still depends on establishing whatever authority Reason has for her exploring, estimating, and accumulating. (II, 676) His thinking must follow the course of the evolution of the animal passions subsumed beneath whatever spiritual and intellectual power men may have; it must explore the relationship of this evolution to beauty in nature and in art, and

to happiness, "things supreme in themselves, eternal, unnumber'd" (I, 35) those existences crowding (I, 679),

I, 683
> activ presences, striving to force an entrance,
> like bodiless exiled souls in dumb urgence pleading
> to be brought to birth in our conscient existence. . . .

The finally chosen title of *The Testament of Beauty* could
hardly have been used until the poem was finished: the poem
itself builds up to and testifies to the triumphant conclusion
that Beauty, that of the natural world and of man's en-
deavours, his creations in art and his potentiality for love,
that this Beauty is "the highest of all these occult influences."
(II, 842) It is the influence of Beauty above all that has led
life from the blind habit of the atom to the potentiality of
spiritual vision. As he was working on it, Bridges' name for
his poem was *De Hominum Natura*[5]; the perspective is taken
always from man; the logical structure of the poem is based
on ideas concerning man's being and becoming. Hence we
find that the second, third, and fourth books are entitled
Selfhood, Breed, and Ethick, the animal passions and the
basic natural law of Necessity as they grow through conscience to spirit.

PART I. *Plato's vision.* (1-41)

As in Book I, the opening lines of Book II are descriptive
of a vision, here the vision of Plato who imagined the Spirit of
Man as a charioteer managing his winged horses. (II, 1-10)
But instead of considering immediately the justification of
Reason in interpreting the myth, the poem explains how
Plato's is to be interpreted and expanded. The charioteer is
indeed Reason, as in Plato, but the horses are not quite the
same: "nor are they, as Plato fancied, one evil and one good"
(II, 35), the spirit and the appetite, but "both are good."
(II, 36) Selfhood is the elder, and Breed the more mettle-

---

[5] Smith. *Notes . . . ,* p. ix.

some. They are rivals, but "both wil pull together as one."
(II, 41) So is Plato's myth amended to the modern non-
theological view, a view further suggested in the character of
Reason, which is not an absolute or eternal nonhuman element like the conscience speaking the word of God. Bridges
notes that Plato has nothing to say as to how the charioteer
mounted in full career, nor of what stuff the reins are woven;
"for not he himself kenneth well of these things." (28) In
Book IV, after the steeds have been discussed in the light
of modern science, practical experience, and man's creative
expression, the Charioteer is shown to be like all else in man,
a part of Becoming as well as Being. This has already been
suggested in Book I, specifically in the section connecting
the animal world with intellectual wonder, which even in
children and savages is the footing of all religion, science,
and art. But in these first few lines of Book II, perhaps by a
slip induced by the Platonic symbols, the two horses are
separated completely from the charioteer, obscuring momentarily the more radical departure from Plato that his treatment of Ethick makes clear.

However that may be, we are again launched by the
account of a vision, but this time the use of it is more limited;
it never takes the fundamental place in meaning or structure
held by Bridges' own. What Bridges had recognized on the
narrowing upland path is structural in the whole of the
poem, and a goal toward which he works; here Plato's vision
and its interpretation are presented as a point of departure.
Bridges' reinterpretation is essential to the progress of the
idea behind the poem.

PART II. *The Evolution of Motherhood from Selfhood.*
   (42-182)

The second and the third divisions of Book I dealt with
the whence and the whither of reality, the essence and the
existence. The being is homogeneous and continuous, the
potentiality of its development is toward Jesus with his divine

compassion. (I, 771) But actually the issue of this potentiality is in doubt. The second division of Book II deals also
with the whence and the whither. Here it is not the whence
and the whither of all that is or may be, but of Selfhood,
which is the first thing, "if ever a first thing wer." (II, 43)
Selfhood rules throughout organic life; consider a plant,
which is of such absolute selfhood that it knoweth not parent
or offspring. Look now upon a child when born, how otherwise than a plant sucketh he and clutcheth. He is like the
blind fledglings in a thrush's nest, and they are food-funnels,
like hoppers in a corn mill gaping. (II, 42-72)

II, 81

> 'tis no far thought that all dumb activities
> in atom or molecule are like phenomena
> of individuat Selfhood in its first degrees.

Here, then, again, this time in respect to Selfhood, we have
homogeneity and continuity through the gradations, atomic,
organic, and sensuous. Because the activity of selfhood looks
in the lower organisms and indeed in the child like a lion on
prowl (77) we are not surprised to find that in the fourth
gradation, consciousness with Reason, denounces Selfhood
as "heartless, and outlaw'd from the noble temper of
man." (86)

But by a natural evolution, not by Reason alone, "Selfhood had of itself begotten its own restraint." (94) Among
beasts of prey and pastoral animals, submission to leadership
and herding together for protection, alike proved curbs to
the autarchy of Selfhood. Parenthood then, in mammal and
partridge, becomes a pretty thing (114) and is the spring of
man's "purest affection, and of all compassion,—the emotion
most inimical to war." (125-27) These results are slow in
coming, but nature's patience becomes reborn in man's virtue, under the care of that motherhood which in Christianity
and art is shown "watching o'er the charm of a soul's wondering dawn." (146) This indeed is the mystic potentiality
of Selfhood evolved through motherhood.

PART III. *The Balance of Dangers and Possibilities.* (183-530)
(183-448) The pictured remembrance, however, the observation of facts in the "real" world, concerning the working
out of Selfhood, are included in the rest of Book II. First let
us ask "how nature wrought when she withheld from life the
gift of Motherhood" (181-82), and in examining the social
organization of bees, a great many sidelights may be thrown
on the life of man. Bees cannot be debarred from vouching
in this case by ignominy of rank (186-87) because in their
complex and well-ordered social system they seem to have
proceeded as our economical bee-minded men would have
us proceed. (188-97). By substituting the goal of cheap production and distribution of common needs for spiritual attainment (205), man's life were cheap as bees. (212) Indeed, all
planned societies, all utopias, "are castles in the air or coun-
sels of despair." (229) Those that are castles in the air he
disposes of by laughing at Plato and Socrates as Aristophanes
did in good jest when he set Socrates "*in nubibus.*" (254)
The despair behind the bees' utopia is shown later to be
lighted by at least a suggestion of the values man himself
holds. But much of the despair of the involuntary and mean-
ingless tragedy of bee-life is paralleled in the life of man even
without a planned economy.

But before showing us the example of the bees' utopia as
a counsel of despair, Bridges develops the analogy of bee
and man by returning to the basic cellular structure of
organic life. (259-447) This analogy reminds us of the homogeneity of existence:

II, 261
> 'tis enough to suppose that their small separat selves
> are function'd by the same organic socialism
> and vital telepathy as the corpuscles are
> whereof their little bodies are themselves composed:
> that this cell-habit, spredd thru'out to a general sense,
> inspireth them in their corporat community.

This process is like the action of the cells "whence the man groweth" (267) and the action of these cells "hath so confounded thought that explanation is fetch'd from chemic agency." (298) By the "unimaginable infinit co-adaptations of function'd tissue" (275-76), when man is born he wakes to a familiar environment, his senses predisposed to terrestrial influences. (II, 318) His evolutionary history comes to his assistance in adjusting to his environment; he welcomes air and sun and milk (320-22) and even the rough contacts which wealth tries to shield him from (326), remembering through a physical memory inherent in his cells. (316) Among his earliest companions were bees. (327-30)

It will have been noticed that the logic of the above follows much less closely the order of the text and less completely the context: we have come to the section where Bridges has tried to link up his knowledge of the bee world with his beliefs about social organization: where he limits himself to the biological matter in which he was proficient, the line of thought is clear. But at the end of his discussion, he himself comments on the undiscriminating inclusiveness of his ideas, and the comment is humorously self-critical as he compares himself to an old black bear eating "grubs, bees and honey and all." (II, 443) He did not apparently recognize the reason for the conglomeration of "grubs, bees and honey and all." We can name it as his not having analyzed his fear and scorn of socialism, and his incomplete analogy of a planned economy with the beehive. Nearly all the poem is thought through and presented both logically and aesthetically, but here the fundamental groundplan of thought is faulty.

However, the section following the one discussed in the last paragraph, begins, with only apparent artlessness, with several scattered ideas about honey, related to man's acquaintance with it throughout his history all over the world. It is in considering them, his usual method again, that he realizes that he has not told the whole story about bees;

really he has come to a wiser affection than his poem is
suggesting. He has come to understand the function of bees
in the economy of nature, and to watch their activities with
appreciation. (II, 365) He sees in their ministry to "the
beauty and fertility of her [Nature's] vegetant life" (340)
another of the points of contact between the gradations; here
the organic life of the bee and the conscient life of man are
joined. The lyric section beginning, "Nay, whether it be in
the gay apple-orchards of May" (II, 345-75), characterized
as one of the great digressions, is the chord uniting these
two kinds of life. Warmed and made flexible by this feeling,
we see into the life of the bee, no doubt exaggerating, perhaps
even inventing, the suffering and sacrifice of their "six unsabbath'd weeks of fever'd toil." (381) "Not one liveth to
sing her *nisi Dominus*" (379) and the Queen-bee is scrapped
like a worn seed-barrow if she slacken her depositing. (II,
415) We have perhaps foolishly travestied this story, yet men
as well as bees respond to the influences of spring and "feel
the exhilaration of the voluptuous air that surgeth in our flesh
to flood the soul." (425) The connections are tightened when
we remember that man-society as well as bee-society has its
tyrants and their mass-massacres (431-41), but socialism is
never re-scrutinized in the light of these musings.

(448-530) The previous section has shown Selfhood where
Nature has withheld the gift of motherhood, and the conscience of feeling in joy or pain. We come now directly to
man as an individual to see how Selfhood may work itself out
both creatively and destructively. In a way, this section is as
exalted in its tone as the section on Motherhood, but it shows
a profound sense likewise of the depth of tragic life to which
man may fall when he becomes a prey to his destructive
passions.

From childhood on, the development of selfhood is colored
by Reason, "the channel of man's spiritual joy" (448), but
also the measure of his suffering. (450) In children the suffering often is "the dread boding of truth," "torments of terror,

fears uncommunicable." (460, 458-59) "Yet for the gift of his virgin intelligence a child is ever our nearest pictur of happiness" (462) in his tireless play with the world of wonders and with "the marvellous inventary of man," (467) the cypher and the alphabet and the scientific commentary on Nature's book. After the preliminary growth, he willingly passes through the sword gates of Eden into the world beyond. (477) His life is now at flower, nor hath he any fear, in spite of the fickleness of fortune. The rude shocks of his life will be brushed aside as they are in art, "wherein special beauty springeth of obstacles that hav been overcome" (495) and he will live "in the glow of a celestial fire." (II, 503) Such is man potentially and his deeds

II, 507

> strewn on the sands of time, sparkle
> like cut jewels in the beatitude of God's countenance.

But without faith, his course may be altered toward self-destruction. (II, 516 f.) In the slavery of their sorrow men then imagine ghastly creeds of despair. (521-30)

PART IV. *The Danger, War; the Possibility, Spiritual Beauty.* (531-1001)

At this point occurs one of the most difficult of all Bridges' transitions, and misunderstanding of it leads to a quite mistaken view of the value of the thought as structure as well as of the actual truth of the conclusions reached. After the passage just quoted, there is a three-line break in the text, and the next section begins with capitals as though to indicate a major shift of subject:

II, 531

> THE Spartan General BRASIDAS, the strenuous man,
> who earn'd historic favour from his conquer'd foe,
> once caught a mouse foraging in his messbasket. . . .

It is instead, like a shift of physical position to renew one's strength to continue what now turns out to be a long course of thought, or conversation. Let us now have done with generalizations and get down to the problem in all its complexity. The story of Brasidas is told with the overtones of emotion left from boyhood when the story was first read and also of emotion surrounding his present affectionate response to a modern mouse which scampers over his page as he writes. After telling the story and taking pleasure in it, Bridges talks about the various virtues of warriors and the variously good effects or necessities of war. Then, it is said, he digresses as usual to speak of Reason, Beauty, and Art, his thought "swaying to and fro between the claims of Reason and Instinct."[6] The fact is that the exploring mind goes too far from the central problem for clarity, but the material presented is always related to it. All of this material leads to the conclusion that war is indeed a vice, although it springs from the same sources as Art; the closing key of the book is one of foreboding that Reason will lose control of the wild brute's madness. (II, 991 f.)

The clue to the elements of meaning in lines 531-1001 lies in the contrast already presented (502-30) between the potentially wonderful effects of Selfhood when a man lives in the glow of the celestial fire, and the danger of his self-destructive passions expressed in war. The whole final section, nearly half the book, is pertinent to the subject of man's judgment of war, which like spiritual vitality, springs from the basic urge of Selfhood. The final conclusion as to how we are to decide about this, is the same we find briefly stated at the end of the poem, "by Beauty it is that we come at WISDOM" (IV, 1305), and it is in "the conscience of spiritual beauty" (II, 871) that we must judge war.

But in exploring the subject of war, men's minds are seen to be in confusion: logic pulls this way and that, depending on where you start; feelings pull this way and that, depending on whether you are experiencing war as a pestilence or reading about it when Time and the Muse have purged the

[6] Smith. *Notes . . .*, p. 21.

old tales of far-off things of their unhappiness. (II, 652-54)
Beauty resides in motives of combat and in the warrior, yet
the flimsy joy of the uproarious city could not still the fear
which was profounder than any caused by the War's darkest
dismay. All these contradictory evidences are laid before us
in the four hundred and seventy lines, as they arose from
the mind of the writer of them; he is musing over ideas as
they occur to him; he is allowing both sides their full time
for the presentation of their case. The confusing thing is that
it is apparently Art and Beauty and common sense that speak
for War, and Reason against it. Can we allow Reason to
declare against immemorial practice and the good favor of
man? (II, 690) The soldier who has fought in the South
Pacific or the absolute pacifist may be ironically amused at
the idea that the problem can be stated in these terms, but
the majority have difficulty in holding a true course in the
ambivalences of war. Logic, religion, and experience combine to complicate the problem, not to solve it. Beginning
in a dramatic way with Brasidas, the poem lays before us the
experience of the mind traditionally bent toward the virtues
of courage and self-sacrifice yet honestly trained to the realistic view.

(531-692)   It finds, for instance, in looking over the historical record, much of value clinging to the idea of war in
the old stories. That of Brasidas, for instance, who saved the
mouse because of its courage, suggests that courage ennobles
man also. (531-54). Although men startle at bloodshed, the
duty of mightiness is to protect the weak; savagery must call
out war. (557-66) Children play at war and love to read of
war in the magnificent chronicles of *Judges* and *Kings*.
(568-84) The great historians likewise "jaunt on their pranc-
ing pens after their man of war" (595) and magnify prowess
and condone cruelty. (599) Man has even written of Heaven
as a sanction and exemplar of war (615) in the stories of
Zeus, and even "like false moneys" (619) have been passed

on to the fold by the church. When Milton described the war in Heaven, he created in the mind tragic sympathy for the great devil as he confronted undismayed inevitable ruin (626), like old Methusalah breasting the great flood. (628-39) Poetry has always honored the selfhood of war, although now she prefers the other steed, Breed. Time and the Muse have purged these old tales of their unhappiness. (652-60) On the other hand there are always dregs remaining; there is "contamination at core of old brutality." (665) Our conclusion in looking to the past, must be apparently that we may never

II, 676
> explore, estimate, and accumulate
> those infinit dark happenings into a single view
> that might affect feeling with true judgment of thought . . .

We have on the one hand, the condemnation of War by Reason, and on the other "the immemorial practice and good favour of man." (690)
(693-868) What is the authority of Reason, who claims authority in being "the consciousness of things judging themselves" (698), and proclaims again apparently as a contradiction, that she has learned

II, 699
> that Selfhood is fundamental
> and universal in all individual Being;
> and that thru' Motherhood it came in animals
> to altruistic feeling, and thence-after in men
> rose to spiritual affection. . . .

The problem lies really in the mixed constitution of Mind. Reason must comprehend and harmonize (710) the dark inconscient mind whose potency is the stuff of life (716), Reason which is still unperfect (714) and variable in power and worth (724). It is the younger born of mind (733) and sometimes powerless when it does not call on the active and

rich personality (719) of inborn faculty (740), as we see
sometimes when philosophers treat of art. (752) Even the
twin-gifted Plato, whose doctrine of ideas takes no hurt at
heart from logic, was guilty of a crude offense, to Aristotle's
mind. (759-73) Reason herself must own to existences beyond
her grasp, "powers unseen and unknown" (774); man, un-
ravelling the physical rays of life, knows that this analysis
"hath not approach'd the secret of their living power." (783)
The imagination of awe and ecstasy felt by the astronomer
in transport of spirit (789) is proper and common in man,
and the beauty perceived by the sense has seemed the revelation of the Maker of All. (784-803)

Reason begins to see an independence of spiritual perception from abstract intelligence, tracing the first from the dark
working of animal instinct and the second from man's awakening mind. The bridge between the two, the harmonizing
of them, has been all thinkers' hope from earliest time.
(804-24) But one has to look to see whether Reason in her
denunciation of war, has really harmonized the divergent
elements of conscience, or whether she is depending too
much on one of them, "the spiritual perception vague and
uncontroll'd." (813) It is clear that Art has made a fruitful
union between spiritual emotion and sensuous form, the
soul's depth being engaged in Art by material appearances.
The ability to sense the effect of Art, goes back to untrained
men and even to animals, as we can see in their response to
music. This response owes nothing to later developments of
consciousness, that is, to developed reason. Therefore there
must be eternal essences or wholes so to move them, the
powers unseen which are the fountains of life. We may name
these powers Ideas as did Plato, or rename them Influences.
Why Bridges equated the words *Ideas* and *Influences* with
Santayana's term *Essences*, as he does here, our information
does not make clear.

(869-1001) The authority of Reason lies in her ability to

become conscient of these essences, of which Beauty is the highest, and she has become conscient of them. She must learn to harmonize them. In denouncing war, she recognizes the value of the animal instinct, here Selfhood, and the beauty of some of its evidences; she recognizes also the ugliness of other evidences. War is like virtue in some ways, but a careful distinction between this and a final judgment must be drawn. War is finally, "in the conscience of spiritual beauty, a vice." (871)

This conclusion is not presented as "philosophy," although Bridges has been led to depend on the authority of two philosophers, Plato and Santayana, for acceptance of his keystone, the doctrine of Ideas or Essences as existences independent of Reason. The whole section (like the poem) is the record of a mind stepping toward truth, as Keats expressed it; it is the dovetailing of various experiences into a whole. As in the discussion of socialism, room is allowed for the expression of temperamental and educational bias. Here he allows his temperamental and environmental affection for the great epic writing of the past, and a sentimental attachment to the social class of retired generals, to halt his thinking on the way to his final and clearer judgment. Even after his reason tells him that war is a vice, he must look again at what he feels.

There has been so much in his experience pointing to justification of war that he cannot yet let go his acceptance of it. "Wise thinkers do homage to good fellow-thinkers, nor disregard the general commonsense of man" (I, 457), he has said earlier. War is "nativ in the sinew of selfhood, the life of things" (873); its old glory is heroism, self-sacrifice, discipline. (878) A true soldier is one "compact at heart," "a man ready at call to render his life to keep his soul" (901), and compared to the common concourse of men "who twixt care of comfort and zeal in worldly affairs" (896) he stands aloof like the Greek statue in the politician's garden among the parasols and silks. (882-901). "All *virtue is in her shape so lovely*" (902) that doubt stirred up by this glimpse of virtue seems connected with his deepest faith; at the least flash of beauty (923) we seem to be in the presence of God. (920-27) But he comes to final victory. He sees that many men exult in the exhilaration of danger with no check of evaluation; and he remembers, as all modern men must, unatoneable sorrows and unforgettable horrors. (II, 958) Man dares not forget that it was his crowded uncleanness of soul that developed a war like the ancient plagues of Athens and London. (II, 991-1001) The honesty and emotional power of this final passage are the greater for the struggle with his confusions, which he has finally recognized and resolved.

Book II has proceeded with the analysis of man's nature, its inherent being, and its process of becoming. The basic factor of his personality appears to be Selfhood. This factor is perhaps even to be related to the first gradation of existence, the atomic. In the development through the other stages of this drive or impulse (Bridges uses the word "instinct" occasionally, believing no doubt that the English language existed before post-MacDougall psychologists) he finds possibilities of the most spiritual of human relationships, Motherhood; he finds that man in its expression may live in the glow of a celestial fire. And he finds a possibility that if Selfhood be made subservient to too complex and rigorous a corporate life, the ensuing slavery may be a horror. But he finds also that Selfhood unbridled of Reason, is the root of the terrible evil, war, which may indeed be the field of exercise of spirit, but which we may not be able to cure or stay. Reason's comment on war apparently being confusing, Bridges again as in Book I, must challenge Reason for her authority. Not directly or logically but by a dovetailing of fact, feeling, and vision, Reason then emerges with the recognition of the union of spirit and sense, a recognition always accompanied by Beauty, the highest of the eternal influences.

BOOK III.

PART I. *Justification and Limitation of the Way of Reason.*
(1-324)

The discussion of Selfhood is followed by that of Breed, the younger of the steeds in the reinterpreted vision of Plato. In it we find the familiar evolution of ideas: the origin, character, and potentiality of this arch-instinct are discussed. The opening lines are not concerned with vision, but with consideration of the intellectual process responsible for the division of the material behind Bridges' revelation of homogeneity and continuity from the realm of being, through the various stages of becoming. Quite clearly and quite fairly, he shows the kind of artificiality there is in abstracting ideas from phenomena, an artificiality useful in giving firm foundations to thought, when the possibility of uncertainties and disagreements are allowed for. "Whatever abode Philosophy thinketh to build" (III, 5) rests on the foundations whose plans are kept stored in the folios. (13) So Reason, divining purpose in Nature, abstracts her main intentions and places under them "the old animal passions ancillary thereto." (17) But the real complexity in Nature's economy is contradictory to this artificial simplicity. For instance, the appetite of hunger, a part of the urge of Selfhood, is in one sense the base of all living activities. (21) But only folly calls it an end in itself. (30) As "from the terrifying jungle of his haunted childhood" (40) man withdrew, and from supply of need, fell to pursuit of pleasur" (42), his luxury created an artistry of eating which "rotteth and stinketh in the dust-bin of Ethick." (139) But this luxury is nevertheless constantly confused by intermingled good and bad. "The agreeable superfluities of life" (65) are not censurable, and good wine may almost be compared in its power to exhilarate the mind and to expel care, to the music of precious violins. (98) But when these delights are compared with "the supreme ecstasy of the mountaineer" (126) who wanders into God's presence, we realize that no heavenly or earthly Muse attends the Epicure. However that may be, the Epicure's passion, like War, comes from Selfhood. There is further, another confusion in that some would derive War from Breed. (142) (151-219)   Nevertheless, the distinction between Selfhood and Breed is a good one; Breed "is to the race as SELFHOOD to the individual" (152) and their purposes are different. The purpose of Breed is achieved in animals by a more special kind of apparatus on which propagation (as we find in plants) need not have depended. For the full effects of sex in man, we must therefore look further than to propagation. Examining the fertilization of plants by Spinoza's microscope, we have found that unlimited power to vary offspring in character by the atomic mechanism of sex "by mutual inexhaustible interchange of transmitted genes" (173) is its fundamental purpose in man. Yet this knowledge throws no light on our way to a purposeful and wise self-breeding. (178-79) We still may follow our instinctive preferences and allow Beauty to create our happiest espousals. Next, examining likewise the evolution of sex, although its origin lies in darkness, like all origins (187), we find first in plants

III, 196

> no separation of sex; plants in the next degree
> show differentiation at puberty with some signs
> of mutual approachment: next in higher animals
> an early differentiation, and at puberty
> periodic appetite with mutual attraction
> sometimes engaging Beauty: then at last in man
> all these same characters . . .
>   by Reason transform'd
> to'ard altruistic emotion and spiritual love.

Finally, following Breed in man as we followed Selfhood to War and Gluttony and also to mother love and spiritual ecstasy, we find Breed "to be the sublimest passion of humanity, with parallel corruption." (211)

(220-324) In higher natures, poetic or mystical, sense may be transfigured, as it was with Dante. His meeting with Beatrice was "thatt awakening miracle of Love at first sight." (220-25) " 'Twas at thatt silent meeting his high vision came." (238) To Lucretius, love came with a frenzy of beauty (246); in his worship of the naked goddess he attributed the creation of all Beauty to her. (251) Shakespeare, too, asserted "beauty to be of love the one motiv." (270) This high beauty of spirit, born of physical beauty, when once it is wakened in the mind, "needeth no more support of the old animal lure." (285) The full majesty of love may be found in lovers of no physical beauty and the love which subsists only in the flourish of the flesh may provide tales of despair. (288-99) Love's true passion, then, at its highest, "is of immortal happiness" (300) and in the understanding of this, the late Greek poets foreshadowed the spiritual message of Christ. However, sensuous Beauty is not therefore torn from its throne (318); it may be accorded honor even above the pleasure of Virtue. (324)

PART II. *The Best Relationship of Man and Woman.* (325-1001)

(325-496) What can we find in the development of this lure of bodily beauty in breed to explain our present conceptions of marriage? As always, Bridges gives hints and suggestions from his knowledge of biology, anthropology, and history, and interpretations according to his predisposition. First, he generalizes his experience. (Not his personal experience.) The allure of bodily beauty exists for both men and women, but for the woman whose instinct deeply engages life, grave and responsible, celibacy without impoverishment of will or intellect is more rare than for the man. (325-34) Perhaps originally the conditions were reversed and "primacy of beauty may hav once lain with the male." (341) Conceptions of beauty change, and changes in men's customs and habits bring with them new beauty, as we see even in the change from oxteams to the threshing machine. Although much beauty has been lost, when the threshing machine is at work "a warm industrious boom" "spreadeth far afield with throbbing power" like the great sounds of an organ in a cathedral. (350-84) But whatever reversals may have taken place in prehistoric times, Eve delving or Adam spinning (388), love poets have established the code of man worshipping the beauty of woman, and the code that poets should be men. When women write love poetry they are "drown'd in man's tradition." (404) Even Sappho "hath this falsification of her true soprano." (410) "For tho' true loves are mutual and of equal strength" (421) man finds elation in the physical beauty of woman and "the woman's choice hath been by a deeper purpose led." (430) When the roles were reversed as with Sappho in her Lesbian loves (471) "the euphony of her isle's fair name whisper'd an unspoken and else unspeakable shame." (472-73)

The connection here between the Lesbian brand of sexual perversion and Bridges' belief that women can scarcely be expected to write poetry, is not clarified, but the general position that Lesbianism is a treason against nature (462) fits in here. It is woman's deeper purpose in love, the selection of a father for her children, that has created in man his attainment of spirit; even the dignity of his masculine intellect was first of her making by the "fostering environment of her lovingkindness." (457) This ideal is the foundation of Christian marriage which to most of the readers of this poem, it is assumed, "wil seem a stablish'd ordinance as universal, wholesome and needful to man as WHEAT is." (478-81) Although monogamy was established early, yet it had to fight two tough battles before it came into its own as an ideal for womanhood. These battles were fought against the idealizations of the pagan poetry of Selfhood and War, and against the poetry of sex without marriage.

(498-740)   These two wars are to be called here the Wars of the Essenes. The first began with the Northern invasions, when the Huns swept down on the old land of the Goths. They were like a sudden eruption of nature (515) and from this eruption sprang sagas and epic rhapsodies (499), just as in the earthquake some new valley is formed with a volcanic moraine to produce a blossom'd Paradise (519); the poet often feels that his joy is "a thread of beauty eterne" in mortal change, and himself a flower fertilized "on the quench'd torrent of Hell." (529-33) But the songs which sprang from the fiery ordeal of these invasions "glorify'd the memory of successful lust, and stirr'd anew the fierce delight of battle and blood." (543) The priests denounced the bards, and then rewrote the old pagan tales for their own purposes. (566) This process continuing, we now have King Arthur christened and losing "keenness of sense and true compact of character . . . whereas time was when good St. Andrew strode forth in plate-mail." (578-81) Before the fight was won, however, "in rescue of womanhood from the ravish of war," the young poetry of Breed, not reconciled to marriage, produced a second conflict. (582-87)

This love poetry stemmed not from the Huns but from the Greeks, whose gracious emblems, once drowned in the fall of Rome, now of their buoyancy struggled up here and there. (594) The first impetuous result of this early Renaissance was that "man marveleth stil whence [the poets] came, or by what spontaneous impulse sang." (615) They rose like a cloud of water birds and settled in Languedoc with Raymond of Toulouse. Their song was as though "some far glimpse of the heav'nly Muse had reach'd and drawn the soul by the irresistible magnet of love." (634) And Provence became a land of delight; its names are magical and one would live forever there as in any of the other fabled lands. (659) There "thatt liberty and good-will which men call toleration" (678) resided, and even the Manichees were there harboured safe. (683) The presence of these heretical Manichees finally brought on the Albigensian War, a crusade preached by the Church; the result was the ruin of Ray-

mond's land and the escape to Italian cities of the Troubadours' worship of love. Blending with the worship of the
mother of God, it there assured the consecration of marriage,
and the New Life, into which full soon Dante was born.
(736-40)

(741-923)　After this historical survey, selected and idealized in detail and significance, the essential influence of
Beauty in Breed and in marriage is considered with some
of the difficulties involved. Selfhood could have developed,
of course, without Beauty, but it did not; the vision of beauty
awaited man and "led him in joy of spirit to full fruition."
(III, 754) So with Breed, Beauty has transfigured love, preventing the falling off of the animal wont as Reason developed. (763) What if Science has nothing to say of this
Beauty? How should Science find Beauty? Its limitation here
points to the vexing philosophical question which Leibnitz
proclaimed solved by imagining two independent worlds
that move "in pre-establish'd harmony twixt matter and
mind." (779) But in the world of experience,

III, 783
　　That ther is beauty in natur and that man loveth it
　　are one thing and the same. . . .

Female beauty has been and remains the common lure in
human marriage and becomes the ladder of joy whereon
"slowly climbing at heaven he shall find peace with God."
(792) As wonder to intellect, so desire of beauty to the soul;
mortal mating requires that physical beauty and spiritual
both be present "mingled inseparably." (799-800)

　This is the ideal, hope for which is a joy in itself, an ideal
of harmony not to be set aside because in common experience
marriage so rarely attains it. It is but the weakness of democracy to set aside the ideal because some "left to themselves
might feel fuller content admiring common things or ugly."
(835) Success in marriage depends not on the animal func-

tions, but on qualities of spirit and mind that are correlated
with them. (853) The old Hebrew poet in his mighty myth
of Eve's creation from the body of Adam pointed to this
condition. Adam's wholeness came again only through union
with her. This myth was law even to those stern ascetics who
execrated the body; they thought no ill "in taking women in
marriage, . . . as comrades indispensable, of spiritual aid."
(881) These old myths may tell us much of the nature of
man, and if we attend to them we find vestiges of his stony
asceticism (893) as well as of his love of fleshly pleasure.
(891) At this point in Bridges' thought it is difficult to detect
the slightest reason behind his juxtapositions. Lines 899-923
evidently intend to show that the idealization of aristocratic
motherhood, or is it womanhood? a kind of ascetism, accounts for the difference between Shakespeare's ideal women
and the baser sort. The phrases descriptive of the Mistress
Quicklies and Overdones are fine:

III, 916
    so they might goodtemper'dly and in laughable wise
    hobnob with ugliness, and jest at frightfulness,
    and keep the farce up mirthfully in the face of death.

But what they have to do with the best relationship of men
and women is hard to imagine.
(924-1001) Though part of Adam was returned to him in
Eve, in the story, in actual fact we cannot say that woman
gives back to man in marriage any ultimately separable
thing. (928) All our qualities are combinations of our basic
elements, Selfhood and Breed, just as starch, oil, sugar, or
alcohol (935) are all carbon and hydrogen in different combinations. (941-43) But still, it is not helpful or realistic to
talk about the disposition of vital elements under a few
common names, alike in both sexes; "Tis easier thought" that
there has been an adjustment in long elaboration of qualities
between the sexes, qualities no longer subservient to the

impulse of Breed. (944-48) The great difference between men and women is that as men were led by Reason along the path of science to search the earth, women stood erect "from light's fount to drink celestial influences." (966) This faculty is returned to him by her; she gives her faith in the hope of beauty, when man seeks truth among the stones. (964) It is "the strange perversity of creation's self-reproach" (990) that as man's spirit comes more and more out of slumber into vision, he loses heart the more "at the inhumanity of nature's omnipotence" (978). But earnest, honest thinkers who deem this the final truth must remember that Reason and spiritual sense alike come from nature. Spiritual joy aroused by the beauty of nature "sanctioneth to the full the claim of faith" (993) which woman has given man. The claim of faith is confirmed by Christ also in his rich poetry, and if his words are not Truth, there is something better than Truth. But such an idea would be the supreme vanity of vanities, the last infirmity of man's noble mind. (995-1001)

PART III. *Conclusion.* (1002-1137)

Book III ends with summary and illustration of this assurance. The poem says again that all gradations from blind animal passion to the vision of spirit come of nature, and exist at different stages of the evolution of the race and of man as an individual. However,

III, 1025

> no two men will be found wholly alike,
> nor any one man always consonant in himself. . . .

Besides this variation, Love will be studied from all its perspectives, and none will be found to be true wholly in itself; men will deem of love differently. (1030-39) But if any one interpretation can be thought better than another, then that ideal will be found in few, not many. It will, however, be an everlasting hope. (1045-51) By it, man will grow to find his will and pleasure in the highest

III, 1055

> by the irresistible
> predominant attraction, which worketh secure
> in mankind's Love of Beauty and in the Beauty of Truth.

We find the proper expression of these great truths in Art, which explores nature for spiritual influences as does science for nature's comforting powers. (1060) The plastic arts, to be sure, rarely reach the soaring vision of poetry or music, or the depths of meaning achieved by philosophy. (III, 1067) However, Titian in his picture of two women at the well, presents the two diverse essences of sacred and profane love in their values and contrast; at least we may so follow the figures he has composed here. The values of each are balanced, and in the final touch, although the interpretation of allegory is always fanciful, the child stirs to and fro both images together, illustrating the beauty which comes from the intermingling of flesh and spirit.

The conclusion of this book takes a firm step ahead toward confirming the sense of joy and security which had been communicated by the original vision. Book I, it will be remembered, ended apprehensively; the Great Light was seen to shine only in great darkness; through the dazed head of the Sphinx the lion's voice seemed to be roaring louder and louder. That is, spiritual potentiality and destructive passion appear to be on a precarious balance. Book II closed with modern man's profound fear that he may not be able to cure or even check the plague of war, the unbridled expression of Selfhood. Book III closes in faith that man's love of Beauty will hold him steady in his search for truth. This love of beauty is firmly bound to him in the relation of man and woman in love, a relation so close to the physical base of life as to be indistinguishable from it, and so powerful in the spirit that in higher natures sense may be transfigured quite. Plato's second steed has indeed been reinterpreted.

BOOK IV.

Part I. *The Potency and The Insufficiency of Vision.* (1-90)

Book III having been largely dominated by the idea of Beauty's relationship to the second of the animal passions, the opening section of Book IV restates the theme of the joy and fulfillment brought by Beauty in love and art. The opening of Book IV returns again to the emotional attitudes of vision, after Book III's more intellectual beginning. Beauty, one with the wisdom of God which brooded over the deep before creation, calls out love in every mortal child, like the prolific miracle of spring in every wintry stalk, to flush his spirit with the pleasurable ichor of heaven. (1-11) Even when the airy vision passes away, the effect is less earthly than that of any other after-attainment of the understanding. (21) It came so to Dante, it comes so to every lover of art; as it came to the poet with the experience of great music. (36) The dream looks out of the boy's eyes as it does from the Christ child's eyes in the great paintings. (45-51) But it is true of the Race as with children,

IV, 58

> this glimpse or touch of immanence,
> being a superlativ brief moment of glory,
> is too little to leaven the inveterate lump of life;
> and the instincts whose transform'd vitality should lust
> after spiritual things, return to their vomit. . . .

Nature's promise is in all, but her full potency is rare; Reason, therefore, has had to harmonize the conduct of life, and by that Science called Ethick, has mapped "a pathway of happiness thru' the valley of death." (87)

Part II. *The Complexity of Ethick.* (91-760)

(91-154) Ethick implies a sense of Duty in man; whence did it arise and how has it developed? It has come indeed from the most remote origins, being the self-conscience of the prime ordinance (106)

IV, 107

> that we call Law of Nature—in its grade the same
> with the determin'd habit of electrons, the same
> with the determining instinct of unreasoning life,
> NECESSITY become conscient in man—....

It is so universal that some have thought it a special faculty underivable from animal bias, "whereby the creature kenneth the creator's Will." (96) It is to gentle souls a sound that gives all silence the joy of his presence (98); to savage men, a horror. (99) Here again we find the gradation from the electrons' habit to the conscience of God. For the expression of the complete unity and continuity of all reality, we may use the symbol of the chain with links interdependent and joined into a ring, as art uses the coiled snake for a symbol of eternity. (IV, 112-22)

Throughout the Ring made by the interdependent links runs Duty (125-30) and the conscience of it is the creative faculty of animal mind potential of Vision. It is the natural law, running from the structure of blind atoms through to what we know of man's highest development of spirit. This natural law which in man is his sense of responsibility, provides the final and closing links of the chain: the first-born atoms are linked thereby to Universal Mind, which is God.

Here is the statement of the justification of the preliminary vision set forth in Book I. That vision was in a way wordless, detail-less, invisible, inaudible; its meaning lay beneath the pattern of the landscape and the joy of the flowers. It was accompanied by the sense of rebirth, a prolific miracle, and also by a sense of security and comfort in the domination of nature's secret urge. We have traced various and constant reëxperiencing of this sense of wonder and security throughout the first three books. At the end of the poem we will find the tentative and broken articulations that try to express the meaning of the experience. Here, the conclusion is expressed by the symbol of the chain made into a ring by the interdependent and continuous links. It is important for the philosophically trained mind to recognize that the argument is not closed by the attempted method of logic; the method of logic is not used here at all. A symbol is used, a symbol similar to the one familar to us of "the coil'd snake that in art figureth eternity." (115) Words in syntactical sequence have no power to express the full significance of the vision: the sequence of this poem, that is the whole poem in its completeness, is left to the reader to contemplate. It is like the circle, separate and complete in itself, something different in any other form, and incomplete if divided into parts.

However, with the symbol of the Ring of Being, Bridges does not give up the attempt to follow Reason as far as she can go in justifying this symbol. More completely than any other mystic who has expressed his vision in words, except perhaps Dante, Bridges trusts Reason's way, the way of observation and experiment, the way of historical consideration, and the way of orderly thinking. For him, all roads lead to Rome. The exceptional quality of this poem is that it gets to Rome by way of them all. Far from turning at this point from the way of reason, from the subject of thought and the science of Ethnick, Bridges devotes the central portion, its largest number of lines, to Mind in men, which is that self-conscience to which animal mind has awakened in the becoming of man. Indeed, he goes on immediately from the presentation of his symbol of unity, to analyze in his accustomed manner: the absolution of Reason, the reëntering of the spirit of man into eternity, is not for all to see. "But any man may picture how Duty was born, and trace thereafter its passage in the ethick of man." (131-33)

Having told us what it is then, this sense of Duty, we look for its first manifestations in animal life and then follow its development in human history. We may easily find how the duteous call was developed in the course of nature (148) by considering the black ouzel building her nest. Asked why she made such a pother with that rubbishy straw, her answer would be, surely, "I know not, but I must." If she did not pursue her nest-building she would not be able to hatch her eggs, and the following spring she would know that the "must" was really an "ought." Then we must inquire how this call was shaped from physical to moral ends, with "OUGHT-NOTS" placed beside the "OUGHTS." (152)

(155-361) It is clear that education has much to do with the form our moralities take. (155-59) Duty has been extended to the moral field of conscience, just as Selfhood extended to affection, and Breed to spiritual love. We find the beginnings of this extension in birds, dogs, savages, although some repudiate any sanction coming from motives engaged in animal welfare, because true spiritual combat is unknown to brutes. (172-74) But since utility need not be denied even on the higher plane of spiritual conduct, denial of the relationship of the conduct of animals to that of man's, because of its utility, is not necessary. (176-82) Denial of use to Ethick, and denial of any sanction by Science, are alike wrong. Ethick, like Beauty, may be "unknowledgeable in scientific sense" (185) but introspection and observation of men show it up as clearly as they show up our persistent search for truth. If all men were perfect, none would seek virtue, no doubt, but also if all men were omniscient, none would seek knowledge. (187-89) However, we go hunting after truth insatiably, though of absolute truth we have no inkling, only a faith; and so we find ourselves going after true happiness in even fuller cry, calling it "Satisfaction of soul." (197) Thinkers generally, "who plot intellectual approaches to the unknown" (201) either lean unconsciously upon Ethick, or incline graciously toward it.

(208-361) We can make no exclusion in this examination of Ethick; even though good disposition needs education by beauty, we must believe that good is inherent in man. (208-14) It is true both that the terms Right and Wrong are pertinent to man's condition on earth, and that his first ethic was a rudiment. (219) Even in "the change of customs that the herd adopt for comfort and to insure what they most

value in life" (221), we see a moral tendency upward. (223)
But such customs when they become habits of order, like
social codes, will outlast their turn and become either gar-
ments outgrown or strong fetters. (225-30) In this phenomenon we see the division in level between social ethic and
individual ethic which soars "away to where the Ring of
Being closeth in the Vision of God." (247) Bridges is speaking, of course, of the potentiality of individual ethic, not of
its universal achievement. We need teachers to show us the
sharp distinction between these two ideas, because neither
Politick nor the Church has ever seen it clearly; social ethick
with its legalized virtue is but the rudiments in primitive
groups of what the higher ethick may be. (232-69)

We need such teachers especially *because* Socialists
"preach class-hatred as the enlighten'd gospel of love."
(IV, 272) This connective *because* is, of course, a false one;
if we disregard it for a moment, the continuation of the
thought is reasonable enough. Should these Socialists look to
history for confirmation of their creed of social virtue and
its progress, they will not find it. From the time the Chaldean
King ordered his grooms, bodyguard, and women of his
harem all slaughtered to accompany him to the mansions of
the dead (277-337), through the long history of Suttee custom permitted to continue in India, to the murderous behavior of Henry VIII, which did not lower him in the esteem
of the folk, although the personal ethick of the individual
judges him despicable, the story is the same. (338-55) Our
crusade against the slave trade was waged against a background of filth in Victorian slums; our present cry of liberty
is heard while Industry is even worse fed and shut out from
the sun. "In every age and nation a like confusion is found."
(356-61) There is a nice logic in this historical survey that
has been missed by commentators previously; all will agree
that individual ethics and social ethics are frequently not on
a par, and that is what the historical material is all about. But

the one illogical connective has been seized upon. Bridges believed emphatically that socialism will never be of value in equalizing the two virtues. Had he made more here of his belief that class-hatred cannot be the instrument of improving social ethics, and less of his belief that socialism in itself is a bad kind of social order, we would not have been so put off by his exploiting the poetic values of the archeological material. We could have seen its bearing, whether we agreed with his beliefs or not.

(362-760)   We have traced "Duty from the selfhood of individual life growing to reach communion with life eternal." (365-66) And in Breed we saw pleasure intensified by love, until it issued in the love of God. But as in the discussion of the different traits of men and women, it would be bookish to insist on a strict division between Selfhood and Breed in searching for the base of Ethick. Since the relation of Pleasure to Duty must be considered, we must investigate Pleasure; not only can we see the relation of Pleasure to Breed, but we must also see that Pleasure has its stronghold in Selfhood, because man's greatest pleasure is the pleasure of life. (362-71)

This Life-joy works along the scale of all functions and motions as the energy of the organism struggles for Selfhood; it is the lordly heraldry of the flower, the pride in vigor of the animal, and, in man, "the grace and ease of health alike in body and mind." (381) Its power and importance give reason to the hedonists' claim of "Pleasure for pleasure's sake." (389) But philosopher and man in the street are agreed in recognizing that some pleasures are bad and that men are honored for risking death for honor's sake. (395) Pure hedonism being thus confuted, the problem of Ethick moves on to distinguishing good and bad pleasures. (407) Indeed some have swung completely away from any acceptance of pleasure as a guide to conduct, and have come to believe it virtue's insidious foe. (410) We must consider how this came to be. It is by a process we have seen working in the love of food; Reason, coming to be conscient of Pleasure, and abstracting it as an idea, developed it in the wrong direction, setting it up as an end in itself and inventing vices for its indulgence. Moralists, then, themselves going too far, banished Pleasure from Ethick, banning it as the pollution of virtue instead of merely setting up a danger signal. (425-33) The justification in the true ascetic for his fear of pleasure, is that "the sublimation of life whereto the Saints aspire is a self-holocaust" (442) and the bent that draws them to this sublimation is such delicacy of sense that a pin-prick or a momentary whiff may set free a force which can distract them wholly. (449) Nevertheless, for their ecstasy they must use the song of Nature; it becomes "the rëincarnation of their renounced desire." (458)

But so solidly founded is this "intrinsic joy of activ life" (461) that its repudiation is folly. "This mortal sensibility" (463) ranges "from mountainous gravity to imperceptible faintest tenuities" (465). The imponderable fragrance of the jasmine at the window is but one of a thousand angelic species, indeed of a legion: these perfumes are like "love-laden prayers and reveries that steal forth from the earth." (487) Such influences as these must not fall into neglect, being to the soul deep springs of happiness, the very existence and nature of God. (501-06) But others have been too vain of their reason, and have disclaimed all complicity with human emotion, and made distinctions between pleasure and happiness. (521-28) The name "happiness" is but a wider term, however. Nature is wronged by the belief that this animal life-joy is not a stepping stone to an elevation of man's pleasures as he realizes his higher energies. (533-39) As Aristotle says, it is the energy of whatever faculty in man apprehends things noble and divine, which apprehension is the perfect happiness. (545-49) The confusions of thought may be sponged from the treatises here (566), and the idea will emerge clear if we will only see

IV, 558
>   Spiritual, Mental and Animal
> to be gradations merged together in growth and mix'd
> in their gradations, and that the animal pleasure
> runneth thru'out all grades heartening all energies. . . .

Although all this is solidly founded, and the distinctions of good and bad hold for the great virtues, the conduct of lesser affairs has been provided with no rules. (567) Here the disposition of the man is the deciding factor: "in thatt uncharted jungle a good man wil go right, while an ill disposition wil miss and go wrong." (576) Comedy has commented "in humorous compact with philosophy" (584) on these missteps, and has been a branch of the education which is necessary for good conduct in the main. (582-94) We see, then, that "all promise of spiritual advancement" lies in these two things, good disposition and right education. (595-97) "First then of Disposition"—(598) There is no security and little hope unless either there is more good than bad in man's make-up, or unless there is an inherent unity and harmony of good to outweigh the surplusage of bad in man. (598-603) We may see that Nature herself has "inclined man's disposition to the virtuous choice." (605) Aristotle has pointed out the strong impulse to mimicry in the child; the relation of this characteristic to morals escapes notice, although it is suggested in the *Ethics*. (614) Surely the child will imitate most what attracts him most, "and must therefore be drawn and held by the inborn love of Beauty inconsciently, of preference to imitate the more beautiful things." (620) If "wellbred in good environment" (629) "in the proud realization of Self common to all animals" (631) he "wil know and think himself a virtuous being" (630) and "be his own ideal." (633) We see, therefore, that there is no more intrinsic need in the education of the child than is the food of Beauty. (643) "And since the hunger of mimicry is so strong in him" (648), without beauty he will draw infection and death from evil (649-50) if he does not have it. The hurt a child may take from contact with evil rather than beauty in his earliest years, led Christ to caution men lest they quench the nascent flame of the Holy Spirit in children (652-59) by denying and blaspheming it. The working of this flame, "the attraction of the creativ energy" (663), permeates, indeed is, "the ultimat life of all being soe'er." (664) Its influences, by the delicate and subtle dealings of nature (660), work where the intellectual faculty is matured, as in Science, and when it is yet unborn. Science, intent on her own invisibles, dreams "to arrive at last at the unsearchable immensities of Goddes realm." (665-73) A child responds to it as he responds to music, and may be taught it readily. (674-87)

Although "of intellectual training 'tis not here to tell" (688) we may stop to see how in education the awakening mind in thrusting out its finely adapted tentacles, finds itself caged in a fusty crypt (695-700). "How should not childish effort, thus thwarted and teased, recoil dishearten'd bruised and stupefy'd?" (708-10) Some repair may be done later to this early damage in intellectual life, but in spiritual life we find that "ev'n the soul wash'd pure of absorb'd taint may take a strange gloss of the lye." (720) It is clear that the effort of struggle tarnishes somewhat the purity of virtue. The colt that with least effort holds his course, and the more graceful of the two runners, are the preferable choices (722-30), yet nevertheless the difference between the best and the least is not great. "The elect are oft in straits extreme" (752) and it is the training in good habit of struggle that gives the appearance of ease which we at first mistook for untried grace.

PART III. *The Nature of Thought.* (761-1267)

The certainty of accent of the foregoing is perhaps due to Bridges following so closely in the footsteps of Aristotle. As he concludes this section, he again for the final time, feels it necessary to examine the relation of Reason to other methods of finding Truth. Now we come to the secret penetralia of ethick lore to ask the questions that even Socrates could not answer, how man thinketh, how thought thinketh itself, how Reason hath the right to rule in the province of thought. (761-80) All life operates through coördinations among disparate parts, and in man the coördinations may be acquired with reasoned purpose, or be innate, or spontaneous, or inconscient like the coördinations of the food organs. (781-94) The main coördinations are self-working; those that have been acquired become habit, as we say. But whatever their original character, they all act in response to external stimulants, the stimulants ranging from material contact to thought. (795-809) These coördinations are made in the corporate mind (813),

IV, 818

> thatt fluid sea
> in which all problems, spiritual or logical
> aesthetic mathematic or practic, resolve
> melting as icebergs launch'd on the warm ocean-stream. . . .

Where the process works best, there we consider genius to be. All stimulus then passes through the indeterminate territory where the boundary is said to lie between matter and mind, and becomes resolved into thought, art, or action. Now this spontaneous life oweth nought to Reason (834); everything there, every Essence, has an existence of its own, Beauty, Courage, Mirth, Faith, Love, Poetry, Music; but to Reason, whose idea is order, all things come for judgment. (837-52) This fact allowed Pythagoras to reduce all things to number, the starry atoms in the seed-plot of heaven, for instance (854), and we see thereby also the triumphs of mathematics and philosophy. The coming to Reason for judgment is a part of the development of Selfhood toward realization. (872)

The mind, then, we have seen as a kind of reservoir, a fluid sea, with Reason able to judge and order the essences in it and proceeding from it. We can think naturally of man as a unique creature with mind and body distinguishable though inseparable. His body is "the machinery of our terrestrial life evolving toward conscience in the Ring of Reality," and his mind is that evolved conscience. (888-91) And that Mind, human Intellect, is formed of the essential ideas. These ideas, identical here with Santayana's essences, as Guérard points out,[7] come to man through the senses, the mind being that all-receptive conscient energy, that ultimate issue of the arch-creative potency of being, wherefrom the senses took existence. (898-904) Thus I come to think that if the mind held all ideas in plenitude

IV, 906

> 'twould be complete, at one with natur and harmonized
> with as good harmony as we may find in nature.

But this notion of completeness in man's mind, like all attempts to bring all colors into one pure white light, fails by a ray or two, because no one man can have hit on all ideas. Besides this, men are only to a degree tuned to take cognizance of them. (917) For this reason, all men are different, and groups of men become incomprehensible to each other. (928) For the same reason, men also run near to the average, "for the animal ideas are common property and . . wil stand-out as the mean statistical features." (940-42)

We can see now, too, how simple natures, having less to harmonize within themselves, achieve a supreme beauty of harmony, like the inviting embrace of the major triad, the sweetest of sounds. (952-57) So Man, in art, having less infinite resource of delicacy and strength than nature, can blend more perfectly than Nature, every essence that he does know of, spirits summoned by him "from the heart-blaze of heaven to the unvisited deep." (971) And the power by which he blends these elements is the creative power of Nature herself, exercised over fewer deliberately chosen and therefore

---

[7] *Robert Bridges*, p. 225.

more amenable materials. In the mind of the artist, nature's method is used; the Ideas which have come to him from his senses

IV, 982

> being come to mortal conscience work-out of themselves
> their right co-ordinations and, creativly
> seeking expression, draw their natural imagery
> from the same sensuous forms whereby they found
> entrance. . . .

This method is purest in music, but we can see its details better in poetry. Its method cannot be artificially imitated, but we find grades of art; in some, considerable disorder; indeed even a jingle may seem to man a hymn to God. (1005-6)

On the whole, in contrast to the harmonizing power of art, the debit of failure is heavy in Reason's accounts, although she can remedy some of the disorder. (1007) Since we do not discredit all medicine because doctors do and must often fail, we can still allow Reason her claim. (1025) She will diagnose the common ailment of Mind a lack of harmony. (1028) The constituents of man's nature are "able among themselves at strife to make a fool, and in co-ordination a sage." (1041) Will, then, may be good when there is a harmony but it may be bad like a Demagogue's and have similar harmful influence when there is a strange coördination or the tyranny of one idea. (1045) Here again I have reached the position of seeing "that all human activities may be order'd equally for ravage or defence." (1060) When Reason herself asks me how I trust her mere ordering of life to make for happiness, I can only answer by my good faith in what I have writ. (1064)

(1065-1267) The mind of man has been shown to have come from inconscient existences ordered toward spiritual conscience by growth of reason. Reason itself will eventually rise to awareness of its rank in the Ring of Existence and will order "discreetly the attitude of the soul seeking self realiza-

tion in the vision of God, becoming at the last thatt arch-
conscience of all." (1076)

At this point a comment is necessary on the position
Bridges has reached; it has been incorrectly objected to both
as inconsistent and as pure primitivism. Carefully read, with
reference to other pertinent passages, it is clear that Bridges
has been considering throughout the evolutionary stages of
Reason: when Reason must be assisted by or even discarded
in favor of other processes of mind, it is because of the im-
perfection of the stage to which it has grown, because of its
mistakes in spite of its possibilities. (I, 151) When considering the process of intuitive or immediate solving of logical
and aesthetic problems (inspiration) he has indicated the
immense activity of that part of the mind underlying full
consciousness. He described it as owing nothing to Reason.
He began by telling us that Reason is still a-fumbling at the
wards (I, 463) and now he is prophesying the potential
future stature of Reason to which it has not yet arisen. As
in all other respects he does not see the different basic parts
of life as antagonistic, although in their development by different paths they sometimes produce antagonisms. Reason
will finally learn how to utilize all the potentiality of the mind
and will become at last a part of the great vision of God to
which we now attain occasionally without its full help.

This great vision is of course the religious vision toward
which men have turned in various ways, often incompletely,
sometimes even destructively. The cause of our turning is
our love of wisdom and beauty, its force that of Duty itself
(1093); the true bond between man and Nature's God (1088-
90) is a right understanding of his creation. (1086) This
right understanding is to be found "in thatt habit of faith
which some thinkers hav styled *The Life of Reason*." (1088)
Guérard has pointed out Bridges' use of the title of Santayana's work; Bridges left it to Santayana to elaborate meta-
physically the equation of faith and reason; he has said
enough about his personal faith in what he has writ.

Here are the springs of religion, which has sometimes "aborted" (1095) in dolorous superstition, so old a trouble that Lucretius is still unrefuted: so much of religion can persuade to evil. (1106) But the godless world we have today has been produced by materialists, in all its grime of murky slums, slag-heaps and sooty bushes. (1118) In sickness of heart and hankering after lost beauty, men are beginning again to rebuild in garden cities and to replant the fair lands which our industrial grandsires disaforested. (1121-22) We see here amidst the blank tyranny of ugliness (1128) that man is eternally athirst for God and longing for religion to return to him. He is indeed a spiritual rather than a rational animal. (1132) Prayer, although not allowed by Philosophy to have a place in Ethick, is "the heav'n-breathing foliage of faith" (1138) and faith is the humanizer of man's brutal passions. (1134) This activity of man is worth consideration. In the present state of the emergence of Reason to full power, Philosophy in "filtering out delusions" (1140) has been afraid of superstitions and so has given no place to prayer in Ethick. But prayer for its constant use by man and its effect in solacing and clarifying self-knowledge, can claim "a place among the causes of determin'd flux." (1153) This exercise is very difficult; its bodily postures may seem foolish in themselves and its words undignified, until man's language grows "from makeshift unto mastery of his thought." (1180) But he may learn by its fine musing art to redeem his soul. (1181)

This will to prayer and the power of prayer alone can with its spiritual gleam hearten the herd. (1188) Mere ideas have the power to infect large groups of people, and may do so producing "exuberant difformity of disorder'd growth." (1191) Indeed, even crowds at football games become ugly, and any observer may find himself carried away, philosophy and all. (1213) But if he join the folk when "they kneel in the vast dimness of a city church" (1219), or even watch the prayer of alien religious groups, he will feel his spirit "drawn into kinship and their exaltation his own." (1233)

Great as is the power of communal prayer, religious solitaries may by the intensity of their contemplation generate ideas of even higher radiance. (1237-46) It is indeed only if our thinking machinery can be a part of the same emergent evolution (1260) as we find in unconscient things whence conscience came (1258) that it can hope not to perish with the body. (1262) It must evolve to Being higher than animal life (1264)

IV, 1265

at thatt point where the Ring cometh upward to reach
the original creativ Energy which is God,
with conscience entering into life everlasting.

Part IV. *What the Vision Means.* (1268-1446)

This is the end toward which his faith in the homogeneity and continuity of Being and Becoming has come. The thought of the four books of this poem has been an explanation of what lay behind the vision at the beginning of Book I. What lay behind that vision, was all the knowledge and wisdom accumulated by study and experience, by processes ranging through observation, feeling, logic, and insight applied to all he had come to know and believe. Having shown the disparate experiences of a lifetime, the mind behind the poem returns again to personal faith in joy.

Thus the last section of the poem begins with an autobiographical experience:

IV, 1268

'TWAS at thatt hour of beauty. . . .

IV, 1279

'Twas at sunset that I, fleeing to hide my soul
in refuge of beauty from a mortal distress,
walk'd alone with the Muse in her garden of thought. . . .

He found himself telling a dream, and wondering that he could tell it so tellingly. (IV, 1293) But indeed he wondered also whether the poem with its subject matter of thought

(1281) was not another of Reason's old inveiglings, filling up the connections of one concentric circle and another with pseudo-logical connections, as once in theology she peopled

IV, 1302
>   the inane that vex'd her between God and man
>   with a hierarchy of angels; like those asteroids
>   wherewith she later fill'd the gap 'twixt Jove and Mars.

Although he fears he is tedious, as tired he drops from the race and hands the staff to the next man, he is sure now however that by Beauty we come at Wisdom, not by Reason at Beauty. But here he breaks off knowing the goal was not for him, trying to tell what cannot be told.

He closes with an ennobled summary of the evolution of God's love as he has before traced it from the mother's embrace. He loses nothing of the firm foundations of scientific knowledge as he has understood and presented it throughout the poem, but writes with the highest poetic passion at the same time. He concludes in the thought of God as the very self-essence of love. (IV, 1439)

CHAPTER THIRTEEN

THE POETIC STRUCTURE

The preceding chapter has given a slightly new version
of the paraphrasable thought of *The Testament of Beauty*.
The corrections of former paraphrases are somewhat tentative and there will no doubt be future rephrasings and re-
interpretations. This study, however, has revealed much of
Bridges' method of thinking and its structural use, as well
as some of the reasons for the weakest links in his inner logic.
On the whole, he is not an original or impeccable philosopher, but he has reached conclusions not completely out of
line with all modern philosophy. He has come to them in a
way philosophers do not recognize; he does not abstract ideas
and pursue their relationships to a logical end. Instead he
examines what his life experience has brought him and as-
sesses it all in the rule of thumb way many thoughtful, intelligent, and gifted persons use.

The process of his thinking leads him to the same position
as have the experiences of his life and his contemplation: the
position expressed by the metaphor of the vision of beauty
and order seen from the top of the downs. But the significant
thing about the movement of the poem is that we are shown
the process leading up to it, a living organism of thought.
He is not developing a systematic philosophy, but on the
other hand, he is not merely celebrating his faith that "God
is seen as the very self-essence of love." (IV, 1439) He is
arriving at this faith. Instead of thinking of this religious
sense of unity as a center, a heart, to be worshipped in lyric
joy, he moves in toward it from the outer world of diversity,
giving homage to that diversity. Every stage of it is presented
with respectful care and loving wonder: rock, plant, animal

256

organism, blind forces, the groping of consciousness through man, man's individual experience in growth, and his corporate experience from primitive societies to the present. He moves in toward this centre, not from one direction, in a line, but as one does in a maze, by curved passages blocked often, but necessary to explore. They lead, if the clue is held, to the last lines:

IV, 1441
> self-express'd in not-self, without which no self were.
> In thought whereof is neither beginning nor end
> nor space nor time; nor any fault nor gap therein
> 'twixt self and not-self, mind and body, mother and child,
> 'twixt lover and loved, God and man: but ONE ETERNAL
> in the love of Beauty and in the selfhood of Love.

This is the language of pure religious mysticism, but in this poem there has been no tunneling under impassable factual or philosophical barriers, no dismembering of the Sphinx to conceal her. Many alleys of thought had to be followed before it was clear that they were blind. Logic will not recognize this method; it is strange to poetry, and the mind is too limited in knowledge and too perverse with pre-judgments to follow readily at first.

Perhaps it would be better to say that this method is strange to the practice of the poets whose long poems we most admire. It is at heart the poetic method, and more widely, the method of art. It is a method of style and structure that builds up details into revealing groups and arranges these groups into a self-existent whole. This arrangement makes sense and uses logic where logical connections exist and are understood, but it admits a lost connection or a significant juxtaposition where logic fails. Because the reins of argument are held loosely, it is especially necessary for this long poem to have other means of amalgamating the disparate experiences into a whole. It is clear that a myth in the usual sense is not one of them, as in *Prometheus Unbound*, nor the personal history of the poet, as in *The Prelude*. There is no map, as in *The Polyolbion,* no calendar as in *The Seasons.* Indeed Bridges has used not one but several methods, and future students of the poem may well find more than are set down here.

However, the several which are described in this chapter are so closely inter-related in what has been called the "keeping" of the poem, and so clearly appropriate to its basic ideas, that they are probably the most significant. Together they are like the framework of steel on which the color burns. By them the fabric is "clamped together with bolts of iron," "a thing you could not dislodge with a team of horses."[1] The first is related to the storytelling aspect of the poem, the presentation of objects or ideas as persons in a narrative, with changes of tone and rhythm that suggest voices or a voice modulated by what is being told, as has been shown. This voice, further, varies significantly from book to book, the changes an emotional accompaniment of the developing thought. The second is the idea of evolution, the basic philosophical idea of the poem; it is used as a pattern in a way analogous to Milton's use of the Ptolemaic cosmogony. The essential differences are first, that Milton's was spatial and Bridges' in a sense temporal; and second, that while Milton knew his framework was no longer intellectually acceptable, Bridges believed firmly in emergent evolution. The third is the continual presence of Reason incarnated as a person. This person is born, has a childhood, becomes a youth of promise but incomplete efficiency, and will one day be the agent with our spiritual sense, in closing the Ring of Being. The fourth is the most important of all, the traditional framework of the vision poem, the journey in search of Truth, a journey on which the life force travels from the structure of atoms, the race from its primitive jungles, and the individual from his wonderful but often terror-haunted childhood to his moment of vision.

[1] Woolf, Virginia. *To the Lighthouse* (New York, 1927), pp. 75, 255.

a. The Voices

The framework of the vision journey in search of truth is of course traditional in literature; in *The Testament of Beauty* it accounts for much that has been underestimated or misunderstood. Its main function and effect will be discussed in the last section of this chapter. Here, however, more or less introductory to the three main aesthetic structural mechanisms, the device should be related briefly to the structure of sounds in the poem. This subject was hinted at in the first division of the book. There it was suggested that a proper reading, acknowledging the end-pause and avoiding an accentual pattern, had the effect of releasing various tones of voice. The result is the emergence of a storyteller who is obvious also, once recognized, in the use of homely diction and ironic asides, and in a few personal anecdotes. The storytelling quality is also strengthened by the constant presentation of ideas as people arising, springing up, being born, and the like, or where there is no personification, by the use of action verbs that give a dramatic effect even to facts and argument. By the same and other methods, the traditional visions of literature likewise have the effect of a story being told. *The Vision of Piers Plowman* begins with a narrative. To paraphrase: "In a summer season I clad myself in shepherds' clothing and went wide into the world. By a brookside, I slumbered and then began to dream. I beheld a tower."[2] And in *The Pearl:* "I entered into that garden green where my Pearl was lost. It was August; I slid into a slumber and thence from that spot my spirit sprang."[3] *The Romaunt of the Rose, The Hous of Fame,* and of course many others, including *The Inferno,* start off similarly.

The medieval analogies of the vision in *The Testament of*

[2] *Prologus*, pp. 1-14.
[3] Loosely paraphrased from Gollancz's translation, stanzas 4-6, *Pearl, an English Poem of the XIVth century*, edited . . . . . by Sir Israel Gollancz (London, 1921).

Beauty are significant, and more will be made of them, but
there is a condition in *The Testament of Beauty* that so far
as I know does not exist in the others. Not only is a voice
speaking through the metre and tonal inflections throughout
the poem, but as the poem progresses in its subject matter
from the Introduction through the analyses of the steeds Selfhood and Breed, to speculations concerning the Charioteer
Reason, there is a significant and progressive change in the
temper of the poet as it is echoed in the sound of his voice.
The gradations of voice from explanation to prophecy that
recur as the meaning dictates in each book, are handled in
larger outlines to rise to the prophetic climax of the poem
as a whole. In developing this point, one must talk about the
content of the books, because the voices can only be heard
in the reading, but at every possible point the development
of the sound to express the progress of the idea will be suggested. The emotional continuity and development of the
poem is felt thereby in a fashion analogous to the emotional
rise and fall in a tragedy. Here the pattern is not of rise and
fall, but of questioning and speculation to ultimate serenity,
a serenity informed by passion. "Our stability is but balance."

The first book is always chosen out as the most lyric, and,
by association of *lyric* with *poetic,* as already discussed, it is
usually chosen as the finest. The second and third are rivals
for the next place: in spite of lyric passages and much brilliantly romanticized history, they are considered a falling off
from the first. To one critic, Book II is a little dull, to another,
Book III shows Bridges' defects as a thinker and a poet. And
inevitably Book IV is deprecated as dry and austerely bare
of poetic ornament. Now there may well be difference of
opinion as to which of these books is "best," but the general
aesthetic question of the relative values of Bridges' four books
is not relevant here. The attempt will be made to describe a
determinable difference in the tone of voice in these books.
Critics have apparently felt this difference even though they

may have come to the wrong conclusions about its nature
and effect.

Book I as has been seen, starts with its generalizations, its
truths, written in grave beauty. The various parts of these
truths, facts, or expositions are constantly interwoven with,
and lifted by, the great lyric passages. In fact, the philosophical discoveries and the religious faith are both expressed
with lyric power. Bridges has taken great pains in Book I to
develop in the reader a flexible frame of mind, to accustom
him to sliding from lyric outburst to scientific fact or generalization. There are, however, few extremes of tone; the
lyric expression of delight is mellowed by a deeper happiness, and the faith is a faith on trial.

I, 771

> So it was when Jesus came in his gentleness
> with his divine compassion and great Gospel of Peace,
> men hail'd him WORD OF GOD,

but

I, 786

> ... the great Light shineth in great darkness,

I, 789

> While loud and louder thro' the dazed head of the SPHINX
> the old lion's voice roareth o'er all the lands.

There is some reminiscence, some argument, some quiet
simple exposition, and some recounting of history as the
storyteller would do it. The reader becomes accustomed to
the tones, while he is attracted into the poem by its dominant
lyricism and spared too striking contrasts.

Book II begins with Plato's myth of the charioteer and
the two horses. The sound is almost like a chant:

II, 1

> THE VISION OF THE SEER who saw the Spirit of Man.
> A chariot he beheld speeding twixt earth and heaven
> drawn by wing'd horses, and the charioteer thereon

upright with eyes upon the goal and mind alert
controlling his strong steeds, that spurn'd the drifted cloud
as now they sank now mounted in their heav'n ward flight.
   Thus Plato recordeth—how Socrates told it
to Phaedrus on a summer morning, as they sat
beneath a lofty plane-tree by the grassy banks
of the Ilissus, talking of the passions of men.

But almost from the beginning, the tone changes to questioning. Selfhood, Plato's good horse, is shown to have such force and inhuman drive that Reason denounces it as heartless (86) as it turns to "the wild brute's madness" in war. (995) Yet this Selfhood also is the joy of life in spring

II, 424

           even as with us
who feel the exhilaration of the voluptuous air
that surgeth in our flesh to flood the soul . . .

and the font of mother love:

II, 159

Nor count I any scripture to be better inspired
with eternal wisdom or by insight of man
than the four words wherewith the sad penitent hymn
calleth aloud on Mary standing neath the cross:
EIA MATER, it saith, MATER FONS AMORIS.

In this dichotomy of love and fear, the voice of Book II is more confused in its emotions, less joyous, than that of Book I. It has a less lyrically unified tone, less musical in its expression of elation concerning his happiness. There is a dual tone, the love of life's potentiality, and fear of the unbridled steed, by which the movement of thought and feeling progress beyond the Introduction. However, Bridges' knowledge that even without Reason Nature begets her own restraint:

II, 95

like as small plague-microbes generate their own toxin
in antidote of their own mischief . . .

keeps the voice from panic, and allows time and space for reasonable consideration. This consideration is pursued with knowledge and humor, sometimes in combative debate, and sometimes with humble tentativeness: these tones emerge from the individual passages as has been shown.

It is interesting in coming to Book III, Bridges' discussion of sex, to find a marked change in attitude toward this second animal passion. At least a part of this change is communicated by the sound, detected by listening to the inflections of the voice. An *a priori* notion that the eminent Victorian, traditional in his poetry, aristocratic in his background, and sheltered in his life by the silken coverlets of wealth, would only approve of sex along the general lines of Margaret Fuller approving of the universe, requires to be carefully taken apart. In the first place, Plato's second steed Bridges describes as "livelier and of limb finer and more mettlesome" (II, 40) than his first. In the second place, there is no suggestion of fear that man may be destroyed by this second steed if he is not controlled. It is Selfhood that has produced war, "faln from savagery to fratricide." (I, 734) It is true that Breed has "a parallel corruption." (III, 212) If it has sanctified fools it has also degraded heroes. (III, 215) But the feeling of the book as a whole is one of wonder at what love can do to man; "love's true passion is of immortal happiness." (III, 300) Added to this is the secure faith that marriage is "as universal, wholesome and needful to man as WHEAT is." (III, 480) Much of the material from which these conclusions are drawn is concerned with the idealized love poetry of the Provençal Troubadours and of Shakespeare's more ideal songs and sonnets. But the physical aspects of Breed command in him a delighted understanding of the intricacies of its scientifically observed detail. He thinks of Spinoza

III, 168

> perfecting the tool that invited science
> to ever minuter anatomy, until she took skill
> to handle invisibles . . .

that is, the "inexhaustible interchange of transmitted genes." (III, 174)

Without discounting the spiritual waste of the misuse of sex by excess or perversion, he has none of the fear of it that unbridled Selfhood aroused in him. There sounds amused contempt rather than horror or even much moral censure in his rendering of Sappho's "lascivious pleasure" (III, 471), and there is only mockery in his phrase describing one of her poems as "thatt muliebrous dump which gave Catullus pause." (III, 409) There is on the other hand, considerable condemnation of the "austere asceticism" (III, 712) of the Manichees, although asceticism too is shown to be deep-rooted in the origins of man.

To make clear the rather unexpected tone of this book, the details of the thought have been given in perhaps a misleading way. Many readers have seen here evidence of what is felt to be Bridges' limitation as a poet; they feel that he knows his science, but that his interpretations of human behavior and part of his expression of the whole create a schism preventing a complete unification into poetry. It is believed that the lack of fire of the traditionalist, the idealist, and the gentleman has prevented the melting out of the clear metal of poetry. The fact of the matter is that the tones reflect perfectly the surprisingly fresh ideas of Bridges. Further, they carry the poem on to its conclusion concerning the function of Ethick in man's behavior. The attitude of mind represented by these tones leads directly into Book IV. Sexual life has been so conclusively discussed in an unheated voice, its joys and its wonders seen equally in its physical and psychological intricacy and its poetic and idealistic expression, that we are prepared to find Ethick not moralistic or compulsive or frustrating, but the final release for the creative spirit.

Of course in Book IV we have the lecturer and the thinker as well as the seer, although this book is above all the book of spiritual vision. For full comprehension of it, one must have learned the tones of voice; they are quieter here; a well-

known and sympathetic person speaks without emphasis; he
has laid the foundation of understanding. Therefore the style
becomes less that of varied inflection of the human voice,
although it is never lacking, and more that of rich and fluent
expression of the complexities of idea. The poetic values
come to be especially those of brilliant imagery, and in general there is a movement to the lines which is sonorous and
serene like the organ music of Bach. Even in this book the
oral effect is still present, and the variety of tone still a
pleasant and affecting part of reading, but the utterance is
deeper, and yet too, more tentative. The search is over, the
journey done. The experience remains human, not divine. In
the final sections the rare personal revelation of Bridges himself increases:

IV, 1306
                        and now with many words
      pleasing myself betimes, I am fearing lest in the end
      I play the tedious orator who maundereth on
      for lack of heart to make an end of his nothings.

His conclusion however breaks from him in his now tried
faith:

IV, 1436
      Truly the Soul returneth the body's loving
      where it hath won it . . .

IV, 1445
                  God and man: but ONE ETERNAL
      in the love of Beauty and in the selfhood of Love.

Many readers will find it impossible to believe that the
claim here of a significant progressive change in voice tones
really provides this poem with part of its structural firmness.
What has been said is of course not proof; until the reader
himself hears the tones as progressive and structural he can
only reserve judgment. In *The Testament of Beauty* the

larger structural outline of the sound element is not so much
fluctuating, as progressive, and gives significant power to the
poem as an organism.

b. The Metaphor of Evolution

In a sense one may feel the presence of a voice echoing
the increasing certainty that in the power of love the human
consciousness may rise to the vision of God, as a metaphor
in this poem. Even more, one may consider the use of the
idea of evolution, the personification of Reason, and the journey in search of truth, metaphorical. Perhaps the concept of
the myth might almost be extended to cover the kind of
framework given to this poem by them. The word "myth"
should not be pushed so far, however, although there is much
in modern critical parlance to countenance it. The "voice"
would be a part of a myth only if the man speaking were
developed into the idealization of Man. On the contrary, the
voice is that of the particular person discovered at the centre
of the material relating to the nature of man, as shown in
Chapter ix. The idea of evolution would be part of a myth
only if there were also an entity "Life" coming to birth, growing and being translated to the realm of vision. This entity
does not exist in the poem. In the personification of Reason,
perhaps, there is better justification, and in the Journey to
Truth, the word "myth" comes still closer to what is actually
in the poem. However, a myth properly demands more of
plot and inter-related character than one finds even in this
device. The three taken together, on the other hand, provide
sufficient objective correlative to bring *The Testament of
Beauty* well out of the rank of those reflective poems which
depend too much on abstract rhetoric to be poetically alive.[4]
The next three sections of this chapter will show the completeness and the function of these three methods of objectification in creating a living organism.

[4] Matthiessen, F. O. *The Achievement of T. S. Eliot*, p. 80, where it is so
ranked.

The most closely related of these to the thought of the poem, and the only one, I think, previously noticed, is the theory of evolution. This present section will try to make clear that this theory is not only at the intellectual base of the poem, but that, used specifically and metaphorically, it is a structural device aesthetic in its effect, and not dependent at all on the logical development of the idea of evolution as a philosophy. This cannot be shown by a chronological run-through of each book, because of the complexity of the method. The pattern can be described in general terms and then shown in its application to each book and to the succession of books.

The kind of structure developed by use of the idea of evolution could be described probably by analogy to a musical form, perhaps even by analogy to a particular composition, if one knew musicology well enough to make a proper choice. In each book the four stages of evolution are recognized, the atomic, the organic, the sensuous, and the self-conscient. (I, 427-28) Each book takes one of these stages as particularly its own, progressing in order of books from the first stage to the last. Further, from book to book, the development from one stage to another advances after a review of the stages already considered. This makes a kind of circular progression, somewhat of the sort Conrad imposed on his materials in *Victory,* and Wilder in *The Ides of March,* the exact pattern of which varies with each book.

BOOK I.

The state of affairs in Book I is somewhat different from the later ones. It is an introduction, of course. As Guérard expresses it: "It establishes the evolutionary naturalism which is to be the philosophical basis of the poem."[5] It discusses particularly, however, the qualifications of Reason as a judge in all our questionings and the apparent failure of Reason to insure social progress. But the idea of evolution

[5] *Robert Bridges,* p. 192.

begins to appear as a structural principle. The pattern, although not essential as yet, is sketched in. First, we have the preliminary mention of the four stages, just quoted. Those lines are the most succinct statement of the crucial ideas more elaborately expressed in the same section. No possible experience of man

I, 369

> hath any other foundation than the common base
> of Nature's building:—not even his independence
> of will, his range of knowledge, and spiritual aim,
> can separate him off from the impercipient. . . .

Second, the factual details of this evolutionary progress are restricted to atomic structure and to very primitive organic life. The sections quoted in Chapter ix, as the strictly scientific material of Book I, deal with the physical base of music (I, 74), with the existence of self-propagating organisms (I, 165), and with the natural flower-bud as but a differentiation of the infertile leaf. (I, 415) The conclusion of Book I questions whether the same miracle of potence to infinite regeneration will develop safely in man. We are not yet far along the path of evolution in this introductory book.

BOOK II.

After the introduction, we have in Books II and III the discussion in order of emergence, of the two animal passions. (III, 17) These passions are symbolized by Plato's myth of the horses, with a significant change of meaning. Selfhood is "the elder and stronger" (II, 39), the closer to those forms of life that are yet undifferentiated as to sex, and therefore comes first in the discussion of the foundations of highly evolved animal life. First, this book traces again the four stages of being from the atomic to the potential highest consciousness. Instead of merely mentioning them, with some slight elaboration, however, Bridges in this book proceeds immediately to give all he knows concerning the four stages in the development of Selfhood. He shows it first in its lowest forms on that borderland between plant and animal, speculating also as to an even more remote origin in atom or molecule. (II, 80 f.) The chief movement is then forward from the plant, which sucks and plunders, to the child who "with his first life-breath" clarions for food. (II, 44-69) The furthest spiritual reach of Selfhood is presented in the state of Motherhood "with the unseen universe communing" (II, 165) and in perfect young manhood. (II, 503) The defections of Selfhood toward despair and war are given full discussion, and like the first book, this one ends in question of man's management of his inheritance.

To be consistent, discussion of the structural use of the theory of evolution in Book II should go on at this point with an emphatic "Second" to match the "First." The establishment of the four gradations from atomic to self-conscient in the impulse of Selfhood is quite obvious, of course. The distinction between the potential spiritual heights and the undoubted dangers toward which this passion can lead man is likewise clear. These ideas make up the first part of the generalization of the pattern suggested at the outset. But the second part of the pattern is not so clearly followed. It demands the concentration of the evolutionary material in one of the stages of evolution and it is true that in Book II the stage so emphasized is the organic; much of the biological material of the book deals with the cells and the selfhood of the primitive organism in seeking out food for self-preservation. It is true, too, that man as an individual has scarcely yet appeared for consideration; man in society, on the way to the heartless, senseless organization of the beehive is very important here. The logic of the structure would ask that man in society be shown in his parallel involvement in destructive wars. War is here to be sure, but the opportunity for structural consistency is missed by the emphasis on the individual rather than the social compulsions causing war. Hardy would have emphasized the social compulsions, and so made the poem structurally firmer at this point. However, Bridges did not consider war as a social phenomenon to this degree; thought twenty years after the publication of *The Testament of Beauty* is sharply divided between the rival ideas that war springs from the neuroses of the individual and that it springs from economic class antagonisms. However the structure of Book II may have slipped in this detail, in general one can readily see that the organic stage of selfhood as it clamors for nourishment and self-protection is concentrated on. The analogy of the organism of the bee-hive intent on self-preservation intensifies this concentration.

It is here that one may consider the structural peculiarity that the opening lines of Book III deal with the pressing forward of the hunger drive to its humorously belittled conclusion in the Epicure, although eating as an end in itself is admitted as a development of Selfhood and apparently should have been included in Book II. Previously it was shown that according to the inner logic of the poem, this so-called digression had as its ostensible purpose illustration of the basic artificiality of tracing all phenomena to isolable and mutually exclusive sources. Here it might be noted that Epicureanism is a complex, not primitive phenomenon, and as such has better place in the sensuous stage of individual development, that is in Book III. The exclusion of this material from Book II makes it more obvious that biological evolution in this book is not extended to man's later development. However, one should not claim that Bridges intended thus to insure the purity of his outline.

BOOK III.

To pass on to the next book, we again find the stages of being from the atomic through the conscious, and the main emphasis of the material on the stage successive to the previous book, that is, the sensuous. For the first part of the pattern, after the lines dealing with the love of food, we begin with the biological, not the atomic base, and are immediately made aware of the full potentiality of Breed in such nature's as Dante's. (III, 220) The faint adumbration of such an exalted experience every man is capable of. Second, there is a brief return to the atomic stage of being in the reference to atomic mechanism in sex. (III, 171) From here, we are led to the course of the evolution of Breed from the simplest kind of reproduction to the most complex conscient passion, transformed by Reason to altruistic emotion and spiritual love. (III, 193-204) In exploring the relationship of men and women on the highest level, we find that there is a very complex differentiation between the sexes which cannot be ascribed wholly to Breed, and that in marriage the woman gives back to man his faith in spiritual beauty. The main emphasis in the discussion of their relationship is thus laid on the state of marriage, founded on sexual passion and evolved through the lure of sensuous beauty to a spiritual experience.

Speaking structurally, this book then, discussing the later born of the passions, carries its history back as far as science can. We are shown its aberrations and corruptions (III, 394 f.) and also its possible transfiguration. A further progression is made by devoting much of the book to the difficult emergence of Christian marriage, a relationship demanding the concentration of man's mature life, whereas the previous book had shown the best development of Selfhood in the youth.

BOOK IV.

In Book IV we leave the steeds which represent the basic animal passions and come to the realm of thought to consider the science of ethics which deals with the "manage of the charioteer in Plato's myth." (IV, 89) The idea of evolution is still traceable in the pattern found in the other books; first, there is the repetition of the original sequence, the gradations of atomic, organic, sensuous, and self-conscient; and second, the return to origins for understanding of the theme of the book, with the emphasis here on the highest evolutionary stage, conscience (consciousness) as it approaches Universal Mind. However, because of the nature of the subject matter, the evolutionary idea is stressed less than in Books II and III; in this book, the personification of Reason, and finally, the journey, emerge as the major threads for the structure of the poem. This is in accordance with the nature of poetry; a mechanical device, a formula, applied indiscriminately throughout, would tend to destroy the life of the poem which a more organic method creates.

The expected pattern by which the idea of evolution has held the other three books together is imposed on Book IV in a particular way; the first rather than the second chord is especially emphasized. In this book, the statement of the continuity of all the gradations, the chord that dominates all the books, is the key passage, philosophically, of the whole poem. Its twenty-one lines are crucial:

IV, 112

> Reality appeareth in forms to man's thought
> as several links interdependent of a chain
> that circling returneth upon itself, as doth
> the coil'd snake that in art figureth eternity.
> From Universal Mind the first-born atoms draw
> their function, whose rich chemistry the plants transmute
> to make organic life, whereon animals feed
> to fashion sight and sense and give service to man,
> who sprung from them is conscient in his last degree
> of ministry unto God, the Universal Mind,
> whither all effect returneth whence it first began.

The application of the general truth to Ethick then is made in familiar terms; we are shown the extension of the basic form to the realm of vision:

IV, 123

> The Ring in its repose is Unity and Being:
> Causation and Existence are the motion thereof.
> Thru'out all runneth Duty, and the conscience of it

is thatt creativ faculty of animal mind
that, wakening to self-conscience of all Essences,
closeth the full circle, where the spirit of man
escaping from the bondage of physical Law
re-entereth eternity by the vision of God.

The second chord, the return to primitive forms for the origin of the main subject of the book, and the full development of that subject, may be detected also. The chief difference in its presentation here is inherent in the subject; the nature of thought is shown to be biological, even chemical, at its base, but its full understanding must be through psychological and philosophical study. Further, although mind and its coördinator, Reason, are together still evolving, they are appreciably near the position in the Ring of Being where their Being and not their Becoming are eternally significant. The evolution of the sense of Duty from "the prime ordinance that we call Law of Nature" (IV, 106) is still the firm foundation behind the revelation. The sense of Duty is

IV, 107
                     in its grade the same
with the determin'd habit of electrons, the same
with the determining instinct of unreasoning life,
NECESSITY become conscient in man. . . .

But the knot that Leibnitz cut was real; there is a Sphinx in all systems. The final link in the Ring of Being cannot be touched as yet, because although Reason will eventually become conscious of its true powers,

IV, 1075
                     and wil itself decree
and order discreetly the attitude of the soul . . .

the poet himself must rely on his faith:

IV, 1305
          Verily by Beauty it is that we come at WISDOM,
          yet not by Reason at Beauty . . . .

IV, 1310

> Wherefor as when a runner who hath run his round
> handeth his staff away, and is glad of his rest,
> here break I off, knowing the goal was not for me
> the while I ran on telling of what cannot be told.

Thus by repetitions, progression, and variation when required by the material, the idea of evolution is used in
The Testament of Beauty to give structural unity to its
diversity.

c. The Personification of Reason

In some sense, a little hard to define, the idea of evolution
may be called an extended metaphor, almost a myth, used to
impose a pattern on the varied experiences of this poem. This
section takes up an even more obvious kind of metaphorical
framework, the personification of Reason. Of all the methods
of unification used by Bridges, this personification and the
related dramatization of all the facts and speculations into
little narratives comes the nearest to Matthiessen's and Santayana's notions of the essentially dramatic quality which
poetry needs to give a living body to ideas. Bridges, if he
does not exclusively think in images as Matthiessen asks of
the poet, predominantly thinks in dramatic fictions of one
kind or another. These range from the constant use of the
pathetic fallacy (the dance of young trees, rye curtseying in
array to the breeze of May [I, 299-301]) to the creation of
a large company of more or less extended personifications of
ideas, emotions, and natural objects, which arise, give witness, declare, and what not. It might be possible to make
something of the structural use of several of these personifications, but that of Reason is the key to all the devices of this
kind one might find. There is no other so complete, so sustained, so continuous. Although several others are present
throughout, Reason is the protagonist. The person Reason
appears from the beginning in two roles, one, that of judge
of all the ideas as they are ranged up for consideration, and

the other, that of a human being in the process of matura-
tion. The poem progressively determines the final character
and authority of Reason, and shows the steps of its emergence
in organic life, its growth and final absolution, when it becomes aware of its true power.

A word or two should be said of Beauty, the titular heroine
of the poem, and of the vague personifications of Mind,
Wisdom, Intellect, Logic, and Science. In the first place,
there is no evolutionary change associated with these ideas;
they are not related to that part of the philosophy of the
poem and in no detailed way follow the outline of the poem.
In the second place they occur as often as not as abstractions,
and not even capitalized. With Beauty especially, occasionally the personification is clear:

III, 317
                      nor sensuous Beauty
torn from her royal throne, who is herself mother
of heav'nly Love. . . .

IV, 1
BEAUTY, the eternal Spouse of the Wisdom of God. . . .

But the human characteristics of this titular character are
muted: "Beauty is neither growth nor strength." (I, 715)
It should be pointed out, however, that personified or not,
the idea of Beauty hovers over the progress of the poem,
never failing of its high function of idealizing those powers
which have the possibility of working for ill as well as good.
Where Beauty is engaged, the issue is decided for idealization.

As for the treatment of Mind, Intellect, and Logic, the first
thing to be said of course is that they are loosely associated
with Reason, and as critics have noticed, they are apparently
"confused with" Reason. The distinctions are certainly not
clear, although I have not found any real contradictions of
the passage where Bridges answers his own question:

IV, 881

> *What the Mind is,* this thing bidden to know itself?
> First I bethink me naturally of every man
> as a unique creature, a personality
> in whom we lucidly distinguish body and mind,
> and talk readily of either tho' inseparable
> and mutually dependent, together or apart
> the created expression of Universal Mind.
> And of the body I think as the machinery
> of our terrestrial life evolving towards conscience
> in the Ring of Reality; and thence of the mind
> as thatt evolved conscience, the which in every-one
> is different, as the body differeth also in each.
> And human Intellect I see form'd and compact
> of the essential Ideas, wherewith soever each man
> hath come in contact personally, and in so far
> as he is kindly disposed to absorb their influences
> to build his personality. . . .

Rather than a confusion, one finds after a study of the personification, a kind of summing up in the figure Reason, of the various aspects of man's conscience (consciousness). Wisdom is the spiritual goal toward which Reason is working, or developing. The tool Logic may be used clumsily or in the wrong place (I, 463) but the goal of Reason is the vision of God. Mind is the vessel, Intellect part of its contents, Wisdom a condition of being. Reason is the evolving condition of conscience (consciousness), treated as an organism like man, presented as a person.

Reason's two roles were distinguished at the beginning of this section; they are connected in that Reason's authority as judge must depend on its maturity. However, at every stage, even when Reason is manifestly insufficient for some aspects of its task, it is the power by which we make distinctions and arrange our experience. In following the inner logic of the poem, one has found Reason at crucial points, the final judge, yet made aware of its limitations. The two roles are thus hard to separate, and if the personification is examined in detail and consecutively, they must be spoken of together. For this reason we must go through the poem book by book again, emphasizing not the development of the thought, but the presentation of a personality; if this distinction is to be clear in the reader's mind, he must attend with some strictness to the phraseology, especially to the verbs of action.

BOOK I.

Reason is on trial in Book I, and in a way the book proceeds by bringing forward the evidence; at the end of the book, the case rests. This figure of speech is suggested by the use of the terms of legal bankruptcy at Reason's first appearance. Man's Reason is

I, 57

in such deep insolvency to sense,
that tho' she guide his highest flight heav'nward and teach
    him
dignity morals manners and human comfort,
she can delicatly and dangerously bedizen
the rioting joys that fringe the sad pathways of Hell.

But the alliance with the senses gives us the miracle of music, and through Reason we become conscious of pain and pleasure:

I, 202

if Reason's only function wer
to heighten our pleasure, thatt wer vindication enough. . . .

Science too has vindicated the appeal to Reason. (145) But however characteristic of humanity our conscient Reason is, she shows serious limitations. Although the marvel of nature,

I, 450

pure Reason left to herself
relieth on axioms and essential premises
which she can neither question nor resolve, things far
beyond her, holding her anchor in eternal Mind. . . .

In the practical test also, Reason may disappoint us:

I, 463

> this picklock Reason is still a-fumbling at the wards,
> bragging to unlock the door of stern Reality.

When we turn to the history of Europe since the birth of Christ, we must feel that "nascent Reason seemeth to hav hoodwink'd Mind." (530) Yet we might have expected better:

I, 523

> Reason, shamefast at heart and vain above measure,
> would look to find the first fruits of intelligence
> showing some provident correction . . .
> to'ard social order . . .

I, 609

>   'tis mightily
> to the reproach of Reason that she cannot save
> nor guide the herd. . . .

Knowledge has of course accumulated (698) and Science has comforted man's animal poverty (722), creating miracles like radio music. (724-30) But in spite of Reason, it is the old lion's voice that roars now through the dazed head of the Sphinx. (789-90) Reason is the "prescriptive oracle" (146) but undeveloped, faulty, and not sufficiently influential.

BOOK II.

In Book II we find that Reason becomes the charioteer of Plato's myth:

II, 14

> the charioteer is REASON, and the whip in his hand
> is not to urge-on the steeds nor to incite their blood . . .

it is on the contrary to "hold them obedient to the reign of his Will." (18) Plato does not tell how Reason ever mounted the chariot in full career:

II, 29
> Yet truly is he portray'd fearless and glad of heart,
> his lash circling o'erhead, as smiling on his steeds
> he speaketh to them lovingly in his praise or blame.

Plato's personification is in marked contrast to Bridges' in its authority and power. Bridges sees Selfhood in its natural and uncontrolled state denounced by Reason (85) and controllable only by Reason (92), but Reason is not all-powerful. In savagery and childhood are torments of terror, often the dread boding of truth "against which man's full Reason at grips may wrestle in vain." (461) Faith alone can keep mortal despair from possessing his soul. (517) Recognizing Reason's limitations we may hesitate to accept its denunciation of War against popular testimony. (690) We must inquire of Reason "whence hath she fetch'd her high authority." (691) Reason is at first a little vague in her answers; to these questions she replies,

II, 697
> "I who hav never doubted of my authority,
> "who am the consciousness of things judging themselves—
>
> .   .   .

II, 703
> What then am I
> "in my conscience of self but very consciousness
> "of spiritual affection. . . .

The answer not being good enough, "my thought went harking back"

II, 709
> on its old trail, whence Reason learn'd its troublous task
> to comprehend aright and wisely harmonise
> the speechless intuitions of the inconscient mind;
> which, tho' a naked babe . . .
> is yet in some sort nearer to the Omniscient
> than man's unperfect Reason, baulk'd as thatt must be
> by the self-puzzledom of introspection and doubt.

That dark inconscient mind (716) holds a treasure that can be used by Reason to increase its power and worth. (722)

II, 725

> For I think not of Reason as men thought of Adam,
> created fullgrown, perfect in the image of God;
> but as a helpless nursling of animal mind,
> as a boy with his mother, unto whom he oweth
> more than he ever kenneth. . . .

a younger born (733) who cannot stand apart to "judge of all and of himself to boot." (735) He is sometimes a "servant and drudge" (736) and barren without the creative gift. (741) "In its naked self" (751) it is powerless, as we see when philosophers treat of art. But when Reason "will collaborate actively and eagerly" (742) with the influences which outreach Reason (801) and own "to existences beyond its grasp" (805), then Reason, "our teacher in all the schools" (804), "the waken'd mind fashion'd to'ard intellect" (809), will face "in a new perspective to'ard spiritual sight." (811)

II, 863

> The authority of Reason therefor relieth at last
> hereon—that her discernment of spiritual things,
> the ideas of Beauty, is her conscience of instinct
> upgrown in her . . .
>   to conscience of Beauty . . .

And so we can accept her judgment of War as a vice. (871) But Reason itself must "dissipate its own delusion" (981-82) that it is war only that brings suffering and horror. And further it must be recognized that Reason has not played its part in preventing war:

II, 994

> Reason hath lost control of his hot-temper'd steed
> and taken himself infection of the wild brute's madness. . . .

Bridges' hope for Reason's control over our civilization is muted here at the end of Book II, but one feels strongly that one has acquired strength from her struggles with these ideas; it is understood better why she goes wrong when she does, and her function as harmonizer of the various potentialities of mind to the enrichment of life and the better ordering of it has emerged strongly.

BOOK III.

The guiding function of Reason is made clear at the beginning of this book. It is she who planned the footing for the "lofty temple" Philosophy erected to "shrine her faith." (6) It was she who divined purpose in Nature, and subsumed under her main intentions "the old animal passions ancillary thereto. . . ." (17) But she can go very wrong in constructing such ideas and in developing the passions in the wrong direction. However, properly used through science, the thinking of man has explored the mysteries of sex, and has shown us how all its characteristics

III, 202
>   promoted and strengthen'd
> to a constant conscient passion, by Reason transform'd
> to'ard altruistic emotion and spiritual love.

Reason can lead in either direction.

When we become aware of the intermingling of sense and spirit in spiritual love, "we are driv'n to enquire of Reason how it came" (335) that bodily beauty is involved even in the holiest love. It seems that Reason has always dealt with evolutionary changes to bring out their beauty (354-84), and in this process, sensuous beauty becomes spiritualized. (792-94) Through this long section, the figure of Reason drops out, the effect of growing conscience (awareness) when Reason functions best being its chief concern. This effect is best expressed in marriage, the consideration of which demands treatment of the differences between man and woman. Reason reappears here as a person, in her less reassuring and more faulty aspect. It is suggested that Adam was given Eve as "his paregoric and comforting cure" (927)

after he was launched by Reason on "his sea of troubles."
(926) And the consequent development of man and woman
in spiritual matters is a story more favorable to woman than
to man because of the influence of Reason upon him; "man's
Reason drew him whither science led to walk with downcast
eyes." (958)

BOOK IV.

This book finally evaluates Reason as both judge and personality. In spite of its limitations, Reason understands and
harmonizes the intimations of the soul. (78) Parallel with
the education of spirit which has mapped out its own science
of conduct (83), Reason has matured to the power of manhood, tutored by Nature's discipline. (80)

The evolution of the sense of Duty, "NECESSITY become
conscient in man" (IV, 110) shows Reason finally in the
"absolution" of the vision of God. (130-31) "This absolution of Reason is not for all to see," but with its guidance

IV, 132
    any man may picture how Duty was born,
    and trace thereafter its passage in the ethick of man.

The story begins with the black ousel, building her nest,
impelled in her task by "I MUST." (140) If she could "take
persuasion of Reason to desist" (141) the results of yielding
would be a realization later that her conduct should have
been guided by "OUGHT." (141-46) Reason then is the guide
in the later shaping of the call of Duty "from physical to
moral ends." (149-50) Now taking for granted that Reason
is "matured to the power of manhood" (80), Bridges continues his argument without recourse to his metaphor of the
evolving person. There are, however, scattered references to
a personified Reason throughout the discussion of the philosophy of Hedonism which show that Man has not yet learned
to use Reason properly; his Reason indefensibly abstracted
pleasure as an idea, in the pursuit of which he "invented

and indulged vices unknown to brutes." (418) "Vain of his Reason" (522) he has made misleading distinctions between pleasure and happiness. (522-70) Aside from these, it is not until we reach the next section of this book (761f.) that the personification emerges again. It was Socrates who taught that the lamp of Reason should be turned "inwardly upon the mind" (771), but even he did not know

IV, 775
> how in thatt province
> Reason hath right to rule; nor of what stuff the reins
> can be, wherewith the Charioteer bridled the steeds. . . .

The lamp of Reason again shows Bridges the intricacies of the coördinations in the unconscious mind (781-833) whose "spontaneous life oweth nought to Reason." (834) By the same lamp, he sees that Reason's claim to be the "very consciousness of things judging themselves" (836) is extravagant. Beauty, for instance, "is not Reason's idea." (840) But we come here to see that the province where she has a right to rule is that of order:

IV, 845
> and surely Reason's property wil be
> the idea of Order;—and if so, I think to find
> how by the very natur of her own faculty
> she was deceived to imagin its universal scope;
> for since all natur is order'd (nor none wil deny
> that 'tis by Reason alone we are of such order aware),
> all things must of their ordinance come in her court
> for judgment. . . .

Here at last, perhaps, we may see the Reason that was on the defensive in Book I, although throughout the poem still in active duty, now judge in her own court.

Socrates evoked Reason "to order and disciplin the mind—" (865) and the scientist Bridges now asks

IV, 879
> what the Mind's cóntents are; how disorder'd; and why
> ther should in the good mind be any disorder at all.

Reason here must also be allowed "her claim to rule" (1025), this time as physician, who like other physicians, is not infallible. There will be in the mind

IV, 1009
> such disorder as Reason can perceive
> and may hav skill to amend; tho' we grant her art
> valid in principle and salutary in effect,
> the debit of failure is heavy in her accounts.
> Yet we discredit not all Medicine because
> ther be incurable maladies that end in death,
> nor yet because the leech . . .
>
> .   .   .
>
> wil hav recourse
> to palliativs and sentimental assurances
> of favorable conditions, exercise and air. . . .

We can accept, then, Reason's diagnosis that "the common ailment of mind [is] a lack of harmony." (1027) A further step in her growth is her own recognition of her liability:

IV, 1062
> Reason herself here questioneth me how I trust
> her mere ordering of life to make for happiness—
> whereto my answer is my good faith in what I hav writ.

The intellectual conclusion of the poem comes now, tentative in its human suggestion. We have seen

IV, 1065
> How the mind of man from inconscient existence
> cometh thru' the animal by growth of reasoning
> to'ard spiritual conscience . . .

and now

IV, 1073
> Reason (say I) will rise to awareness of its rank
> in the Ring of Existence . . .
> and wil itself decree
> and order discreetly the attitude of the soul. . . .

This relationship of Reason to religion (1080-1447) is expressed with increasing reliance on the method of vision; the personification drops out, and the mental process gradually dissolves into mystic utterance. Reason is still fallible in men, but its potentiality for man lies in its ability to reënter "eternity by the vision of God." (130)

In its absolution Reason loses its human character; like man it attains immortality by rising from its earthly machinery. The conclusion of its justification as a judge and its evolution to fulfillment brings the personification structurally to a close at the place in Book IV where the framework of the Vision-Journey draws the poem to its final completeness.

d. The Vision-Journey

By far the most important element in the structural unity of this poem is its use of the vision as framework. Most of the quarrel of critical opinion with its formlessness is proved irrelevant when this is realized: the lack of logical connectives, the juxtaposition of various kinds of experience, the apparently miraculous sense of completion and joy are all a part of the psychological state of the moment of vision. The same characteristics joined with a local habitation, that is, the fiction of someone telling the tale of a sleep, a dream of journeying toward truth, with the vision of glory at its end, make up the pattern of the dream-poem convention of medieval literature. The particular justification in *The Testament of Beauty* for the use of the traditional form lies in the vision as a psychological phenomenon.

Bridges did not have to be a psychologist with considerable reading in his field, nor even a religious mystic who was accustomed to the experience of trance sustained as was, we believe, that of Dante or Saint Francis. To be poet was enough. But it is quite clear that he had at hand the various evidences of the psychologist, the mystic, and the literary historian. Perhaps also he used his experience as a physician. He must often have observed the mental process of the patient who with awakening rationality tries to fit the facts he knows into the pattern of order and ecstasy of those eternal seconds anaesthetic has provided. The various kinds of vision may some or all of them be fallacious, but the combinations of memory, logic, and brilliantly felt emotion are unmistakable. *The Testament of Beauty* conventionally framed by the vision-journey, is a glorified and extended version, structurally, of this mental and spiritual experience. Once this is grasped, one can see how reasonable, if not logical, the arrangement of material is; feeling, information, descriptive details, the facts and interpretations of the various disciplines, and the faith in order and beauty that is the mark of the mystic, are all cast into this traditional form by a powerful creative operation utilizing its appropriateness to the full.

Bridges' variation on the type of the dream convention consists in its meticulous homogeneity of detail, and the reinforcement of the framework by many other structural devices. Readers of the previous section dealing with the structural implications of the theory of evolution will remember that the final stage of the "gradations" from the atomic through the conscient was always that of spirit, and usually of vision. This was true even of Book I, where the emphasis was on the atomic level; the jostling ripples of the atoms of the air were received by the enthroned mind "as heralds of high spiritual significance." (I, 77-81) It was apparent, too, that the course of evolution seemed to be a progress, or even a journey, toward a goal. Certainly we find it in the following passage which is always pointed out as crucial in Bridges' thought:

II, 204

the high goal of our great endeavour
is spiritual attainment, individual worth,
at all cost to be sought and at all cost pursued. . . .

In going through these passages dealing with the attainment of a spiritual goal, we find the symbol of the journey and the path fused with that of the dream, and the dream, waking or sleeping, attended by a feeling of the miraculous and the serenity of the mystic in his moments of vision. It will be unnecessary here to try to disentangle these elements, because their mixture is familiar not only in this poem but in all examples of the dream and vision convention. The preponderance of these merging symbols and their connection with almost all the other symbols, light and dark, for instance, has already been discussed. The subject of this section is their structural use in a familiar tradition.

That there are echoes of the medieval poems of vision, former commentaries have pointed out; Guérard even stresses the character of "the conventional invocation" and "the traditional palinode of medieval allegory."[6] But he is so concerned with admitting and admiring Bridges' traditional methods, that his simple statement obscures the original and radical effect in *The Testament of Beauty* of what in a really conventional treatment would be stale. Starting off with the invocation to Prudence, one may find it a little chilling at first reading, but not flat. With the poem behind it, so to speak, as the opera is behind the overture to give it richness when one knows it well, this invocation, with the navigation metaphor prominent, becomes resonant with the dangers and joys of the journey from the earliest beginnings to where the spirit of man reëntereth eternity. After the invocation, the main direction of the poem is established by the traditional dream-journey-vision of medieval literature, a tradition which through Dante goes back to the journey or voyage of classical epic. As Dante changed the spirit and content of the journey to suit his medieval purpose, so Bridges has changed the spirit and content of the medieval to suit his modern needs. The echoes and reflections of the earlier great examples are all there, indeed, to enrich and clarify *The Testament of Beauty*, but when the theme is closed in the concluding passages of the poem, although the echoes yet remain, the

[6] *Robert Bridges*, pp. 194 and 229.

individuality of Bridges' vision, its modern personality, makes the word "traditional" almost a distortion of what is the true effect.

Specifically, I think, only the opening lines of *The Inferno* have previously been noticed as analogous to the journey element in *The Testament of Beauty*. Reference to several others makes clear the dominance of this device in the shape and personality of the poem as a whole. Beginning with *The Divine Comedy* we read:

i, 1

> In the middle of the journey of our life I [came
>   to] myself in a dark wood [where] the
>   straight way was lost.

i, 10

> I cannot rightly tell how I entered it, so full of
>   sleep was I about the moment that I left the true way.

i, 28

> After I had rested my wearied body [a short
>   while,] I took the way again along the desert strand . . .

i, 37

> The time was at the beginning of the morning;
>   and the sun was mounting up with those stars,
>   which were with him when Divine Love
>   first moved those fair things. . . .[7]

With the coming of Virgil as his guide, Dante then starts on the long journey toward Paradise where he comes to understand the Divine Love he mentions at its beginning. That Dante was glowing within the mind of Bridges as he wrote Book III, is of course obvious, the Dante both of *The Divine Comedy* and *The New Life*:

III, 242

>   and on those feather'd wings
> his mighty poem mounted panting, and lieth now
> with all its earthly tangle by the throne of God.

[7] *The Inferno of Dante Alighieri* (London: Temple Classics, 1912), pp. 3, 5.

It is clear that Bridges in proceeding with his poem, leaves "the earthly tangle" of an actual, materialized journey; but it is clear too that the metaphor of the journey to truth ending in vision not only hovers continually over the poem but holds it firmly in shape. In the several examples of the dream in Chaucer, and in *The Vision of Piers Plowman,* we find the preliminary sleep and the fiction of a story told, but these poems are not so close to Bridges' practice as the Dante, or as another dream poem, *The Pearl.* In *The Pearl,* the journey growing from the sleep is reduced in size to the pleasant walk of *The Romaunt of the Rose,* but as in *The Divine Comedy,* the poet sees his Paradise, here the New Jerusalem across the river, and his Beatrice, here Marguerite, the Pearl.

The intermingling of the navigation metaphor with the journey, so prominent in *The Testament of Beauty,* is not a part of these medieval poems, but the medieval mind seized upon the imaginative suggestiveness of sea voyaging in other literature, the voyage of St. Brandon, for instance, and the story of Constance. In his use of the navigation theme, however, Bridges was reflecting more the voyages of Ulysses than the aimless wandering among insignificant wonders and perils of medieval voyage literature. The great difference between the Greek and medieval sea voyages lies in the superior sense of the need for knowledge and skill in navigation. Important and fine and charming as they are, St. Brandon and Constance would never have had a landfall on their own initiative; even God as captain of their vessels seems to anyone who has but sailed a catboat, rather a landlubber. Bridges, however, gives us the feel of the hand upon the tiller:

II, 451
               and in the lowest
pain can be felt no more than mid the dancing waves
a pleasure-boat feeleth the hand on her tiller
that keepeth-up her head to th' wind and her sails full.

One must grant that this sounds more like yachting at Cowes than sailing into the western seas through the Pillars of Hercules. However, by frequent use of the navigation metaphor,[8] the two kinds of journeys are related, and the invocation to Prudence takes its place within the framework of purposive traveling:

I, 1

> MORTAL Prudence, handmaid of divine Providence,
> hath inscrutable reckoning with Fate and Fortune:
> We sail a changeful sea through halcyon days and storm,
> and when the ship laboureth, our stedfast purpose
> trembles like as the compass in a binnacle.
> Our stability is but balance, and conduct lies
> in masterful administration of the unforeseen.

The specific and detailed use of this device to further the organic unity of the poem can be made clear in several ways; first, the evolution of the stages of existence from the atomic to the fully conscient can be shown book by book in terms of the journey to realization; second, the beginnings of the successive books form a pattern; third, the beginning and end of the poem, even more than the beginning and end of *The Divine Comedy*, define the poem as a search for truth; foreshadowed in the opening lines, and repeated and amplified in the close, all the themes of experience gather within this metaphor, or myth.

First, the reading of the subjects of each of the four main divisions of the poem in terms of the road upward through the stages of existence is easy enough and must have occurred to many. The words "road," "path," "journey" are many times repeated as the figurative vocabulary of this evolution. Book I is clearly the examination of Reason's pretensions as interpreter of man's toilsome journey "from conscience of nothing to conscient ignorance" (I, 435), Reason itself being a recent development on this path. In Book II, man trying to see his way between intellect and spiritual

---

[8] About thirty references.

sight is "disconcerted twixt their rival promises" and he becomes "doubtful of his road." (II, 815-16) In Book III, man's perversion in making pleasure in food an end in itself is "a road whereon the brutes already had broken ground." (III, 33) The most significant of them all occurs in Book IV:

IV, 761
> AND here my thought plungeth into the darksome grove
> . . wherein
> I hav wander'd often and long and thought to know my way . . .

The course of the journey of man himself can be expressed as follows:

III, 40
> From the terrifying jungle of his haunted childhood
> where prehistoric horror stil lurketh untamed,
> man by slow steps withdrew. . . .

These few examples of a constant habit of terminology are of course more the evidence of the permeation of the text with this metaphor, already discussed in Chapter x. The marking off of the significant divisions of the poem is achieved by the journey in search of truth seen in vision; the most important passages relating to this idea are the structural posts, as it were. The opening passages in each book are vital to see as part of this device.

Book I opens with the invocation to Mortal Prudence, just quoted; the beginning of the "story" follows with the dramatic narrative of the walk on the downs from which familiar haunts were seen estranged by beauty. This passage will be analyzed in detail when the beginning and end of the whole poem are shown as part of the vision idea; but it must be recognized that this walk in fine early summer weather, the presence of the garden, even the upland region to match the Malvern Hills of *Piers Plowman,* emphasizes the medieval mystical element in the vision. At the beginning of Book II, the literary reference changes from the medieval to Plato's

The Testament of Beauty

vision of the seer who saw the spirit of man. (II, 1) There is considerable aesthetic and philosophical interest in this switch from the medieval Christian tradition of vision which was established in Book I. The contrast is particularly marked after the conclusion to Book I with its echoes of *The New Testament*. In this next book, Reason takes hold in the analysis of the bases of man's personality in the animal passions; the attitude and method of Plato is more consonant with such a subject than would be that of the Christian visionary. The variation of material and mood is also interesting in itself and saves the metaphor from being mechanical in its extension. The medieval tradition is constantly reappearing, however. And further the emphasis on the "goal" of Reason driving the steeds from his chariot, and to the evolutionary element throughout, keeps alive the idea of the journey, which is not a part of Plato's myth. There is a further variation at the beginning of Book III. Here there is an increase of the rational, in the interpretation of the steeds as abstractions:

III, 1
> HAVING told of SELFHOOD, ere I now tell of BREED
> the younger of the two Arch-Instincts of man's nature,
> 'twer well here to remember how these pictured steeds
> are Ideas construed by the abstract Intellect.

The content, however, of Book III continues to give preponderance to the medieval in the continuous treatment of Dante's vision of love and the love poetry of the Troubadours; the metaphor of the medieval convention still flourishes, too. The opening lines of Book IV, are, in effect, the epitome of all these ideas. We have the return to the bursting out of the wintry stalk with the prolific miracle of Spring (IV, 7), to the Dantean vision (IV, 14), to the use of the words "goal" and "clue." (IV, 16)

The greatest significance of the dream-journey framework can be seen in the beginning and end of the whole poem. By these sections the poem is enclosed in its proper shape. When this is once grasped, the expectation that the poem will, or the feeling that it should, proceed from one end of a philosophical system to another, that it have the kind of progression and logical consistency of a treatise, are set aside forever. As well expect *The Divine Comedy* to be a *Summa* in its style and structure, as to expect *The Testament of Beauty* to be *Scepticism and Animal Faith* or *The Life of Reason*. Further, when this fact is imaginatively grasped, and the poem is seen as the whole testimony of a lifetime which led to the joy and recognition of a vision, one no longer asks that all its material shall be either lyrically consistent or expressed with the plot and character machinery of a story. The poem is neither a lyric nor an epic, and must not be judged by either standard.

By now, familiar with the phraseology of the vision, if the reader will return to the poem and read the first fifty-six and the last one-hundred and seventy-eight lines, he will see its structural force for himself. But the tale should no doubt be made complete here.

One begins again with the invocation, but only to point out the importance of the last two lines:

I, 6

> Our stability is but balance, and conduct lies
> in masterful administration of the unforeseen.

The psychology of the moment of vision is expressed here in in the word "balance." All know that revelation fades, that the pattern of interpretation breaks up when new circumstances occur:

> Making it momentany as a sound,
> Swift as a shadow, short as any dream,
>
> .   .   .
>
> So quick bright things come to confusion.

It is with the next lines that we come to the key of the poem, one indeed that unlocks more than the secret of the traditionalism of Bridges. It is the key to the tone, the meaning, and the structural firmness of *The Testament of Beauty*. After detailed study of the poem, the opening vision can be seen holding it all in solution. There is nothing strange in the claim of a music critic that every note of an overture is related by significance and mathematics to the whole composition; Conrad has said the same for a literary composition: "a work that aspires . . . to the condition of art should carry its justification in every line."[9] Here the claim for the rich aesthetic importance of the first fifty-six lines of *The Testament of Beauty* is made in the same spirit. The following are the important ideas relating to the vision motif which becomes the coördinating factor of the structure.

We begin with the idea of the journey, already suggested by the lines "we sail a changeful sea," this journey being the climbing of a hill. Throughout the section there is marked English reference, more specifically to a neighborhood not far from or uncongenial with the garden of the poem's centre. We are made aware of this by the localization of the seaward South Downs, and at the top, a garden planted years ago. These opening lines refer to three experiences, the present one, late in his life, an earlier similar climb to a downland height, and one in boyhood when the quiet driving power of a factory engine room filled him with the same confidence in natural forces. The journey, then, is also from boyhood to old age, the boyhood and old age of the central figure of this poem described in an earlier chapter.

On the uplands reached by the narrowing path, as any man may, he rests to view the lowland he has left and he sees his familiar haunts both patterned and estranged by the beauty of distance. The landscape is mapped out by Reason's ordering like the whole experience of the poem, the perspective showing a beauty which, like Wordsworth's feeling for the probably unworthy picture by Sir George Beaumont,

<hr>

[9] Conrad, Joseph. Preface to *The Nigger of the Narcissus,* opening sentence.

was "the light that ne'er was seen on sea or land." But the experience was a double one: without the special intensification of the vision, without man's ordering, the beauty of the earth's wild loveliness, the blue sky and the soft air would be enough. The vision of the pattern of life, and the intense perception of the central force in the common flowers and the weaving mill, were alike. The relationship between man and nature is happy wherever the secret strength of nature is felt; during these moments man is aware of the unseen company (I, 691) of things which govern thought. (III, 135) The beauty felt throughout this experience is part of the conviction of its truth; "Beauty is the highest of all these occult influences." (II, 842)

In his use of the journey-vision convention, then, Bridges has set forth both the idea that life is a journey spaced off by moments of vision in which one looks back with wonder and sees with joy the Being, the essence of things, and also the beginning and end of his own personal journey and its discoveries. Between the beginning and end of the poem the theme is kept alive and progressing, as has been shown. Hardly a page of the poem is free from some mention of vision, and no page is without some use of the related symbols. However, the progress through the poem is more particularly obvious in terms of Reason. It is through Reason that the sensuous becomes conscient, and by the ordering of Reason that the Ring of Being is perceived and understood. When the way has been traversed, the search and the discoveries come to their particular end where the vision of ordered beauty has been confirmed by thought. No claim is ever made, however, for an absolute homecoming to truth such as one finds it in *The Pearl,* for instance, or in *The Divine Comedy.* "Our stability is but balance." The more certain view is possible only for a much more authoritarian mind than Bridges'. He had neither the philosophical assurance nor the theological faith necessary for the positive all-inclusive answer. In Book IV he is still analyzing and inquiring, although the state of rest is approaching by the time we are halfway through.

This state of rest is one that recognizes all experience; it is not quite an ironical contemplation nor even a "mingling of the approbative and the satirical," but it is surely "the balance or reconcilement of opposite or discordant qualities."[10] It is the reformulation by experience of the great commonplace.[11] The passage at the centre of Book IV beginning "And here my thought plungeth into the darksome grove" (IV, 761) provides the chord in a minor key which introduces the poem's mystic close. By its imagery and cadences faith in sensuous beauty is joined with philosophic thought, ignorance with knowledge. A careful scrutiny of the diction in the light of the analyses of imagery in Part II will show how concentrated here are all the essential means Bridges used throughout the poem to bring his diverse properties into keeping. A practiced reading of the lines will reveal the most poignant music, where the voice of the poet takes on its most compelling register.

The tone here is that of continuous experience of the mind through a long life. In casting back to the beginning of the poem, one is aware of the contrast between the noontime glowing light of those sun-soaked hours on the downs, and the obscure shadows of the paths of philosophical meditation in the tradition and in the company of the great thinkers of the past. There is no fear there, although the penetralia are secret; there has been a great clearing in the darksome grove, and the way of vision was seen when "the path was narrowing and the company few." The discoveries of the retracing of the remembered paths of ethic lore relate to Selfhood and Sex, to Reason, Beauty, Art, and Prayer. These discoveries are presented as the result of a life of Reason consonant in all its parts; the final ordering may be like that

[10] Brooks, Cleanth. *Modern Poetry and the Tradition*, p. 29, quoting Richards; and p. 40, quoting Coleridge.
[11] Tillyard. *Poetry Direct and Oblique*, 2d ed., p. 43.

of theology when it filled the inane between God and man
with angels, or like that of astronomy when it filled the gap
between the planets with asteroids. It is, however, Reason's
order which may be expressed in conjunction with the metaphor of light in darkness:

IV, 865
> and 'twas thus Socrates
> coud evoke Reason to order and disciplin the mind—
> the divine Logos that should shine in the darkness . . .

This is a hopeful use of the metaphor to supersede the fearful
questioning at the end of Book I: "But the great Light
shineth in great darkness." (I, 786)

At the end of Book IV we have the closing of the circle
with the restatement of the themes of the opening lines, and
a complementary autobiographical passage rich in the symbolic use of personal experience, time of day and geographical location. The hour is an hour of grief, the time is sunset,
and the garden is the refuge; natural beauty and the personal
sorrow lead to the final revelation:

IV, 1279
> 'Twas at sunset that I, fleeing to hide my soul
> in refuge of beauty from a mortal distress,
> walk'd alone with the Muse in her garden of thought. . . .

IV, 1287
> Then fell I in strange delusion, illusion strange to tell;

IV, 1291
> for being in truth awake
> methought I slept and dreamt; and in thatt dream methought
> I was telling a dream; . . .

> . .

IV, 1297
> for my tale was my dream and my dream the telling,
> and I remember wondring the while I told it
> how I told it so tellingly.

The whole section is as rich in repetition of metaphors and

themes as the first section was rich in their first establishment, and it is, further, a richer bed of reference to the great
literature of religion, the dream-visions, the *Old* and *New
Testaments,* with all of which our minds have become saturated like

III, 570
>   all these diverse stuffs thru' the dark centuries
>   [which] lay quietly a-soak together in the dye-vats. . . .

Of the briefer references, it will be enough to call attention
to the clear echoes of the opening lines of *The Vision of
Piers Plowman* in IV, 1297-1300 above, the loose Alexandrines falling into the movement of

>   In a somer seson, whan softe was the sonne,
>   I shrope me in shroudes as I a shepe were. . . .

The conclusion of *The Paradiso,* however, will bear a longer
quotation, to bring out the relationship of Bridges' journey
toward truth discovered in vision with that of Dante's.

xxxiii, 52
>   because my sight, becoming purged, now more
>   and more was entering through the ray of the
>   deep light which in itself is true.
>   Thence forward was my vision mightier than
>   our discourse, which faileth at such sight, and
>   faileth memory at such great outrage.
>   As is he who dreaming seeth, and when the
>   dream is gone the passion stamped remaineth,
>   and nought else cometh to the mind again;
>   even such am I; for almost wholly faileth me
>   my vision, yet doth the sweetness that was
>   born of it still drop within my heart.

xxxiii, 82
>   Oh grace abounding, wherein I presumed to fix
>   my look on the eternal light so long that I
>   consumèd my sight thereon!
>   Within its depths I saw ingathered, bound by
>   love in one volume, the scattered leaves of all
>   the universe;

substance and accidents and their relations, as
though together fused, after such fashion that
what I tell of is one simple flame.[12]

The conclusion of *The Testament of Beauty* is in comparably religious and mystic terms; substance and accidents of life's experience are similarly fused into "ONE ETERNAL in the love of Beauty and in the selfhood of Love." (IV, 1445) In this fusion of self and notself, mind and body, God and man (1444-45), the Ring of Being and the dream vision are complete.

[12] *The Paradiso of Dante Alighieri* (London: Temple Classics, 1912), pp. 403, 405.

CHAPTER FOURTEEN

CONCLUSION

The body of this book has demonstrated at considerable length the extraordinary aesthetic unity of *The Testament of Beauty*. To the aesthetic philosopher, this procedure, if accurate and convincing, is enough.[1] But it is additionally important to many that the unified poem be "worth" something in relation to a world of human values as well as to the world of aesthetic values. Some readers insist on some sort of constructive residuum in the realm of human beliefs or human experience; many critics believe that such a residuum is in itself a part of the aesthetic make-up of the poem. The purist would not see such a belief as philosophically demonstrable, or even pertinent. Some of the severest minds in present-day criticism, however, either implicitly or explicitly demand of a poem that its unity be not mechanical, that is, cut off from human spiritual value, or morality in the widest sense. They find what they are willing to call a moral value in the aesthetic excellence of the poem. This, too, the aesthetic philosopher appears unwilling to do. Although the critic of a particular poem cannot stop to decide philosophical issues in philosophical terms, it is important that he be firm in his method of analysis, avoiding the fallacies a pure impressionism or relativism may fall into. But it is important, too, that he concern himself with the sanctions for his analytical activity. He may be very tentative about it, and he must be as inclusive as possible: in fact, the greater the variety of readers he can induce to follow his discussion to its conclusions, restating them if they must

---

[1] Wimsatt, W. K., Jr., and Beardsley, M. C. "The Affective Fallacy," *The Sewanee Review* (January, 1949).

in their own terms, the more effective his method may seem to be. To be specific, the holders of various shades of opinion must be convinced that no view need invalidate the foregoing analytical procedure, that all schools may learn something significant from it. If *The Testament of Beauty* emerges as "great" for the religious mystic, the Jungian, the Marxist, and the royalist among the partisans, and for Hughes, Elton, and Guérard, through Winters and Brooks to Wimsatt and Beardsley among critics, a high evaluation of the poem will seem the more sound. It would be the supreme practical justification for the poem to be accepted by all shades of interpretative judgment, as well as in all ages. To change the emphasis of a statement tending to establish the permanence of the great work of art in spite of shifting tastes and beliefs: "a structure of emotive objects so complex and so reliable as to have been taken for great poetry"[2] by any sensitive and trained student will not suffer in the light of many and various views, be they aesthetic, psychological, sociological, or religious. A quite tentative justification for the careful aesthetic analysis of *The Testament of Beauty* contained in this book follows.

The connecting link between the feeling that the formal aspects of a poem are satisfying and a belief in its value beyond that of artistry, is very difficult to forge. Just how the power of the poet creates truth as well as a poem has not been clearly defined, and perhaps it cannot be; but the faith that he does create both in one might be expressed in the following way:

It is the conviction of all serious artists and critics that the full creative power is never brought to bear on the trivial, the sentimental, or the permanently destructive. The poem that stands up to the scrutiny of the preceding pages cannot be an empty shell. By the power of the imagination, which is both a psychological capability and a special craftsmanship, an interpretation of mankind which is out of key with twen-

---

[2] Wimsatt and Beardsley. *Op. cit.*, p. 25.

tieth-century civilization becomes a profound truth. The logic of this is elusive, but the force of the belief inescapable. There is, however, a little more that must be said about this in justice to the serious attempt made here to present *The Testament of Beauty* first as sophisticated art, and finally as a great poem.

In the opinion of many, the question of significance in art, even that of moral value, has passed from the realm of moral codes, or philosophical or theological systems. But this is in no sense to say that the ultimate value of the poem depends only on its formal aspects. There is no tendency to return to the narrow and jejune notion that ornamental or dream-inducing beauty is evidence or object of excellence in poetry. Indeed Arnold's idea that it is an advantage to a poet to write of a beautiful world, and the belief that beauty of image or cadence justifies itself, have been expressly denounced.[3] In this light, *The Testament of Beauty* must not be relegated to a backwater because Bridges' belief in the superior importance of individual attainment to social progress, and his religious faith in joy, create an atmosphere that appears to belong more in a dream-world than in our own. Nor can the incidental beauties of the poem be allowed to give it undue importance.

What have we then to tie to, if the significance of the poem is not connected with the doctrines of its paraphrasable message or with its beautiful world? The extreme position is really a religious one, though it is seldom expressed in theological terms. The theologically inclined are as doubtful of it as the rational or the practical. In this view the literary act is "conceived as a sort of raid on the absolute and its result as a revelation."[4] In more sympathetic language: "there are two worlds, one the world of time, where necessity, illusion, suffering, change, decay, and death are the law; the other the world of eternity, where there is freedom, beauty,

---

[3] Brooks. *Modern Poetry and the Tradition,* pp. 18f., and 34f.
[4] Quoted by Eliot. *The Use of Poetry,* p. 120, from Rivière.

and peace. Normal experience is in the world of time, but glimpses of the other world may be given in moments of contemplation or through accidents of involuntary memory. It is the function of art to develop these insights and to use them for the illumination of life in the world of time."[5] The art of poetry fulfills this function by the use of deep-springing rhythms, metaphors, or symbols, and the creation in miniature of a perfect, eternal world of beauty, that is, the poem. The artist must, then, be somehow gifted so that he may perceive truth directly, and communicate it wordlessly, if in music or painting; the poet must go beyond the logic of words, his communication to be inexpressible in other words than those used originally. He creates, as it were, a new indefinable word by the choice and arrangement of words in a line, and, in the whole poem, a further word.[6] The Believer will go further than this, and call this created word The Word, or Divine Truth. But at this point the line of thinking has diverged from literary criticism to revelation; the logical justification for the extension in this direction is tenuous. The material of the poem, however interpreted, does not in itself lead as far as this. We must have other grounds than the poem for believing that the poem (or the poet) goes out of our world to be associated with values pertaining to a self-existent world, whose authenticity must be self-evident. The position taken by this book does not preclude this extension of authority for those who wish it, but it depends in itself on no divine or other supra-human sanctions.

In some sort, no doubt, the leap from observation of facts to statement of value is always an act of faith. There is no bridge from one side to the other that all travelers will trust themselves to. But if the critic holds to the full implication of the description of a poem as having a life of its own created from a fusion of its materials, with significance in its whole-

[5] March, Harold. *The Two Worlds of Marcel Proust* (Philadelphia, 1948), p. 246.
[6] Winters, Ivor. *Primitivism and Decadence*, pp. 2-3.

ness for human beings, it is clear that he is depending on
some kind of teleological sanction. If it is not theological or
sociological it is probably psychological. It may be defined,
if loosely, and may be accepted as a base by those who go
further toward the sanction of God or Marx. It is only individual and only human, but it involves us in the consideration of the power of sounds and symbols and wholeness to
affect us deeply and relate us to something not ourselves. We
accept as a psychological truth that when we are receptive
to this power, our feelings are moved, our spiritual perceptions are enriched and sharpened and our intelligences satisfied. The acceptance of this truth does not demand adherence
to any particular psychological party line.

Sensitive readers of poetry feel the inexpressible effect
of the rhythms and cadences both Eliot and Housman believe to penetrate "far below the conscious levels of thought
and feeling, invigorating every word; sinking to the most
primitive and forgotten, returning to the origin and bringing
something back, seeking the beginning and the end."[7] Or, as
Housman puts it, speaking of the cadence of the line: "In
these six simple words of Milton—

'Nymphs and shepherds, dance no more'—

what is it that can draw tears, as I know it can, to the eyes
of more readers than one? . . . Why have these mere words
the physical effect of pathos when the sense of the passage
is blithe and gay? I can only say, because they are poetry,
and find their way to something in man which is obscure and
latent, something older than the present organization of his
nature, like the patches of fen which still linger here and
there in the drained lands of Cambridgeshire."[8] These effects
may have something to do with our origins in an ultimate
reality; perhaps the reader is responding to the vibrations of
a heavenly harp, or perhaps to the rhythmic motion of the

[7] Eliot, T. S. *The Use of Poetry*, p. 111.
[8] Housman. *The Name and Nature of Poetry*, p. 45.

salt sea from which we took our life. Ignorance of the final truth does not affect a conviction that the power of rhythm and cadence in a fine poem has a spiritual significance as well as a deeply exciting effect. This power appears to relate the human being to something more permanent and thus in one sense more valuable, than himself.

The same state of suspension of final justification may exist in the realm of imagery. Coming down at least from Samuel Butler, running through Jung and emerging in a strong current in Yeats, is the belief that the poet (or anyone sufficiently gifted with imagination, or willing to relax the bands of logical thought) has wisdom at his hand in the great racial memory. He dips into this reservoir and brings out not ideas or facts, but images or symbols representing man's universal and eternal experiences. We may be moved unaccountably by the great symbols in literature, as we find them for instance in Pericles' lament in the storm:

> A terrible child-bed hast thou had, my dear;
> No light, no fire.

However, the connection between this emotion and a mystic or anthropological doctrine or even of any kind of doctrine, is unnecessary to make. Stauffer expresses a similar reluctance to link the two: "One need not accept Yeats's belief that any significant past event or emotion passes into the Great Mind, lives in the Great Memory, and may be evoked by symbols."[9] He does not thereby reduce the importance to poetry of the symbol, nor the seriousness for human beings, of poetry. Symbols are a universal language and the illumination of the mind caused by their effective use provides a link between their aesthetic value and their emotional significance.

Neither the aesthetic nor the spiritual effect of the wholeness of a poem is usually felt as strongly as the effect of sound or symbol. Both the creation of poetic rhythms and symbols and the reader's response to them are likely to be

[9] *The Nature of Poetry*, p. 169.

more immediate and to appear more self-evidently valuable. The spontaneous seems to be a gift from somewhere and therefore to have a supra-human power behind it. Expression of feeling by rhythm and symbol can in itself be emotionally arousing and we believe if we do not understand. Such phrases as "the obscure and latent," "the beginning and the end," we find hard to question. But when it comes to considering the satisfaction caused by structure, one must be silent or prosaic; the effect of the whole poem lies in the whole poem and cannot be recreated by phrases. To fall back on the simple statement "This is right," a proper remark to oneself, is not to convince; the explanation must be reasonable. But whatever the difficulties, we can find some guidance.

There are those who believe that the conscious control exercised and evident in the structure of a very good poem is a moral act in itself, a discipline for both the writer and the reader.[10] There are others who see in the psychic satisfaction of bringing an idea around to a conclusion, or arranging sensuous material in a pattern, a humanly significant activity, one related to the deepest urges of mankind. Both the Gestalt and the several branches of psychoanalytic psychology account for the human value in creating and experiencing wholes, by the satisfaction on a high level of demands of the psyche. But readers may object to the austerity of the first position, and the lack of aesthetic reference in them all. From these positions one does indeed look on Beauty bare, right down to the skeleton, or on Beauty enslaved to a psychological doctrine.

The case for the human significance of the poem achieved by its structural firmness and unity in proportion, may be presented in further ways. Brooks finds honesty and strength in ironic contemplation of spiritual values expressed by structural balance. The finer and more complex view of experi-

---

[10] Hamilton, G. Rostrevor. *Contemplation and Poetry* (Cambridge, 1937), *passim;* Winters, Ivor. *Primitivism and Decadence,* p. 5.

ence is the one which considers, accepts, and then assimilates both extremes. The suppression and exclusion of the negative, of evil, in the interests of moral fervor, is the sentimental view. The integration of all elements into a carefully constructed unity which evaluates by proportion, is the stronger view. Both beauty and significance result from contrasts and balances, a beauty of both color and proportion, in Donne's words.[11] Structure, according to this line of thought, becomes the way of amalgamating opposites to arrive at a firm and mature truth which refuses to ignore inconsistency, ugliness, and evil. But what of the poem which does not take explicitly into its content both sides of the balance? Probably structural precision may be the very mechanism needed to strengthen the expression of a steady fervor, be it love, religion, or patriotism, felt by the poet, if only temporarily, as the very heart of truth which blazes with no hint of dross or shadow. We may prefer poems which express our own complex questionings or the precarious balance we have with difficulty achieved; we will certainly in that case ask for something to raise the passion to a power, beyond the cadences, beyond the symbols.

That the idea behind the poem may be a universal truth and not a paradox, but that it needs the complexity of organization given by a careful and significant structure, is made very clear by Tillyard. To the first point, he even goes so far as to say that beneath the apparent complexity of much poetry, *The Waste Land* as well as *The Iliad,* lies its profoundest meaning, and that when found it turns out to be one of those universal truths which stated directly are of so little value to the modern mind. Tillyard does not hesitate to call these truths expressed in art, great commonplaces. However, the word "commonplace" should not blind the understanding to the real meaning here. Such a truth as it implies is not connected with any over-familiar codes of morals or

[11] Brooks, Cleanth. *Modern Poetry and the Tradition,* especially pp. 33f. Donne, *First Anniversary,* line 250.

religion. "The great commonplaces have something mysterious about them as embodying the utmost wisdom of the race."[12] "They are in perpetual danger of perishing. They have to be refelt continually and reformulated by human experience. They cease to be true unless continually ratified by fresh expression."[13] This ratification includes a reliving of experience, but the fresh expression of the truth discovered in this process must involve the control of experiences as they are relived, "even in the very height of excitement."[14] All the elements of the poem create the predominant thought or feeling the poet's control forces upon us, but the structure is the most important. The reason for this is that the great commonplace suffers from direct statement; it must be implied; it must underlie the whole poem, but be expressed by it obliquely. By some extension of the phrase, the whole poem must be "the objective correlative" of the universal truth, by virtue of its structure (or formula). If the poem by its structural firmness and unity can exist in itself as the creation of a poet's full creative powers, we become confident that here is no aphorism, cheaply repeated. Its truth is a rediscovery by the discipline and illumination of proportion, and we share the experience of its rediscovery in understanding the pattern of the order that has been imposed.

There will be no attempt in this last chapter to reassess the spiritual value of *The Testament of Beauty.* I will only conclude very briefly with what concerns the modern mind, and I believe with justification, when it admits the remarkable artistry of this poem, but then wonders whether its sociological and sectarian views do not force us to doubt the truth of its vision. Is this poem concerned only with a withdrawn and remote life, a luxury item left over from the halcyon days when men could afford to meditate over the changeful sea of personal conduct whose storms affected the

12 *Poetry Direct and Oblique,* 2d ed., p. 42.
13 *Ibid.,* p. 43.
14 *Ibid.,* pp. 46 and 76.

individual and not society? It is true that economic and governmental problems are set aside or ignored entirely: cartels, labor relations, distribution of goods, location of raw materials, the relation of the freedoms with safety, none of these is part of the content of the poem. More seriously, considering the nature of the poem, there is no consideration of the individual as a part of society, his economic instability in a world he never made, the clash between his public and his private responsibilities.

Some ages do not see the fundamental problems of society and the individual in relation to them. But today these problems are exposed to the bitter air; the coverings have been ripped from the naked necessity by the kind of wars that escape their adamantine doors like Blake's winter. Even in the nineteen-twenties Mussolini and the London pavement artists were alike portents. How blind was the poet who wrote, in the latter half of that decade, that the socialist glosses "his soul-delusion with a muddled thought,"

II, 204
> Not knowing the high goal of our great endeavour
> is spiritual attainment, individual worth,
> at all cost to be sought and at all cost pursued,
> to be won at all cost and at all cost assured;
> not such material ease as might be attain'd for all
> by cheap production and distribution of common needs,
> wer all life level'd down to where the lowest can reach. . . .

How confusedly traditional the poet who concludes his Darwinian poem with echoes from the Anglican Church service? And how dangerously sentimental the challenging of Reason's condemnation of War, on the grounds that it is firmly entrenched in the practice and good favor of man? No defense of the views these questions imply as fundamental to *The Testament of Beauty* is even considered here. The question to be answered is whether they are really inherent in any stultifying form in the fabric of the poem.

We know that Bridges' voice did not go up in pacifist protestation during the years of war or after; in his poem he romanticized soldiers, especially generals. He was a communicant in the Anglican Church and it became a family joke perpetuated by him, that a Roman Catholic journal had considered him far removed from Christianity.[15] We know that his warm friend and admirer, Edward Thompson, believed him carelessly ignorant of socialism and narrow in his restriction of significant history to Western Europe. But can anyone following the analysis of the structure of sound, imagery, and meanings in this poem believe that these views actually make up its communication?

The reader who thinks Bridges approved of war and delighted in the idea of the exercise of manly virtues it provides, can not have followed the analysis of the inner logic of the poem given in Chapter xii. He can not have assimilated the emotional evaluations given by the style, either, which is poetically the more important. That this poet loved whatever friend or relative happened to be a retired general and saw in the faces of other soldiers the qualities he admired, is clear from his characterization of the soldier as one who is compact of heart, of sterner virtues, and great modesty, a man "ready at call to render his life to keep his soul." (II, 901) This may appear the reflection of a personal loyalty mistakenly extended to cover a group; but war is never so idealized. It should be clear, too, that Anglican theology as contrasted with Christian feeling, is not basic to this poem. The divinity of Christ, and his Kingship, if one looks closely enough, is seen to be treated as much like a good myth, that is, a metaphor, as is the story of Adam and the creation of Eve. In this story the theology of the Fall and the Atonement is carefully avoided. The theology of the Fall is indeed expressly denounced in another connection:

I, 471

For I rank it among the unimaginables
how Saint Thomas, with all his honesty and keen thought,

15 "George Santayana," *Collected Essays,* Vol. 8, No. xix, p. 150.

Conclusion

311

toiling to found an irrefragable system
of metaphysic, ethic and theologic truth,
should with open eyes hav accepted for main premiss
the myth of a divine fiasco, on which to assure
the wisdom of God; leading to a foregon conclusion
of illachrymable logic, a monstrous scheme
horrendum informe ingens cui Lumen ademptum.

Similarly when "Jesus came in his gentleness" . . . "men hail'd him WORD OF GOD." (I, 771-73) But "wandering unarm'd save by the Spirit's flame" (775) he founded an Empire "in the heart of man." (780) He speaks of the essence of Christ in all friendship, which is love; this is the rife Idea which is the "only deathless athanasian creed" (IV, 1430). The conclusion of the poem breaks into incoherent phrases with an echo of the Church service used for his special purpose.

IV, 1436

Truly the Soul returneth the body's loving
where it hath won it . . . and God so loveth the world. . . .

The structural emphasis on thought, personified Reason, the idea of evolution and the state of vision as the flower or final development from the common base of Nature's building (I, 369), should show how perceptive the Catholic journal's assessment was, if Christianity be assumed to be an exact theology rather than a way of life.

In so far as Bridges' belief that individual perfection should be *at all cost* pursued led him to fear modern man's concentration on social betterment, we may be concerned if he shows limitation of sympathy, rather than objecting to his actual disapproval of socialism. He was undoubtedly ignorant of the best thinking on this subject, but so are some of its proponents; both are to be reprehended. Guérard is right to point out that to a well-to-do man, the pleasure of contemplating goods may be more than the goods themselves, but to the starving man it is the food itself that brings brightness to the eye.[16] Here is a limitation, perhaps a deformity of the

[16] *Robert Bridges,* p. 181.

whole man. But what of the poem? Here again, the structure of meanings in the poem and the stylistic tone belie the specific statement. The foregoing pages have included many passages which communicate Bridges' understanding of the terrors from within and without that man is subject to, and his profound sense of the tragic lot of man throughout history. Man "from the terrifying jungle of his haunted childhood . . . by slow steps withdrew" (III, 40-43), but "dumb shapes of ancient terror abide." (II, 666) His uncontrolled Selfhood may tarnish his mirroring mind,

II, 516

> and mortal despair
> [may] possess his soul: then surely Nature hath no night
> dark as thatt black darkness that can be felt: no storm
> blind as the fury of Man's self-destructiv passions,
> no pestilence so poisonous as his hideous sins.

The passion of Breed that sanctifies fools, may degrade heroes (III, 215), and although the clown may have "his rare moments of revelation and peace" "the saint wil hav his days of humiliation and trial." (III, 1027-28)

The possibility that Bridges' sympathies were limited by his aristocratic and comfortable background is perhaps more serious. The personal vision this poem explores could only have come to a man of health and education whose lines were fallen unto him in pleasant places, it may be said. To survey the history of art, philosophy, and science required the university experience, the medical training, the long life of reading and travel. To rejoice at the constant and ubiquitous potentiality of experience like the winter rose bed to "burst into crowded holiday of scent and bloom," perhaps required a life protected from malnutrition, frustration of ambition, unpleasant surroundings, all the concomitants of poverty. But we must be realistic: the usual effect of security and riches is not this great joy; the protected and the spoiled generally are not our teachers in living. And further, it should not be forgotten that Bridges was a physician in hospitals until he was thirty-eight. This vision whose justification we are subjecting to scrutiny, occurred in a happy moment, if that is not too great an understatement; but its ecstasy is set in contrast with the knowledge of man's great unhappiness and his doubtful future. It is this contrast that a close study of the style and structure of the poem made clear. Through the aching ages, pestilence and war have beaten upon man:

I, 531
>   if we read but of Europe since the birth of Christ,
>   'tis still incompetent disorder, all a lecture
>   of irredeemable shame; the wrongs and sufferings
>   alike of kings and clowns are a pitiful tale.

Mesopotamian inhumanity, Nigerian slavery, Victorian slums have given place to the treadmills of modern industry. Science, it is true, has comforted our animal poverty (I, 722), but in every age and nation confusion and horror are found. Thus it was that even in 1918, Bridges feared for the future of man on earth, for all the intrinsic miracle in the foundations of life. It is out of the paradox of what is and has been against what is and may be that the great commonplace of the poem is relived and freshly expressed.